THE DISTRIBUTION OF PERSONAL INCOME
IN THE UNITED KINGDOM 1949-1963

THE DISTRIBUTION OF PERSONAL INCOME IN THE UNITED KINGDOM 1949–1963

THOMAS STARK

CAMBRIDGE
AT THE UNIVERSITY PRESS
1972

Published by the Syndics of the Cambridge University Press
Bentley House, 200 Euston Road, London NW1 2DB
American Branch: 32 East 57th Street, New York, N.Y.10022

Library of Congress Catalogue Card Number: 72-160099

ISBN: 0 521 08258 7

Printed in Great Britain by
Western Printing Services Ltd, Bristol

TO THE MEMORY OF MY MOTHER

CONTENTS

TABLES

CHARTS

LORENZ CURVES

CHARTS

ACKNOWLEDGEMENTS

My major debt and gratitude is to Professor A. R. Prest of the London School of Economics who for three years was my Ph.D. supervisor at Manchester University.

Professor Prest obtained funds from the Relm and later the Leverhulme Foundations to support this and other similar projects being undertaken at the University of Manchester. He also initiated the very necessary assistance from the Board of Inland Revenue. In addition to this he devoted much time to reading and lengthy discussions on all aspects of my work.

The main burden of the assistance from the Inland Revenue fell on Mr J. Squire, now with the Midland Bank Ltd, who provided me with considerable unpublished material and worksheets and outlined to me the techniques currently used in this field at the Board. The organiser of this assistance was Mr S. F. James of the Inland Revenue. Mr James also gave much useful advice in early discussions and later made many comments on the technical chapters. To both these gentlemen I would wish to express my thanks.

Also I would wish to express my gratitude to the following persons for either the provision of data or helpful comments: Mr J. Revell, Department of Applied Economics, Cambridge University; Messrs Duval and Cochrane of the Co-operative Insurance Society, Manchester; Mr Rogerson of the Co-operative Permanent Building Society, London; Miss C. H. West of the Central Statistical Office, and Mr G. L. Reid, Department of Economics, Glasgow University.

The final acknowledgements are to Mrs R. Rainey, Miss L. Bacon, Mrs M. Caldwell and other members of the secretarial staff of the New University of Ulster without whom my efforts would have remained incomplete.

T. STARK

Coleraine, August 1970

INTRODUCTION

'An' it's the poor what gets the blame'
(Popular Song)

History teaches us that the less fortunate of any community invariably become 'scapegoats' during periods of social and economic stress. Those with relatively low levels of income are no exception.

During the nineteenth century, in the midst of starvation and deprivation, society scorned the growth of Trades Unions, manifestations of equality, Socialism and the like. Crime and disease also were often considered to emanate from the poor. The latter half of the twentieth century, in the United Kingdom at any rate, has witnessed the disappearance of such scorn. The 'scapegoat effect' in some sectors of our society has developed a subtle twist. The low income groups are now accused of being too affluent. How often do we hear complaints of cars, television aerials, washing machines, etc. cluttering council house estates? Every university graduate has at least once commented disapprovingly on the divergence between the social and private returns on education, usually in comparison to a £40-per-week job on a car assembly line.

These are not uncommon sentiments. There exists, I believe, a substantial body of opinion that the size distribution of personal incomes nowadays is insufficiently inegalitarian, though recent and excellent studies on poverty by Abel-Smith and Townsend [1] and Atkinson [4] may have gone some way in reducing the conviction with which this opinion is voiced. Nevertheless it is voiced. The political 'left' of our society is also not slow in mentioning the unearned millions that flow into the hands of the few.

In spite of a few good studies, such as those mentioned above, only a small amount of data exists on the overall distribution of income. Furthermore, casual observation often appears as the only empirical basis for many non-academic opinions on the subject. This is not to say that such opinions are unimportant. They clearly are not. The fundamental equity of our economic and social structure is being questioned. The implications for the burden and system of taxation and for the nature of redistribution and community welfare are evident. For these reasons it would appear essential that our social commentators be provided with some data.

The first attempt to provide the required data which had some degree of reliability was made for 1904 by Sir L. G. Chiozza-Money [18]. This work was directed specifically to the task of measuring the distribution of income before taxation, which corresponds closely to what is defined in later chapters as the 'original' distribution.[1] It is clear that Sir L. Chiozza-Money intended his data to be used for social comment. The paucity of data sources limited the number of income ranges to three: those incomes of less than £160 p.a., those between £160 and £700 p.a., and those above £700 p.a.

These groupings resulted from the nature of the data. In 1904 £160 p.a. was the income tax exemption level and aggregate data on incomes above this level were obtainable from the Inland Revenue. A subdivision at the £700 mark was made possible by data on the tax abatement provisions which operated for incomes between £160 and £700 p.a. Incomes below the tax exemption limit were estimated in a residual manner, drawing heavily on Sir Robert Giffen's Census of Wages, undertaken by the Board of Trade in 1886. In his book Sir L. G. Chiozza-Money terms the three groups Poverty, Comfort and Riches. An interesting, though somewhat arbitrary, social comment.

This was the first complete and tolerably acceptable estimate of the distribution of income in the United Kingdom. It was followed by a similar computation for 1910 by Bowley [7]. The two estimates are compared in table 0.1.

Table 0.1   *The distribution of personal income, 1904 and 1910*[a]

Income range (£)	1904		1910		Percentage of all Incomes	
	No. of incomes (000s)	Income (£m)	No. of incomes (000s)	Income (£m)	1904	1910
<160	18,000[b]	880	18,850	1,055	94.0	94.5
160–	750	245	880	250	3.9	4.4
700>	258	585	212	565	2.1	1.1
Total	19,008	1,710	19,942	1,870	100.0	100.0

Sources: Chiozza-Money [18] p. 42; Bowley [7] p. 22.

[a] The original source tables have been adjusted in order to give comparability.

[b] See [18] pp. 16 and 24. This item includes all manual workers and those assessed for income tax but exempt. It is similar to Bowley's 'intermediate incomes', some of which may be slightly in excess of £160 p.a.

One should not attach too much importance to the precise numbers presented above, but concentrate on the general outline. The startling feature is the very small proportion of incomes subject to tax. Whether we can consider every income below £160 as poor, as did Chiozza-Money, is open to debate. By rough approximation £160 in 1904 was equivalent to £1,000 in 1970 and the average of the range, £49, to £340. This

[1] See chapter 1, pp. 19–20.

suggests that the vast bulk of the incomes in the range would be close to poverty. What can be concluded is that the breakdown of income ranges in greater detail above £160 p.a. is largely irrelevant, in view of the dominance of the bottom or lowest range.[1] The problems that we encounter in later years when the bulk of incomes are assessed for tax were quite insignificant before the First World War.

After that war the proportion of incomes subject to tax increased and income tax law became steadily more complex. This development had two significant effects on the analysis of income distribution in the U.K. First, economists began considering the measurement problems of tax incidence and the redistribution of income. The importance of the latter was on the embryonic development of what we now loosely term the 'welfare state'. The second effect was that income tax data became the main source of information on the size distribution of personal income. In fact the Inland Revenue took on the task of estimating this size distribution (B.I.R. [19]). Its first estimates were for 1918–19 and these were rapidly followed by similar estimates for 1920–1. There was a longer gap before the next set of estimates, which were for 1937–8.

The first two surveys by the Inland Revenue were made in response to specific demands. The first was undertaken for the Royal Commission on Income Tax and the second for the Colwyn Committee (Report of the Committee on National Debt and Taxation). The estimates were of significance only for calculating the yield of possible income tax changes. This was their prime purpose. The jungle of tax law, abatements, etc., not to mention avoidance and evasion, made it impossible to draw any broad or general conclusions. Furthermore, they attracted little attention from the academic economists of the day.

The 1937–8 survey, on the other hand, formed the nucleus of Barna's pioneering study on the redistribution of income [5]. Barna's work examines, in depth, the problems of meaningful statistical measurement. In addition, he constructed a sound conceptual framework for the analysis of the redistribution of income. This present work draws substantially on the concepts and methodology developed by Barna. These are, first, that the number of incomes must be related to the number of persons in the U.K. (this is not the case with the Inland Revenue surveys); secondly, that any study of the size distribution must include as much as possible of total personal income (called 'actual income' by Barna) and, finally, that the distribution of income cannot be considered in isolation from the wealth stocks of individuals and the non-monetary flows that stem from these stocks.

Barna's study unfortunately was hindered in its treatment of some of the

[1] It is interesting to note that few subsequent income distribution surveys have produced 'bottom' ranges of significantly smaller width.

above aspects by the paucity of available data. For example, he was only able to say that there are, on average, 2.57 persons dependent on each income unit[1] which has been assessed for tax purposes. Thus 2.57 times the total number of income units is subtracted from the total population to give the number of persons with incomes exempt from tax, which Barna assumes to be incomes below the exemption limit. Furthermore, 2.57 times the number of persons in each income range gives us an approximate per capita distribution of income. This type of analysis is unfortunately unsatisfactory. A per capita distribution of income cannot be derived as above, since the number of persons per income unit varies directly with the level of income. In addition, some of the incomes not assessed for tax will be above the exemption limit. The number of tax-exempt persons cannot be estimated as a residual, because there will be substantial double-counting with taxable incomes.

Since 1948 the Inland Revenue has periodically produced data on the size distribution of income, classified according to family size. It is this source of data which has enabled us to improve upon Barna's techniques and measurements. By a number of complex and invariably tedious manipulations we are able to link income distribution data more rigorously to population data and to derive income distribution by family size for the whole community, including most forms of 'personal income'. These manipulations and the end-products are outlined in chapter 2 and described in detail in appendix 1. They form the core of the present study.

Unlike Barna, we make no attempt to analyse the redistribution factor. The choice we faced was between a one-year study covering pre- and post-redistribution income and an analysis of the pre-redistribution distribution of incomes over a number of years. The latter was chosen. The years we compare, 1948, 1954, 1959 and 1963 were determined by the timing of the Inland Revenue surveys of 'taxable' income distribution. These surveys are described in detail, along with other current sources, in chapter 1.

The reason for our choice between the alternatives was that there exist three excellent one-year studies for the United Kingdom, but none of them can be directly compared with each other. There is a need for intertemporal comparisons. The studies referred to are Barna's, described above, and those of A. M. Cartter [14] and H. F. Lydall [38]. Cartter's study, which was for 1948–9, is similar but not identical to Barna's. It is defective in that the base data, the Inland Revenue tax distributions, are no more than simple extrapolations of the data used by Barna. The 1948 survey by the Revenue was published too late to be used by Cartter. Cartter's most important contribution is the technique he devised for

---

[1] An income unit is either a single person or a married couple. This is the definition of the income recipient used in the Inland Revenue estimates.

relating the size distribution of 'personal wealth' to that of personal income. This technique permits more detailed and purposeful estimates than that used by Barna. Both economists used the estimated relationships between wealth and income to apportion retained company profits to the 'personal sector'. We shall argue that this is conceptually incorrect and shall use the relationships to apportion capital appreciation. The theoretical justification of our procedure and a description of the calculations and results are presented in chapter 4.

Lydall's study, which was for 1953–4, differs substantially from those of Barna and Cartter. Firstly, it is derived from an extensive sample survey of 'personal savings' in the United Kingdom. Secondly, it does not discuss the redistribution of income. The work contains a wealth of useful and interesting information, much of which is not available for any other year. It also has the advantage that the data can be aggregated and linked to the 'national income' magnitudes. It is unfortunate that this author did not have the resources to conduct a similar survey for other years.

Apart from the studies of Lydall and Cartter, most other works on personal income distribution after the Second World War failed to follow the admirable example set by Barna. The problems of measurement and sources were largely ignored. There was a spate of small studies comparing data for a number of years, such as Paish [56] and R. J. Nicholson [54] which simply used official data as published. The Inland Revenue and the Central Statistical Office themselves gave approval to the broad social and economic conclusions[1] being drawn from their data. It was generally accepted that the size distribution of income was moving towards an 'egalitarian' state. A later study by Lydall [39] even supported this view. This study, like the others, was based largely on 'untreated' official data Its main contribution was a hint at the possible importance of items of personal income not normally allocated to income ranges in official sources. This category of personal income includes national insurance contributions, some forms of income in kind, non-taxable grants, post-war credits and employee superannuation contributions. We make an attempt to allocate these types of income. In addition we also attempt to account for some factors which are not considered as part of personal income in the National Income Accounts, such as subsidised factory products for workers, company cars, etc. Factors such as these, we argue, are relevant to the distribution of personal income. These problems are analysed in general in chapter 5 and an outline of the manipulations and calculations is presented in appendix 6.

It would not be unfair to comment that after Lydall's study for 1953–4, economists ceased to undertake major analysis in the field of income distribution. This may have resulted in part from a general belief that the

[1] See *Economic Trends* [23].

problems of inequality were no longer with us. This pattern was finally broken by Professor Titmuss [70] in a very powerful attack on the acceptability of official statistics. Though Professor Titmuss did not present any calculations of his own, he did return us to the crucial issues of the meaning and measurement of data. In spirit this present study is a reaction to the issues raised by Professor Titmuss. Essentially we are trying to find solutions to the problems of either inadequate or inept data. This investigation differs from other recent studies in the field, many of which are also clear responses to Professor Titmuss's book, in that we try to re-forge the links with the earlier works of Barna, Lydall, etc. We opted for an approach to the study of personal income distribution which still has Inland Revenue data as the nucleus and the national income estimates of personal income as its control. The alternative would have been to adopt the data produced by the *Family Expenditure Surveys*, undertaken initially by the Ministry of Labour and now by the Department for Employment and Productivity, as did Abel-Smith and Townsend [1] in their study of poverty and J. L. Nicholson [53] in his fine book on redistribution. In chapter 1 we put forward some reasons for considering the traditional approach to be more useful.

Those readers interested only in the results of the study are referred to the discussion in chapters 3 and 6. The former covers the adjustments to official data and the latter summarises the influences of 'capital gains' and the income categories investigated in chapter 5. In chapter 3 we are very much aware that data of this type are used for social commentary. We therefore try to steer clear of the temptation to use simple statistical summaries. We argue in that chapter that these are frequently meaningless.

The book is based on a Ph.D. thesis by the author, lodged in the Manchester University library. For reasons of publishing tidiness and cost, many of the intermediary tables in the thesis are not reproduced in the book. The author would be very grateful if any researcher who wishes to make use of these tables would kindly contact him, since subsequent research has led to the discovery of a small number of minor errors in eighteen of the 170 tables contained in the original work. The major difference between the book and the thesis is the extension of the estimates in chapter 4 to cover the years 1954 and 1963. Initially only estimates for 1959 were attempted.

1

SOURCES AND DEFINITIONS

As we outlined in the Introduction, the history of empirical investigations of the size distribution of income in the United Kingdom is not extensive.

Since the last war data sources have improved, becoming more frequent and comprehensive. At the present time there are three regular sources for data on personal income distribution in the U.K. These are: the Reports of the Commissioners of the Inland Revenue [19], hereafter called Board of Inland Revenue (B.I.R.) Reports and referred to by B.I.R. numbers; The Central Statistical Office *National Income and Expenditure Books* [16], hereafter called by their popular title – the C.S.O. Blue Books (this source is an extension of the Inland Revenue data); and the Ministry of Labour [45] *Family Expenditure Surveys*.[1] The *Family Expenditure Surveys* provide data on income distribution only as a by-product of the study of consumption patterns. They have, however, been the source of basic data for much of the excellent work currently being undertaken by Nicholson [53] on income redistribution, and by Abel-Smith and Townsend [1] on poverty.

The base data in our study will consist of the first two sources. We rejected use of the *Family Expenditure Surveys* for a number of reasons. First, as mentioned in the Introduction, we wished to retain a methodological link with earlier studies in this field undertaken by economists. Secondly, we felt that some of the problems encountered when using *Family Expenditure Survey* data were less easily surmountable than most of the problems we would have in adopting the alternative sources. In reaching this conclusion the problems we had in mind were:

(i)   the definition of the income recipient,
(ii) the definition of income,
(iii) comparability over time,
(iv) sampling errors,
(v)   response and participation bias.

Let us consider each of these in turn.

(i) The *Family Expenditure Surveys* (hereafter *F.E.S.*) define the income recipient as the household unit. This presents difficulties when an attempt

[1] Now undertaken by the Department of Employment and Productivity.

7

is made to construct 'control' totals and cross-checking procedures. The number and distribution of households in the survey cannot be easily linked to the number given by the Registrar General. In addition there are some theoretical objections to the 'household' as the basic unit. These are discussed later in this chapter.

(ii) The procedure currently adopted by the *F.E.S.* is to request information on 'normal take-home weekly earnings' which means, to quote Atkinson [4], 'that a man away from work for 13 weeks or less is regarded as continuing to receive his normal earnings when at work'. There is some evidence to suggest that mean 'normal' earnings are about 2% below mean actual earnings (see Mogridge [50]). It is thus impossible to derive reliable annual figures from such data. Annual figures are of course preferable to weekly figures. They not only provide a link to national income data, but also give a much clearer picture of the significance of the distribution of income. Life-span data would be the ideal, but that is quite impracticable. A less important defect of the *F.E.S.* income estimates is that self-employment income is based on the annual income of the latest available year. This is not so with the Inland Revenue data.

(iii) The *Family Expenditure Surveys* were first produced in their present form for the period 1957–9. The codes and definitions varied slightly each year till 1962, since when they have remained intact. These variations would not cause a great deal of trouble. However, the attempt to compare the results with those of an earlier enquiry into household expenditure for 1953–4 would raise a number of problems. This means that if we were to use the *F.E.S.* source we would be unable to extend our analysis back beyond 1957, or 1953 at the limit. There is a clear advantage here for the Inland Revenue and C.S.O. data, which can take us back to 1948.

(iv) The sample sizes for the *F.E.S.* data have varied from 5,000 to 10,000 households. The sampling errors for any given group, therefore, ought to be larger than for a corresponding group in the Inland Revenue surveys, where the sample size varies from 100,000 to 1 million cases. This difference in reliability is particularly important for groups where the sample size is very small in the *F.E.S.* data, particularly the very high income groups.

(v) The *F.E.S.* samples rely on voluntary participation. The response rate is about 70%. There is evidence which suggests that the non-respondents are households of specific categories, generally either the sick and aged or the very rich. Mogridge estimates that there could be a sampling deficiency of up to 6% amongst the higher income groups (see [50], p. 15).

These problems with the *F.E.S.* are serious for a study which aims to tie in income distribution data with population and national income data. They are much less serious for studies adopting less tight constraints, such as Nicholson [53] and Abel-Smith and Townsend [1]. This does not imply that the Inland Revenue and C.S.O. sources are either perfect or perfect for our purposes. They are only more preferable and more adaptable. They still pose many problems, as we shall see.

1.1 THE INLAND REVENUE REPORTS

Since the Second World War the Inland Revenue has periodically undertaken an investigation which it originally called an 'Income Census', and now describes as an 'Income Survey', and which are reported in B.I.R. Reports [19] for the relevant years. The surveys so far have been for the financial years 1949–50, 1954–5, 1959–60, 1962–3, 1963–4 and 1964–5. The first three and the last are the quinquennial major surveys. Since 1962, however, smaller annual surveys have been designed to fill in the years between the main surveys. Before 1962 such information as existed for the intervening years was merely an extrapolation of the previous survey.

Income is defined in the Inland Revenue data so as to cover all income subject to tax, i.e. taxable income. Specifically, it is that income computed for income tax purposes after making certain statutory deductions relating to expenses, schedule A and capital allowances.[1] The types of income not included are all non-taxable benefits awarded by the State, such as national assistance grants, etc. and the first £15 of savings bank interest. The statutory deductions are mortgage interest repayments and other similar annual payments. For data referring to years before 1961 national insurance contributions are included among these deductions.[2] Personal allowances and life insurance relief are not deducted. In terms of taxation practice the definition corresponds to what is termed 'actual' income.

Therefore not all income is covered by the Inland Revenue surveys. Incomes below the effective exemption limits and all types of non-taxable income above these limits are excluded. If for the time being we define income as being 'total personal income' as given in the Blue Books, then table 1.1 provides us with some guidance as to the scope of the Inland Revenue data.

The Inland Revenue surveys embrace roughly three-quarters of all personal income. It must be pointed out that in most cases the income referred to in the surveys means the amount received or earned in the

---

[1] Income before these deductions is termed 'gross income' in the surveys. After deductions it is called net income.

[2] In the 1965 Budget, personal allowances were raised and the deduction for national insurance contributions was abolished. The Inland Revenue informed us that since 1961–2 national insurance has been included in the tax computation and not as a deduction from income.

particular financial year under analysis. The only exception is for schedule D income. Here the assessments are normally based on the amount of income arising in the previous year. In technical terminology the surveys relate only to income 'returned'. It is for this reason that they cannot easily be related to other (non-survey) information in the B.I.R. Reports. The latter generally refer to 'income charged', which will include 'back-duty' assessments, etc. Such items would give a false impression of income received or earned in any specific year.

Table 1.1   *The percentage of total personal income covered by the Inland Revenue surveys*

Year[a]	Income below the exemption limit[b] but above £50 (a)	Other non-taxable income above the exemption limit and income below £50[d] (b)	Coverage 100 − [(a) + (b)]
1949	6.25	16.80	76.95
1954	5.60	16.10	78.30
1959	3.10	20.20	76.70
1963	3.40[c]	20.10	76.50

Source: Information from the Inland Revenue, and the C.S.O. [16] Blue Books.
    [a] We use calendar year data, given to us by the Inland Revenue.
    [b] The exemption limits were £135 p.a., £155 p.a., £180 p.a. and £275 p.a. respectively
    [c] Approximated by taking all income accruing to income units receiving less than £250 p.a.
    [d] The significance of income below £50 is explained in the notes and the definitions at the back of any C.S.O. [16] Blue Book.

The numbers of incomes in the Reports do not correspond to persons, but to single persons and married couples, the latter counting as one income. For the sake of clarity incomes defined in this way will be denoted as (income) units. Titmuss [70] and Cartter [14] both argue that wives with incomes separately assessed are also counted as separate units. This is not true and is categorically denied by the Inland Revenue in the 105th Report. There is no evidence to support the suggestion that the Inland Revenue has deviated in any way from its strict and clear definition of an income unit.

Another area of academic controversy concerns the income of dependents. Dependents are defined as children, relatives or housekeepers for whom a tax allowance is or should be claimed. Professor Titmuss [70] points out that there have been some differences of opinion among writers on the subject about how the Inland Revenue treats the income of children. He also states that 'no information about the statistical treatment of children since 1938 can be elicited from the Board's tables'.[1] The problem is whether the income of children is counted as part of parents' income and also whether children are entered as separate units. Titmuss cites the C.S.O. explanation, that if their income exceeds £50 p.a. then they are treated as separate units. Professor Titmuss asks why, if this is the case, the Board cannot provide any estimate of the number of minors' incomes.

These are serious criticisms of the Board's data. To some extent they are justified, in that the Board has not provided a clear explanation of what happens to the income of minors. On the other hand they are not valid criticisms. First the Board, in accordance with fiscal law, does not aggregate the income of parents and minors unless the income of the latter has been covenanted, etc. by the former. Professor Titmuss confirms this himself.[2] Children who receive an income which still permits an allowance to be claimed on their behalf will not enter the Inland Revenue distributions, since their income will be below the effective tax exemption limit. Children who receive incomes which exceed the statutory limit, as laid down in tax law, and whose allowances cannot be claimed, will be included in the distributions as separate tax units, provided the income is above the effective tax exemption limit.[3] The age of the child is irrelevant in this matter.[2]

Those children whose incomes are below the effective exemption limits will not therefore appear in the Inland Revenue statistics. They will, however, appear as separate units in the C.S.O. distributions, which includes categories in addition to taxable income. Only if their incomes are less than £50 p.a. will they not be entered. Finally, Professor Titmuss is only broadly correct when he states that the Board does not have the data on minors' income. They are able to produce some estimates on minors' trusts and covenants, as we shall see in chapter 2.

The final point of importance concerns the deficiencies present in the Inland Revenue surveys and the comparability between the surveys. Incomparability arises as a result of the different treatment of deficiencies in each of the surveys. Wherever possible the Inland Revenue checks the results of its sample surveys against independent estimates. This has led to the discovery of a number of important deficiencies in the sample data. The three most important types of deficiencies are in investment income;

[1] See Titmuss [70] pp. 63 and 64.

[2] Titmuss [70] p. 63, criticises the Board for not defining the point at which a child becomes an adult. Given the structure of fiscal law this is not necessary. As we shall see later in this chapter (section 1.2), the Board implicitly assumes that all children of over 15 receive an income of some sort.

[3] Since 1963–4 a sliding scale of allowances has been in operation for children's income which marginally exceeds the statutory limit, following the long established practice used for dependent relatives' income. Details on this and the statutory limits (which are well below the effective exemption limits) are given in any Inland Revenue Report.

the earnings of wives and the number of earning wives; and the number of children reported in the family classification tables.[1]

Table 1.2   *The investment income deficiency*

Year	£m	As a percentage of taxable income[a]
1949–50	150(290)[b]	1.8(3.5)[b]
1954–5	72	0.6
1959–60	60	0.4
1963–4	30	0.15

Source: Information from Inland Revenue and
B.I.R. [19] Reports (various).
    [a] i.e. after all adjustments for deficiencies.
    [b] £290m including the basic adjustment on surtax incomes (i.e. £150m + £140m).

The deficiency in investment income is given in table 1.2. It was estimated by the Inland Revenue by comparing the grossed-up sample total with a control total derived from other statistics. This control total was also subdivided so that the deficiencies could be broadly located. In the 1949–50 survey a basic £140m adjustment was also made on the basis of surtax data. Even so, there was a deficiency of £150m for that year. The adjustments for this item in subsequent years have been nowhere as large.

The Inland Revenue observed that investment income as a percentage of total net income fell sharply below the surtax limit. Therefore, on the hypothesis that the deficiency is mainly due to income receivers not reporting investment where tax has already been paid, the Inland Revenue made up the deficiency by allocating it among the income units liable only to standard rate income tax where no investment income had been reported.

The number of units affected by these adjustments was not available to us, except for the 1954–5 survey, where they caused an increase of 307,000 in the number of units receiving investment income. In no year did they cause any significant increase in the total number of units receiving all types of taxable income.

In the 1959–60 survey the above adjustments are incorporated in all tables, whereas in the other three surveys they are included only in the 'after-adjustment' summary tables.[2]

As with investment incomes, the deficiencies attributable to the earnings of wives were particularly great in the 1949–50 survey, but by the time

[1] Much of the material that follows on this subject and on the nature of the corrections adopted was kindly supplied to us by the Inland Revenue.
[2] In the 1949–50 survey the original adjustment to surtax incomes of £140m is incorporated in all tables, but not the £150m adjustment.

of the 1959–60 survey they had been substantially reduced. National insurance statistics indicated that in 1949 there should have been approximately three million earning wives. In fact only 1,416,000 were reported in the survey. So there was a deficiency of 1,584,000 persons, involving approximately £171m.[1]

The Inland Revenue made the adjustment by plotting graphically the number of wives per range and estimating the number of wives to be added by reference to the number of married units. Originally an independent sample had been taken of cases where wives' income had been reported. But this proved to be a fruitless exercise.

In the 1954–5 survey the deficiency in numbers was 1,940,000 wives and the income deficiency £264.6m. The same adjustments were undertaken as in the previous survey. In both the first two post-war surveys these adjustments were incorporated only in the 'after adjustment' summary tables.

Table 1.3 *The deficiencies resulting from the 'earnings of wives' deficiency*

Year	Deficiency (£m) (1)	(000s of units) (2)	(1) as a percentage of taxable income	(2) as a percentage of taxable income units
1949–50	171	1,584	2.1	7.9
1954–5	264.6	1,940	2.3	9.6
1959–60	315.1	111	2.0	0.5

Source: B.I.R. *Reports* [19] (various), and information from the Inland Revenue.

In the 1959–60 and subsequent surveys an important change was made in the treatment of this deficiency. All tables incorporated adjustments based on wives' earnings above the effective exemption limit. To quote the B.I.R. [19] 105th Report, 'The correction was made by adding wives' earnings to selected groups of husbands who had returned no such earnings, the selection being made by reference to the distribution of similar earnings of wives which had been duly returned by the husband'. A sample drawn independently from P.A.Y.E. sources indicated that the extent of the deficiency was about one-third of wives' earnings, concentrated mainly in the lower income ranges. The estimated deficiency was £257.2m and 101,000 units.[2]

The adjustment for wives' earnings below the exemption limit was included in the 'after adjustment' summary tables only. As a result 10,000 units and £57.9m were brought into the distribution.[3]

[1] See table 1.3.
[2] B.I.R. [19] 105, p. 83, paragraph 12, which refers to tables 80 and 103.
[3] B.I.R. [19] 105, table 75.

Identical techniques were used for the 1963–4 survey, except that no adjustment was made for wives' earnings below the exemption limit. In this survey therefore, the 'after adjustment' summary tables correspond to the 'before adjustment' tables in the 1959–60 survey. It is not possible to estimate the size of the deficiency in 1963–4, since all the tables were published after correction.

It is interesting to note that the corrections did not have any effect on the totals in the higher income groups. This is particularly evident if we compare the 'before' and 'after' adjustment tables. There are really no grounds for supposing that the deficiencies are caused by large-scale tax evasion by members of the higher income groups who fail to declare their wives' earnings.

Tables 1.2 and 1.3 illustrate a declining trend in the significance of these deficiencies. The deficiency in income fell from 5.6% in the first post-war survey to about 1.7% in the 1959–60 survey and was probably as low as 0.2% in the 1963–4 survey. The number of income units is quite large, as can be seen in table 1.3. However, these are misleading statistics. The adjustment to units represents largely a change within the total number of units already given and not an addition. If the main criticism of the size of the deficiencies is that they may be some indicator of avoidance or evasion of tax[1] then it is the income totals that are relevant. In this light, the deficiencies are very insignificant. On the other hand, if it is suggested that the deficiencies cause considerable errors in placing income units in the correct ranges or in tracing the proportions of wives' earnings per income range, then the errors in the first two surveys can rightly be judged as large.

The final deficiency is in the number of children in the family classification tables. This has also followed the pattern of being reasonably large in the first survey but diminishing gradually in subsequent years.

The estimated number of children can be broadly, though not precisely, checked against the numbers of children obtained from the Registrar General's statistics. The lack of precision arises from the existence of children over 15 in respect of whom children's allowances cannot be claimed. The eligibility for these allowances depends upon whether the children in question are receivers of income and, if so, whether that income in its taxable form exceeds the limit above which the allowance is reduced.[2] On this basis the relevant 'children's allowance' children over 15 will be mainly those in full-time or part-time education.

Such independent checking suggested a deficiency of about 500,000

---

[1] The Inland Revenue points out that these deficiencies do not necessarily imply a tax loss. Those concerning wives are often the result of husband and wife being in separate tax districts and those for investment income are a result of tax being paid at source. Cf. B.I.R. [19] 105, p. 82, para. 9.

[2] See p. 11, n. 3.

children in 1949–50 and 250,000 in 1954–5.[1] In each case this was accompanied by a similar deficiency in the number of children's allowances. The Inland Revenue state that this deficiency occurs in the lower income groups, where in some families the income may already be protected from tax liability by allowances, etc., so that it is not worth claiming for any additional allowance.[2] For example, they point to a large drop in the percentage of married couples claiming two children in the income ranges £300–£350 and £250–£300. A similar phenomenon is also cited for families with three and four children.

The Inland Revenue could not make any correction for this deficiency in the 1949–50 survey, because there was no alternative information. In 1954–5 an adjustment was made, but it was incorporated only in the summary family classification tables, not in the detailed tables.[3]

By 1959–60 the problem had become almost non-existent. The 105th Report simply states that 'there appeared to be a small deficiency in the number of children for which an adjustment was made'.[4] This adjustment was included in all family classification tables. We estimate this deficiency to be at the most 42,000 children, i.e. 0.3% of all children.

In 1963–4 no deficiency was reported. The difference between the numbers reported in the family classification tables and those estimated in a rough manner similar to that in footnote 4 below was a very small one indeed.[5]

The only other deficiencies recognised by the Inland Revenue relate to the 1963–4 survey. They arise out of administrative problems with Code Cards and Deduction Cards. Code Cards were formerly issued where income was above the effective exemption limit but not subject to tax because of child allowances, etc. Though these cards were being gradually

[1] B.I.R. [19] 94, pp. 96–117, para. 154.
[2] B.I.R. [19] 99, p. 87, para. 4.
[3] B.I.R. [19] 99, table 82, not tables 76–9.
[4] B.I.R. [19] 105, p. 83, para. 15. The Inland Revenue informed us that there were 13,142,000 children accounted for in the family classification tables. We estimated that there should be a maximum of 13,195,000 for the same period. This total was arrived at by taking the June figures for 1960 (3 months after the end of the 1959–60 financial year) of:

1. Children 0–14		12,214,000
2. Over 15 at school		540,000
3. Receiving further education (full-time and part-time, 15–18 year olds)		313,000
4. Trainee teachers and University undergraduates		122,000

The sources were the *Annual Abstract of Statistics 1961*, tables 14, 93, 96, 108 and 115, and various tables in *Statistics on Education 1963*.

This estimate is in fact an over-estimate to the extent that some students are over 21 and others foreign. It is an under-estimate in that the unemployed are excluded. Also the use of the June data means that there will be an excess over the financial year total due to new births. It is, however, only intended as a rough guide.

[5] B.I.R. [19] 105, tables 68–71. These tables give a total of 13,712,000 children. An independent estimate varied between 13,682,000 and 13,894,000, depending on the treatment of 18- to 20-year-olds in part-time education. Some of these may not have had allowances claimed on their behalf by their parents or may have been ineligible for such allowances.

withdrawn in 1963–4 'there were still some in existence'. The deficiency
in respect of Deduction Cards arises because these cards 'are not always
obtained from farmers in respect of their employees, nor in respect of
domestic servants or members of the forces, in cases where an employee's
income is above the Deduction Card Limit (£5 5s. 0d. per week in 1963–4)
but there is no tax liability'. The extent of these deficiencies was small –
170,000 units and £75m in income. They were corrected for in previous
surveys, but not in the 1963–4 survey.[1]

The deficiencies, on the whole, are small, except for 1949–50. That
particular survey we must accept with some scepticism. The others,
though, would appear to be reasonably accurate. In the main, the work
in the succeeding chapters will be using tables in which the corrections
are incorporated. There is no reason to suppose that the corrections made
by the Inland Revenue could be improved upon, or are only wild 'guesti-
mates', as Titmuss implies.[2]

1.2   THE CENTRAL STATISTICAL OFFICE

The C.S.O. data on income distribution are in fact produced by the
Inland Revenue. As far as possible they attempt to cover all forms of
'officially' recognised personal income and implicitly provide a link
between the estimated number of incomes and the Registrar General's
population figures.[3] The model devised by the Inland Revenue in order to
build up the control totals of persons for each of the surveys is given in
table 1.4. The link between the total number of persons and the income
unit universe is far less complicated than many writers have presumed.[4]

The basis of the model is the calculated total number of persons over
15 years of age who are residing or have resided in the U.K. at any time
during the year in question. This is item 10 in table 1.4. From this the
number of married couples, single males and single females over 15
during the year are estimated. Item 11 – marriages during the year –
is not subtracted, since any female married in the year is counted twice,
first as a single person and secondly as part of a married couple. The
result is item 13, onto which are further added those under 15 with incomes
in their own right, namely Minors' Covenants, and those in receipt of
Local Education Authority (L.E.A.) grants. This produces the total
number of all income units, from which those below £50 p.a. are deducted,
to arrive at the numbers with incomes above £50 p.a.

There are two criticisms of this procedure. Firstly, only net migration
is considered, when in fact we should take gross migration. There are,

---

[1] B.I.R. [19] 108, p. 80, para. 6.   [2] Titmuss, [70], p. 61.
[3] C.S.O. [16] Blue Book, 1965, p. 97.   [4] Cf. Titmuss [70], pp. 40–5.

Table 1.4 *The build-up of the control total of persons and income units ('ooos)*

Item	Year			
	1949 ('ooos)	1954 ('ooos)	1959 ('ooos)	1963 ('ooos)
1. Mid-year U.K. total population	50,063	51,064	52,157	53,797
2. Add births from June to December	413	382	423	481
3. Less deaths from June to December	266	267	265	284
4. Net migration from June to December	−5	1	50	−2
5. Net movement of forces overseas from June to December	−5	−15	−9	14
6. Total population on 31 December	50,200	51,167	52,356	54,006
7. Add deaths during year	590	578	606	655
8. Less children under 15 on 31 December	11,331	11,659	12,163	12,458
9. Less deaths of children under 15 during year	39	27	26	28
10. Total population over 15 during year	39,420	40,069	40,773	42,175
11. Add marriages during year	426	393	390	401
12. Less all married females on 31 December	12,260	12,810	13,333	13,550
13. Total number of males and single females over 15 during the year	27,586	27,642	27,830	29,026
14. Add minors in receipt of covenants	15	20	40	60
15. Add minors in receipt of L.E.A. grants	100	120	139	154
16. Total number of income units	27,701	27,772	28,017	29,240
17. Less units below £50 p.a.	1,801	1,532	1,525	1,962
18. Total number of units above £50 p.a.	25,900	26,250	26,484	27,278
19. Item (18) rounded off	25,900	26,250	26,500	27,300

Source: These figures were provided by the Inland Revenue.
Notes: Minors are under 15 years of age. Items 8 and 12 are the mean of two June figures.

unfortunately, no data available for the latter. Secondly, the coverage of minors' incomes is incomplete (cf. chapter 2 and appendix 1).

Likewise, the adjustment of the Inland Revenue survey data to eliminate discrepancies with those presented by the C.S.O. is a relatively uncomplicated affair. In addition to the calendar equivalent of the survey data[1] the Blue Book distributions include:

(1) all units with incomes greater than £50 p.a.,

(2) national assistance grants and benefits paid in the form of non-taxable incomes – for example, unemployment benefits, national assistance, national insurance benefits, maternity grants, sickness and injury benefits and the like,

(3) scholarships and educational grants paid to persons or paid on their behalf (e.g. university fees),

(4) income-in-kind of domestic servants and agricultural workers.

These items are all divided between the appropriate income groups, with adjustments being made for incomes which as a result move into a higher range. The difference between total personal income classified by ranges and total personal income is known as 'unallocatable' non-taxable personal income. 'Classified' total personal income represents the extent of the 'coverage' of the C.S.O. data vis-à-vis total personal income: see table 1.5.

Table 1.5   *The proportion of total personal income classified by income ranges (in percentages)*

Year	'Classified' income (1)	'Unallocatable' income (2)
1949	84.8	15.2
1954	85.6	14.4
1959	83.0	17.0
1963	83.5	16.5

Source: C.S.O. [16] Blue Book, various issues.

Note: Col. (2) in this table is part of col. (b) in Table 1.1. Unallocatable income represents 'other' non-taxable income in that column. The difference between the two columns is non-taxable income above the effective exemption limit.

'Unallocatable' income, as can be seen from table 1.5, is quite a large item and has become slightly larger over the period 1949–63. This large item consists of:

(1) other non-classified income in kind, e.g. free coal to coalminers, etc.,

(2) non-taxable grants from public authorities, such as milk and welfare foods, industrial services for the disabled, grants to schools and universities,

_____
[1] Which the Inland Revenue estimates.

(3) investment income of private non-profit making bodies, of life assurance companies and superannuation funds,

(4) the amount by which the imputed rent of owner-occupied dwellings exceeds the schedule A valuation (in 1963 the whole of imputed rent as a result of the abolition of Schedule A tax),

(5) that part of the income of self-employed persons which is covered by allowances for depreciation,

(6) accrued interest on national savings certificates,

(7) post-war credits,

(8) incomes of persons receiving less than £50 p.a.,

(9) most employers' and employees' contributions to national insurance and superannuation schemes – this item has presumably diminished in importance after 1961–2, since when national insurance relief has not been deducted from income in the Inland Revenue surveys.[1]

Finally, we should note that the C.S.O. publishes distributions for each year. However, only those for 1949, 1954, 1959, 1962 and 1963 stem directly from the Inland Revenue surveys. The others are extrapolations.

1.3   DEFINITIONS

One of the strongest criticisms of official statistics and literature based on official statistics is that the limitations of the definitions of income and units, coupled with the jungle of fiscal law, hide much inequality in the form of tax evasion, tax avoidance, the erosion of the surtax base and so on.[2] If this is the case the 'official' statistics must be regarded with scepticism.

The purpose of this work is to overcome some of these objections – to present U.K. income distribution in the light of several definitions of income; to present it with an unambiguous concept of income receivers, and lastly to tackle some of the statistical problems caused by tax avoidance; hence our chapters on 'capital gains' and 'fringe benefits'.

There is no single concept of income which can be claimed to be perfectly appropriate in all circumstances. As the reasons for constructing distributions of income vary, so the relevant definitions of income also vary.

Thus it is important at this stage to get clear what we propose to measure. Brady [10] has pointed out the dangers of selecting concepts which require broad definitions of income, including large amounts of non-money income and indivisible benefits. This approach requires too many arbitrary decisions and is too readily capable of being geared to any desired pre-selected conclusion on the part of the author,[3] particularly,

---

[1] Cf. p. 9, n. 2 and chapter 5.   [2] Cf. Titmuss [70] and Brittain [11].

[3] Cf. Brady [10] p. 14.

as F. Andic has stated, if these arbitrary forms of income are assumed to accrue largely to the high income groups.[1]

In our study we hope that we have been able to avoid some of the above types of 'arbitrariness' by restricting our terms of reference to the distribution of the 'natural' or 'original' standard of living among the inhabitants of the U.K. The 'natural' standard of living is defined as that which prevails before adjusting for the effect of direct taxation and government 'exhaustive' expenditure. It includes direct transfer incomes from the government in the form of non-taxable money-income benefits, scholarships, etc., but excludes non-money benefits resulting from educational, defence, transport, housing and local government expenditure, etc., i.e. 'exhaustive' expenditure. These latter items would form part of an 'actual' standard of living – the post-redistribution income.[2] The definition of a 'natural' standard of living corresponds to Nicholson's definition of pre-redistribution income plus direct benefits.[3]

A standard of living is defined as representing an income receiver's command over resources, that is, his power to satisfy his desires for current consumption, provision against uncertainty and security for the future, and the expansion of this power over time. No pretence is made to relate income and welfare. Any concept of welfare is to a large extent abstract and as such not appropriate for an empirical study employing a considerable degree of aggregation. The definition is similar to that devised by the Minority Report of the Royal Commission of Taxation [65].

A complete approach would require a study of living standards over a period longer than 12 months – say 5–10 years or even a lifetime. It is necessary to establish a 'normal' standard of living in the Friedman sense. Fluctuating incomes and expectations will influence peoples' consumption and saving patterns and hence the manner in which they plan to utilise the currently attained 'command of resources'. A high money income in one year may not necessarily signify a large increase in this 'command'. It may be only a random deviation from an expected 'norm' and consequently a misleading statistic in a one-year sample. This is a problem we are unable to overcome, though a tentative effort has been made for a narrow group of incomes elsewhere [60]. In the main, though, the implicit assumption that a high current income reflects a high 'natural' living standard will have to be accepted.

With respect to the ownership of wealth the hypothesis put forward is that increases in the monetary value of property owned by individuals constitute an increase in economic power. For example, such an increase may cause changes in consumption or savings plans by directly influencing

---

[1] Cf. F. Andic [3] p. 61.   [2] Cf. Barna [5] pp. 21–4.
[3] Cf. Nicholson [53] pp. 3–4.

'liquidity' preference, expectations and uncertainty. These effects could perhaps lead to a reduction in the holdings of 'liquid' or safe assets or an increase in the consumption of consumer durables or other forms of non-monetary assets.

Some previous works have attempted a similar definition. The Inland Revenue in its 1919–20 survey included 'actual income of companies, which though charged to income tax, is not distributed to shareholders in dividends, but is retained for the purpose of increasing reserves'. Though in the 1919–20 survey this item was unclassified by income groups, it was allocated in later years in studies by Barna [5] and Cartter [15].

The justification for the inclusion of the above item, according to Barna and Cartter, is that increases in undistributed profits are closely correlated to share prices and hence are a reflection of capital gains in the widest sense. There is neither any strong *a priori* argument for, nor empirical verification of such a correlation. This manipulation relies on a hypothetical distribution of dividend income which, it is assumed, would have taken place had all profits been distributed. Furthermore, retained profits do not represent a direct increase in the 'command over resources' of the individual shareholder. Since he does not have the 'income', he has no control over it and also has no 'control' over its possible effect on the value of shares.

According to this line of reasoning a measure of capital gains is more relevant. In this case the accretion in value has occurred and an individual does have 'control' over the accretion, to the extent that he can decide to realise the capital gain or not, or change other economic plans. A capital gain measure is furthermore not limited to shares and equities. All forms of personal wealth (property) will be included when we add this item to the 'classified' C.S.O. income definition.

Further developments will include an attempted classification of 'unallocatable' income and an attempted distribution of 'fringe benefits' (cf. chapter 5) arising out of employment. Fringe benefits are defined so as to include those which are non-taxable and do not already appear in 'official' estimates of total personal income. Such benefits would be: the use of company cars, subsidised company meals, free sports facilities, free travel, and other forms of non-taxable compensation, etc. Fringe benefits directly contribute to either the physical comforts of living or the security of living and are hence an integral part of that standard of living.

The last two additional groups of income probably involve the greatest degree of arbitrariness. Therefore in the following chapters income distributions will be presented excluding capital gains, fringe benefits and unallocatable income and then including each item separately. This is done for three reasons: first, to ascertain the quantitative importance of each group; secondly, to provide continuity with definitions employed by other writers in this field, and lastly to provide information on incomes under a variety of different income definitions.[1]

The final problem of definition is that of the income recipient. It is commonly believed that the most suitable definition is either a family or a household. Apart from the fact that we have no comprehensive statistics on households[2] (or families in a broad sense), a number of theoretical difficulties arise out of such a definition. Both groups can vary considerably in composition over time, especially households (e.g. lodgers, dependent persons, etc.), and these factors could seriously distort statistics on income distribution. The household is, in other words, a variable factor.[3] A family, however, is quite precise if taken, in its narrowest definition, to include a man and/or woman and any child who is dependent upon each or both of them. In adopting this approach it is implicitly assumed that the 'inner' family is the basic social unit. This is a view propounded by one of the most eminent American economists in this field, Dorothy Brady, who argues that 'A man's obligation to care for his wife and minor children may be viewed as one of the fundamental and unchanging features of our society'.[4] Moreover this view was legally recognised in the United Kingdom by the 1948 National Assistance Act, which placed on a person financial responsibility for his/her spouse and children.[5]

This, then, is our definition, which forms the basis of our concept of the income receiver. A narrow definition has been deliberately chosen, so as to reduce the complexity of interpretation to a minimum. Finally, by use of this definition we are able to derive a per capita and per adult equivalent distribution of income. These concepts are discussed in greater detail in chapters 2 and 3.

---

[1] Cf. Brady [10] p. 20: 'The questions involved in defining money income are difficult enough, but relieved of the pressure to produce some grand total of money and non-money income, the estimator can develop methods for basing income distributions on different definitions for experimental analyses. As Kuznets noted, since "our goal is a size distribution so prepared as clearly to reflect income cause" the best definition for this purpose should be determined by empirical tests. It is not over-optimistic to hope that once certain difficulties of data collection are overcome, a size distribution can be based on income defined to include and exclude such items as capital gains and losses, gifts, prices, gambling profits, annuities and insurance settlements.'

[2] The Ministry of Labour [45] *Family Expenditure Surveys* are, as previously stated, not ideally suited for our purposes.

[3] F. Andic [3] p. 63.

[4] Brady [10] p. 11.

[5] *National Assistance Act, 1948*, Section 7(b)a (H.M.S.O.).

2
THE PER CAPITA
DISTRIBUTION OF INCOME

Each of the Inland Revenue surveys classifies income units in each income range according to family status. Family status includes the marital condition of the income recipient and the number of children and dependents for whom he or she is claiming income tax relief. There is also further information on the earning status of wives. These family classification tables, of course, include only income units receiving taxable income. As with all data in the Inland Revenue surveys, the year referred to is the financial year. The C.S.O. data, as previously mentioned, present taxable and non-taxable income distributions on a calendar year basis.

The task at hand is to match these two sets of data. The reasons for attempting this are simple. If we can obtain an 'inner' family classification for the C.S.O. data, then conversion to a per capita distribution, or for that matter to a per adult equivalent distribution, is an uncomplicated process of division which involves only regrouping (with interpolation to avoid overlapping ranges). The process can be set out formally as follows:

Income range	Number of income units per range	Number of units in size groups of: 1 2 3 4 ... n persons	Number persons per range	Aggregate income £m
$y_1 \ldots y_2$	N_1	$N_{11} \, N_{12} \, N_{13} \, N_{14} \, \ldots \, N_{1n}$	Z_1	Y_1
$y_2 \ldots y_3$	N_2	$N_{21} \, N_{22} \, N_{23} \, N_{24} \, \ldots \, N_{2n}$	Z_2	Y_2
.	.	.	.	.
.	.	.	.	.
.	.	.	.	.
$y_n \ldots y_{n+1}$	N_n	$N_{n1} \, N_{n2} \, N_{n3} \, N_{n4} \, \ldots \, N_{nn}$	Z_n	Y_3

where y_i is level of income, $i = 1, 2 \ldots n$,

N_i is aggregate number of units per range,

N_{ij} is number of units of size j in range i,

Z_i is aggregate number of persons per range and is given by

$$\sum_{j\,=\,i\,=\,1}^{n} (N_{ij} \times j)$$

and Y_i is aggregate income per range.

23

The per capita range limits for each cell, N_{ij}, are

$$\frac{y_i}{j} \dots \frac{y_{i+1}}{j}.$$

Each such cell is then regrouped according to these 'new' range sizes. Interpolation is adopted to avoid overlapping ranges.[1]

The principle may be relatively simple to understand. Unfortunately its application involves numerous complex steps. The first is the matching of the two data sources.

The gap between the financial and calendar year data was overcome in two ways. First, the Inland Revenue provided us with a breakdown of the C.S.O. distributions into taxable and non-taxable income units. The former are, in effect, the calendar year equivalents of the summary financial year data presented in the Inland Revenue surveys (see table A in appendix 7). Secondly, we assumed that the family size/income pattern is unaffected by the three-month gap between the financial and the calendar year. This enabled us to apply the family size patterns derived from each Inland Revenue survey to the respective taxable income units in the 'broken-down' C.S.O. distributions. The 'broken-down' C.S.O. data also contained information on those income units whose income was part taxable and part non-taxable. Adjustments were accordingly made to the family size classification patterns, to allow for taxable income units which had moved to a higher income range as the result of some additional non-taxable income.[2]

The next step is to estimate the number of persons 'accounted for' by the taxable income units, after the application of the family classification patterns. The difference between this estimate and the total number of persons in the U.K. (see table 1.4) in each year represents the number of persons 'accounted for' by non-taxable income units. At this stage we were faced with two further problems: first, the family size pattern of the non-taxable income units and secondly the double-counting of income units. The existence of extensive double-counting was indicated for each year by the excess of non-taxable units over the 'residual' of persons supposedly accounted for by these units.

The family size pattern of non-taxable income units above £250 p.a. was assumed to be identical to that of taxable units with a similar taxable income. According to the information available the group of such non-taxable units rose from 7% of all non-taxable units in 1949 to 15% in 1963,

---

[1] See appendix 2.
[2] A taxable income unit is defined as an income recipient whose income may be wholly or partly included in the Inland Revenue surveys. For further details of this adjustment, readers are referred to the author's Ph.D. thesis, pp. 36–47.

that is roughly from 2% to 5% of all income units. The family size pattern for the non-taxable units below £250 p.a. was approximated by using some unpublished sample data provided by the Inland Revenue, in conjunction with the 'residual' of persons still unaccounted for. This last step, however, could not be undertaken until the double-counting was largely eliminated and a meaningful residual obtained.

Broadly, two kinds of double-counting can be distinguished. The first is direct double-counting, which arises from marriages, divorces and deaths of husbands in the current year. In each case the female partner will be entered twice in the distributions, firstly as part of a 'married unit' and secondly as a single (including 'widowed') unit. This type of double-counting is recognised by the C.S.O.[1] It results from the U.K. tax laws, which amalgamate the incomes of husbands and wives. Secondly, we have indirect double-counting. This occurs where persons with non-taxable incomes of £50 or more are also included as dependents or children in the family classification tables. Such people would be:

1. dependent relatives receiving incomes below the maximum income permissible before the dependent relative allowance is rendered unclaimable,
2. adults in receipt of covenants below the effective exemption limit,
3. young persons in receipt of educational scholarships,
4. children under 15 in receipt of L.E.A. maintenance awards,
5. children under 15 in receipt of covenants,
6. young persons, in full-time or similar study, in receipt of unearned and/or vacation-earned income below the effective exemption limit, and also minors under 15 in receipt of unearned income other than covenants, etc.

The number involved for each group of double-countings is given in table 2.1.

A formal attempt is made to eliminate all these types of double-counting except items 2 and 6, and that resulting from the death of husbands. The first, adults in receipt of covenants, is very small indeed.[2] Not all the persons in this category will necessarily be counted twice. If the covenantor claimed tax relief, then he (or she) would be unable to claim the dependent relative allowance, assuming the covenantee to be a dependent relative,

---

[1] C.S.O. Blue Book [16] 1965, pp. 91–2.
[2] Adults in receipt of covenants.

Year	As a percentage of all income units
1949	0.028
1954	0.270
1959	0.380
1963	0.470

Source: Information from the Inland Revenue and table 2.1.

Table 2.1 *The number of income units involving one or more double-counted persons*

Year	Marriages ('000s)	Deaths of[a] husbands ('000s)	Divorces ('000s)	Dependent[b] relatives ('000s)	Scholarships[c] ('000s)	Adult[a] covenants ('000s)	Minors'[a] covenants ('000s)	Total ('000s)
1949	355	189	31.1	1,953.0	—	5	10	2,543.1
1954	326	192	25.4	1,627.4	225	55	20	2,470.8
1959	324	209	23.0	1,473.7	300	80	40	2,449.7
1963	334	225	28.0	1,427.5	387	100	60	2,561.5

Sources: *Annual Abstract of Statistics* (various issues), H.M.S.O.; *Statistics on Education 1963*, Parts I and II, H.M.S.O.; *Education in 1955*, Cmnd 9785 Ministry of Education, B.I.R. *Reports* [19] (Various issues); information from the Inland Revenue.
[a] Extrapolations from the 1951 and 1961 Population Censuses.
[b] Based on the financial year data in the B.I.R. [19] *Reports*.
[c] Includes minors under 15 in receipt of L.E.A. maintenance awards.
[a] By no means all of these are double-counted.

which is highly probable. In this case there would be no double-counting between the number of adult covenants and the family classification tables, though there might be some double-counting involving other non-taxable income units, e.g. pensioners with pensions below the effective exemption limit. In this latter case double-counting will be indirectly eliminated when we obtain the 'meaningful' residual after all other types of double-counting are eliminated. Finally, if the dependent relative allowance is obtained on behalf of the covenantee, then the double-counting with respect to the family classification tables is eliminated under item 1, though there may still be double-counting with respect to other incomes below the effective exemption limit, as above. Since we had no means of distinguishing which of the adult covenants were double-counted and/or automatically eliminated, we decided not to attempt any formal elimination procedure.

With the other item, i.e. item 6, a complete dearth of data meant that even a tentative attempt at elimination was impracticable. However, this omission should also be insignificant. Unearned income of dependent children, if provided by the parents, would be included in the parents' income. If provided by some other body, e.g. a grandparent, it would in all probability be in the form of a trust or covenant. Absolute and contingent trusts are included in the estimates of minors' covenants, i.e. item 5. If the income is from wealth made over to the minor then it may or may not be in the form of a trust, etc. There are no data on such cases.

Some of the income units in item 6 may also be included in the data for scholarships, items 3 and 4. There may be further double-counting between scholarships and minors' covenants. It is impossible to make any allowance for these 'multiple-countings'.

Our final problem concerned the double-counting of wives, resulting from deaths of husbands. As can be seen from table 2.1, these, like our other two problematic items, are only a small proportion of all double-counted units. Again, a complete dearth of data on the income status of dying husbands was the reason that no attempt at elimination was undertaken. However, there are grounds for supposing that a substantial proportion will be eliminated by the 'residual' procedure already mentioned. The reason is that many such husbands will be beyond retirement age, probably with low incomes, which, in conjunction with their survival for only part of the year, will mean that both the married units and the subsequent widows will be in the lower income brackets, below the effective exemption limits and hence non-taxable. This being so, the double-counting will disappear automatically in the 'residual' procedure for estimating the family sizes for non-taxable income units in that group of incomes. The numbers not eliminated will be in all probability no more than 100,000 units each year, i.e. 0.5% of all units. This is, of course, hypothetical, but omissions of this order will have a very insignificant effect on the distribution unless it can be shown that it is mainly the very high income ranges, i.e. above £1,500–£2,000 p.a., which are affected. This would be likely only if these groups displayed an income structure remarkably dissimilar to that of the rest of the community. A cursory glance at table 2.1 indicates that only approximately 8% to 13% of all double-counting income units are left unadjusted, that is 0.75% to 1.2% of all income units.

The principles underlying the methods of elimination differ between the direct and indirect kinds of double-counting. With respect to marriages, the aim is to create one income unit where there were formerly two, and for divorces to estimate a meaningful separation in terms of income ownership during the year. For new marriages the income of brides for the year up to the date of the marriage will be added to that of her husband for the year and her own after marriage. The reverse takes place with respect to divorces, where the income of the wife whilst married (if any) will be subtracted from that of her ex-husband for the year and added to her income received after the divorce.

As we shall see later, these adjustments were carried out meticulously for marriages. A lack of data rendered a similar treatment of divorces impossible. In this case all adjustments had to be made with respect to the earned income of wives only, there being no data available on unearned income. Likewise no adjustment was possible in regard to the change in the guardianship of children after divorce. This may have involved, in some cases, an 'unreal' placing of children in the family classification tables. We also made no allowance for women who divorced and remarried in the same year. Even if the 'divorces' adjustments are to some extent inaccurate, we again stress the 'insignificance' hypothesis. In any one year there are never more than 30,000 divorces, involving at the most 150,000 people, that is about 0.2% of the total population and 0.15% of all income units. We estimate that the amount of double-counting 'uneliminated' or dubiously eliminated in our data involves less than 1% of all units and 0.5% of total population.

For indirect double-counting there are two types of elimination techniques, the choice depending on how we interpret our concept of the 'inner' family with respect to each category of double-counting. For example, if we have two income units x and y, but y also appears in the family classification tables as dependent on x, then we can either eliminate y as a separate income unit and add his income to that of x or we can exclude y from x's family and leave him as a separate income unit.

The latter procedure was adopted for dependent relatives whom we considered not to form part of the 'inner' family. The first procedure was used for the remaining items: scholarships, minors' covenants, etc.

A further snag arose because we were unable to obtain reliable data for scholarships and minors' covenants for 1949. To overcome this we decided to present two types of distributions for each of the years. The type 1 distribution formally eliminated double-counting due to marriages, divorces, and dependent relatives (though informally eliminating much of that due to deaths), and the type 2 included in addition, allowances for scholarships and minors' covenants. The type 2 distributions are presented only for 1954, 1959 and 1963. The type 1 is included in order to give some standard of comparability between 1949 and the other years.

The results of our operations are presented in tables 2.2 to 2.10. There are two forms of table for each type of distribution. One is the per capita distribution and the other is based on the income unit concept, classified by the 'inner' family size. The former is derived from the latter in the manner outlined earlier in this chapter. In appendix 1 we present a more detailed account of the procedures adopted in deriving the above tables: appendix 1 is intended primarily for those readers who are interested in the computational aspects of income distribution analysis.

Table 2.2 *Distribution of income by income units, type 1, 1949*

Income range (£)	Number of units ('000s)	Amount of income (£m)	Average income (£)	Number of persons per unit							Total number of persons ('000s)
				One person ('000s)	Two persons ('000s)	Three persons ('000s)	Four persons ('000s)	Five persons ('000s)	Six or more persons *a* ('000s)	Seven persons ('000s)	
50–	11,811.8	1,873	158.6	8,534.6	2,137.9	683.4	290.0	104.6	60.3	1.0	16,942.55
250–	2,935.5	810	275.9	1,517.0	742.7	419.0	175.5	55.0	26.0	0.3	5,407.50
300–	4,577.3	1,583	345.8	1,274.8	1,411.4	1,000.0	600.8	195.0	94.0	1.3	11,095.90
400–	2,561.3	1,140	455.1	439.9	869.9	586.1	414.5	162.1	87.6	1.2	6,984.30
500–	1,376.0	749	544.3	177.3	533.2	307.4	215.7	88.0	53.2	1.2	3,822.90
600–	679.0	440	648.0	83.9	283.4	145.8	103.2	38.9	23.0	0.8	1,850.50
700–	402.9	301	747.1	55.3	171.2	84.4	60.9	20.6	10.1	0.4	1,065.95
800–	412.8	366	886.6	66.0	175.3	84.2	61.0	19.5	6.2	0.6	1,055.20
1,000–	405.6	487	1,200.7	76.0	165.6	77.0	60.0	20.0	6.4	0.6	1,024.00
1,500–	151.7	258	1,700.7	31.3	62.4	26.0	22.0	7.8	2.0	0.2	375.50
2,000–	118.5	286	2,413.5	26.3	51.5	18.5	14.6	5.2	2.2	0.2	284.90
3,000–	68.4	257	3,757.3	11.8	27.7	10.9	11.0	5.2	1.7	0.1	181.65
5,000–	33.2	225	6,777.1	6.6	14.7	4.4	4.4	2.2	0.9	—	83.65
10,000–	9.0	117	13,000.0	1.6	5.0	0.8	0.8	0.8	—	—	21.20
20,000+	2.0	70	35,000.0	0.5	0.9	0.4	0.2	—	—	—	4.30
Total	25,545.0	8,962	350.8								50,200.00

Sources: See tables 1.4, 2.1, A1.1, A1.2 and A7.1; B.I.R. [19] *Report* No. 95, table 111.
a We assumed an average of 6½ persons per unit for units of six or more.

Table 2.3 *Distribution of income by income units, type 1, 1954*

Income range (£)	Number of units ('000s)	Amount of income (£m)	Average income (£)	Number of persons per unit							Total number of persons ('000s)
				One person ('000s)	Two persons ('000s)	Three persons ('000s)	Four persons ('000s)	Five persons ('000s)	Six or more persons a ('000s)	Seven persons ('000s)	
50–	8,449.1	1,392.98	164.8	6,970.6	1,075.7	197.4	110.4	58.7	36.3	—	10,685.25
250–	1,655.9	453.02	273.6	1,271.8	249.1	71.0	33.0	17.0	14.0	—	2,291.00
300–	3,352.5	1,175.76	350.7	1,905.9	817.0	325.0	174.6	77.7	52.0	0.3	5,941.90
400–	3,371.0	1,515.14	449.4	1,226.2	1,025.8	552.0	343.0	134.0	89.0	1.0	7,561.30
500–	2,837.9	1,556.04	548.3	521.2	1,035.7	622.7	407.0	147.8	102.6	0.9	7,500.90
600–	2,174.0	1,403.03	645.3	314.9	824.3	484.0	336.0	135.0	79.0	0.8	5,953.60
700–	1,465.3	1,093.80	746.4	124.6	593.7	338.0	257.0	94.2	57.0	0.8	4,201.10
800–	1,301.1	1,142.88	878.3	109.7	580.2	275.9	211.4	77.6	45.6	0.7	3,632.70
1,000–	764.6	907.82	1,187.3	115.5	333.6	142.1	118.6	38.7	15.5	0.6	1,981.85
1,500–	234.6	401.67	1,712.1	46.1	93.6	38.5	36.8	14.0	5.3	0.3	602.55
2,000–	162.0	392.37	2,422.0	33.0	67.0	23.5	25.5	8.3	4.4	0.3	411.70
3,000–	98.0	365.72	3,731.8	16.9	39.7	15.6	15.7	7.5	2.5	0.1	260.35
5,000–	45.0	294.63	6,547.3	9.0	20.0	6.0	6.0	3.0	1.0	—	112.50
10,000–	11.0	143.49	13,044.5	2.0	6.0	1.0	1.0	1.0	—	—	26.00
20,000+	2.0	73.65	36,825.0	0.5	0.9	0.4	0.2	—	—	—	4.30
Total	25,924	12,312.00	474.9								51,167.00

Sources: See tables 1.4, 2.1, A1.1, A1.2 and A7.1; B.I.R. [19] *Report* No. 99, table 82.
a We assumed an average of 6½ persons per unit for units of six or more.

Table 2.4   *Distribution of income by income units, type 1, 1959*

Income range (£)	Number of units ('000s)	Amount of income (£m)	Average income (£)	Number of persons per unit								Total of persons ('000s)
				One person ('000s)	Two persons ('000s)	Three persons ('000s)	Four persons ('000s)	Five persons ('000s)	Six persons ('000s)	Seven persons ('000s)	Eight persons ('000s)	
50–	5,456.0	911.56	167.0	4,685.3	582.7	111	62	11	—	—	—	6,512.7
250–	1,691.6	463.39	273.9	1,514.95	119.65	25	14	9	6	3	—	1,987.25
300–	2,657.2	925.65	348.4	2,128.35	375.85	81	38	20	10	2	3	3,471.05
400–	2,616.2	1,177.24	449.9	1,629.05	604.15	212	100	39	16	10	6	4,280.35
500–	2,701	1,483.46	549.2	1,099.0	813.0	425	240	83	28	8	5	5,639.0
600–	2,550.5	1,650.44	647.6	624	814.45	506	310	153	53	26	4	6,423.95
700–	2,253.2	1,684.9	747.7	383.5	712.7	520	400	157	58	14	8	6,263.9
800–	3,000.6	2,668.6	889.3	347.1	1,046.5	690	548	223	91	34	21	8,769.1
1,000–	2,275.7	2,670.33	1,173.4	227.2	960.5	480	379	145	53	18	13	6,377.2
1,500–	445.5	759.65	1,705.2	66.7	170.8	81	79	37	8	2	1	1,222.3
2,000–	289.3	692.96	2,395.3	48.0	108.3	50.4	52.6	22	6	1	1	787.2
3,000–	157.0	592.83	3,776.0	27.0	62.0	25	26	12	4	1	—	421.0
5,000–	65.2	434.6	6,665.6	13.1	29.1	8	9	4	2	—	—	163.3
10,000–	14.0	182.25	13,017.8	3.0	8.0	1	1	1	—	—	—	31.0
20,000–	3.0	100.14	33,380.0	0.7	1.3	0.6	0.4	—	—	—	—	6.7
Total	26,176.0	16,398.0	626.4									52,356.0

Sources: See tables 1.4, 2.1, A1.1, A1.2 and A7.1; information from the Inland Revenue.

Table 2.5   *Distribution of income by income units, type 1, 1963*

Income range (£)	Number of units ('000s)	Amount of income (£m)	Average income (£)	One person ('000s)	Two persons ('000s)	Three persons ('000s)	Four persons ('000s)	Five persons ('000s)	Six or more persons [a] ('000s)	Total number of persons ('000s)
50–	4,174.8	819.01	196.2	4,049.7	84.0	24.7	12.5	3.9	—	4,361.3
250–	1,373.7	376.78	274.3	1,171.5	134.1	29.5	21.7	8.0	8.9	1,712.85
300–	2,286.2	805.83	352.5	1,921.3	245.7	51.7	34.3	17.4	15.8	2,894.7
400–	2,258.8	1,012.67	448.3	1,728.7	377.7	76.3	36.4	17.6	22.1	3,090.25
500–	2,130.3	1,170.96	549.7	1,283.8	534.8	144.1	97.8	39.3	30.5	3,571.65
600–	2,180.7	1,416.55	649.6	991.2	618.9	289.8	177.4	71.4	32.0	4,373.0
700–	2,104.2	1,575.43	748.7	734.0	637.3	345.7	228.0	103.7	55.5	4,836.95
800–	3,815.2	3,418.45	896.0	813.0	1,239.7	757.9	589.5	254.3	160.8	10,240.80
1,000–	4,573.9	5,483.71	1,198.9	479.7	1,796.9	924.0	822.9	335.9	214.5	13,210.85
1,500–	1,263.1	2,122.35	1,680.3	128.2	545.4	248.8	211.4	86.6	42.7	3,521.55
2,000–	463.6	1,100.2	2,373.2	64.6	189.0	79.3	81.7	34.7	14.3	1,273.75
3,000–	212.4	798.31	3,758.5	35.5	85.1	33.5	32.7	18.4	7.2	575.8
5,000–	105.1	698.88	6,649.7	17.1	45.5	14.7	14.7	8.4	4.7	283.55
10,000–	20.0	265.09	13,254.5	3.8	8.7	2.8	2.8	1.9	—	50.30
20,000+	4.0	130.08	32,520.0	1.1	1.7	0.6	0.6	—	—	8.70
Total	26,966	21,194	786							54,006.0

Sources: Tables 1.4, 2.1, A1.1, A1.2 and A7.1; B.I.R. [19] *Report* No. 108, tables 68–71.
a We assumed an average of 6½ persons per unit for units of six or more.

Table 2.6 *Distribution of income per person, type 1*

1949

Income range (£)	Number of persons ('000s)	Amount of income (£m)	Average income (£)
<200–	37,258	4,000	107.3
200–	7,811	1,952	249.9
300–	2,584	890	344.4
400–	982	436	440
500–	459	250	545.7
600–	263	170	645.5
700–	167	124	745.6
800–	219	193	882.9
1,000–	238	286	1,202.3
1,500–	88	151	1,707.8
2,000–	73	175	2,398.6
3,000–	35	131	3,767.9
5,000–	18.8	126	6,666.8
10,000–	3.3	43	12,900.9
20,000+	0.9	35	39,179.8
Total	50,200	8,962	178.5

1954

Income range (£)	Number of persons ('000s)	Amount of income (£m)	Average income (£)
<200–	28,690	3,697	127.7
200–	10,929	2,712	248.1
300–	5,619	1,940	345.3
400–	2,706	1,203	444.6
500–	1,074	587	546.6
600–	620	401	646.8
700–	299	223	745.8
800–	328	290	884.1
1,000–	337	403	1,195.8
1,500–	126	216	1,714.3
2,000–	97	234	2,412.4
3,000–	44	165	3,750
5,000–	23.4	154	6,581.2
10,000–	3.7	48	12,973
20,000+	0.9	39	43,333
Total	51,167	12,312	240.6

1959

Income range (£)	Number of persons ('000s)	Amount of income (£m)	Average income (£)
<200–	18,753	2,612	139.3
200–	14,845	3,622	244.0
300–	7,670	2,659	346.7
400–	4,547	2,022	444.7
500–	2,681	1,460	544.6
600–	1,350	871	645.2
700–	754	562	745.7
800–	739	655	886.3
1,000–	579	685	1,183.1
1,500–	190	326	1,715.8
2,000–	140	332	2,371.4
3,000–	69	258	3,739.1
5,000–	32	214	6,687.5
10,000–	5.8	77	13,275.9
20,000+	1.2	45	35,833.3
Total	52,356	16,398	313.2

1963

Income range (£)	Number of persons ('000s)	Amount of income (£m)	Average income (£)
<200	12,888	1,982	153.8
200–	14,021	3,485	248.6
300–	9,213	3,210	348.4
400–	6,043	2,707	448
500–	4,247	2,338	550.5
600–	2,475	1,599	646.1
700–	1,622	1,209	745.4
800–	1,769	1,565	884.7
1,000–	1,057	1,260	1,192
1,500–	309	528	1,708.8
2,000–	209	499	2,387.6
3,000–	104	392	3,769.2
5,000–	38.7	263	6,624.7
10,000–	7.6	100	13,157.9
20,000+	1.7	57	33,529.4
Total	54,006	21,194	392.4

Table 2.7 *Distribution of income by income units, type 2, 1954*

Income range (£)	Number of units ('000s)	Amount of income (£m)	Average income (£)	Number of persons per income unit							Total number of persons ('000s)
				One person ('000s)	Two persons ('000s)	Three persons ('000s)	Four persons ('000s)	Five persons ('000s)	Six or more persons a ('000s)	Seven persons ('000s)	
50–	8,253.1	1,380.38	167.2	6,749.1	909.2	388.4	104.3	61.8	24.8	15.5	10,728.6
250–	1,063.9	438.98	273.7	1,221.8	249.1	70	32.4	16.8	13.8	—	2,233.3
300–	3,348.1	1,174.24	350.7	1,905.9	817	322.7	173.4	77.1	51.7	0.3	5,929.25
400–	3,335.4	1,499.33	449.5	1,226.2	1,025.6	534	332.1	129.8	86.2	0.9	7,425.0
500–	2,821	1,547.31	548.5	521.2	1,035.7	614.7	401.4	145.9	101.3	0.8	7,435.85
600–	2,180.9	1,407.95	645.6	314.9	824.3	488.1	337.8	135.5	79.5	0.8	5,978.85
700–	1,484.3	1,107.93	746.6	124.6	593.7	347.6	282.5	96.5	58.6	0.8	4,273.8
800–	1,323.2	1,162.32	878.4	109.7	579.3	286.5	218.8	80.7	47.3	0.9	3,720.25
1,000–	774.6	918.41	1,185.6	115.5	333.3	146.7	122.2	40	16.3	0.6	2,021.15
1,500–	236.1	404.05	1,711.3	46.1	93.4	39.2	37.5	14.2	5.4	0.3	608.7
2,000–	162.4	393.33	2,421.9	33	67	23.7	25.7	8.3	4.4	0.3	413.1
3,000–	98	365.84	3,733	16.9	39.7	15.6	15.7	7.5	2.5	0.1	260.35
5,000–	45	294.72	6,549.3	9	20	6	6	3	1	—	112.50
10,000–	11	143.54	13,049	2	6	1	1	1	—	—	26.0
20,000+	2	73.67	36,835	0.5	0.9	0.4	0.2	—	—	—	4.3
Total	25,679	12,312	479.4								51,167

Sources: As for table 2.3, with A1.3, A1.6, A1.7, A1.8 and A1.9.

a We assumed an average of 6½ persons per unit for units of six or more.

Table 2.8 *Distribution of income by income units, type 2, 1959*

| Income range (£) | Number of units ('000s) | Amount of income (£m) | Average income (£) | Number of persons per unit | | | | | | | | Total number of persons ('000s) |
				One person ('000s)	Two persons ('000s)	Three persons ('000s)	Four persons ('000s)	Five persons ('000s)	Six persons ('000s)	Seven persons ('000s)	Eight persons ('000s)	
50–	5,193	889.64	171.3	4,317.3	570.8	183.5	59.2	38	24.2	—	—	6,581.4
250–	1,651.6	452.45	273.9	1,476.95	119.65	24.5	13.5	68.5	6	3	—	1,941.75
300–	2,618	911.96	348.3	2,091.35	374.85	79.9	37.6	19.8	9.7	1.9	2.9	3,424.85
400–	2,609.8	1,174.47	450	1,629.05	604.15	208.3	98.3	38.4	16	9.8	6	4,260.05
500–	2,678.6	1,470.34	549.3	1,099	813	413	233	80.7	27.3	7.8	4.8	5,556.3
600–	2,519.5	1,632.24	647.8	624.05	872.45	492.6	300	149.5	51.7	25.4	3.8	6,312.65
700–	2,231.2	1,668.47	747.8	383.5	712.7	511.1	391.9	153.8	56.9	13.8	7.5	6,176.8
800–	3,039.6	2,706.19	890.3	347.1	1,046.5	710.3	560.3	227.2	92.2	34.5	21.5	8,914.9
1,000–	2,309.6	2,708.92	1,172.9	227.2	959.6	495	391	149.9	54.9	18.6	13.4	6,511.7
1,500–	454.4	773.77	1,702.8	66.7	170.3	85.2	82.3	38.3	8.4	2.1	1.1	1,257.5
2,000–	291.5	696.96	2,390.9	48	108.3	51.2	53.4	22.4	6.1	1.1	1	796.1
3,000–	157	593.63	3,781.1	27	62	25	26	12	4	1	—	421
5,000–	65.2	435.18	6,674.5	13.1	29.1	8	9	4	2	1	—	163.3
10,000–	14	182.5	13,035.7	3	8	1	1	1	—	—	—	31
20,000+	3	100.28	33,426.7	0.7	1.3	0.6	0.4	—	—	—	—	6.7
Total	25,836	16,398	634.7									52,356

Sources: As for table 2.4, with tables A1.3, A1.5, A1.7, A1.8 and A1.9.

Table 2.9 *Distribution of income by income units, type 2, 1963*

Income range (£)	Number of units ('000s)	Amount of income (£m)	Average income (£)	Number of persons per unit						Total number of persons ('000s)
				One person ('000s)	Two persons ('000s)	Three persons ('000s)	Four persons ('000s)	Five persons ('000s)	Six or more persons a ('000s)	
50—	3,848.5	774.14	201	3,452.2	243.3	106.2	23	18.2	5.6	4,476.8
250—	1,306.4	358.55	274.4	1,104.6	134.1	29.2	21.6	8	8.9	1,644.65
300—	2,240.6	790.38	352.7	1,878.6	245.7	50.3	33.6	17.1	15.3	2,842.2
400—	2,248.0	1,007.85	448.3	1,719.7	377.7	75.5	35.9	17.4	21.8	3,073.9
500—	2,124.1	1,167.38	549.5	1,283	534.8	141.8	96	38.6	29.9	3,549.35
600—	2,172.1	1,410.97	649.5	990.2	618.9	285.9	174.8	70.5	31.8	4,344.1
700—	2,097.3	1,568.84	748	734	637.3	342.6	225.8	102.5	55.1	4,807.65
800—	3,800.7	3,404.19	895.6	813	1,239.7	752.6	584.4	251.9	159.1	10,181.45
1,000—	4,572	5,480.21	1,198.6	479.7	1,769.9	924.6	821.1	335.6	214.1	13,201.35
1,500—	1,261.7	2,122.10	1,681.9	128.2	543.3	247.3	211.9	87.4	43.5	3,524.25
2,000—	493.1	1,171.4	2,375.5	64.6	188.2	92.4	92.3	39.2	16.4	1,390.0
3,000—	223.5	832.74	3,725.9	35.5	84.9	37.7	37.2	20.2	8.0	620.2
5,000—	107	709.73	6,632.9	17.1	45.5	15.4	15.4	8.8	4.8	291.1
10,000—	20	265.52	13,276	3.8	8.7	2.8	2.8	1.9	—	50.3
20,000+	4	130.3	32,575	1.1	1.7	0.6	0.6	—	—	8.7
Total	26,519	21,194.3	799.2							54,006

Sources: As for table 2.5 with A1.3, A1.4, A1.7, A1.8 and A1.9
a We assumed an average of 6½ persons per unit for units of six or more.

Table 2.10   *Distribution of income by persons, type 2*

Income range (£)	1954 Persons ('000s)	1954 Income (£m)	1954 Average income (£)	1959 Persons ('000s)	1959 Income (£m)	1959 Average income (£)	1963 Persons ('000s)	1963 Income (£m)	1963 Average income (£)
200	28,741	3,679	128.0	19,043	2,627	137.9	13,097	1,964	149.9
200–	11,118	2,714	241.7	14,511	3,570	246.0	13,711	3,420	249.4
300–	5,644	1,952	345.8	7,669	2,655	346.2	9,174	3,187	347.3
400–	2,704	1,203	444.8	4,574	2,044	446.8	6,055	2,712	447.8
500–	1,080	589	545.3	2,688	1,467	545.7	4,275	2,351	549.9
600–	619	401	647.8	1,359	878	646.0	2,495	1,615	647.2
700–	301	224	744.1	753	561	745.0	1,644	1,223	743.9
800–	328	291	887.1	741	658	887.9	1,800	1,597	887.2
1,000–	338	403	1,192.3	580	685	1,181.0	1,078	1,281	1,188.3
1,500–	126	216	1,714.3	190	326	1,715.7	319	548	1,717.8
2,000–	97	234	2,412.4	140	332	2,371.4	204	485	2,377.4
3,000–	44	165	3,750	69	259	3,753.6	105	391	3,723.8
5,000–	23.4	154	6,581.2	32	215	6,718.7	39.7	263	6,624.6
10,000–	3.7	48	12,973	5.8	78	13,448.0	7.6	100	13,157.0
20,000+	0.9	39	43,333	1.2	43	35,833.3	1.7	57	33,579.0
Total	51,167	12,312	240.6	52,356	16,398	313.2	54,006	21,194	392.4

Sources: As for tables 2.7 to 2.9.

3

GREATER OR LESS INEQUALITY

3.1 INTRODUCTION

The most persistent question in income distribution analysis is whether there has been a movement towards a more equitable distribution or not. The adjustments to the data described in chapter 2 were specifically designed so that this question could be meaningfully tackled. The role these operations play will become clear in section 3.2. In that section we devise a measure of inequality which directs attention to the lower and upper ends of the income distribution. To compensate for this emphasis we shall consider the whole structural pattern of the distribution of income in chapter 6.

Interpretations of official statistics, i.e. the C.S.O. and Inland Revenue data, have until recently indicated a movement towards greater equality.[1] This conclusion has, however, been seriously challenged, in particular by Titmuss [70], who is at great pains to describe the defects of official data. This sort of criticism, though undoubtedly necessary, largely ignores the most important aspects of the question. These are the definition and measurement of inequality.

In many works a definition must be deduced by the reader. The most common of these implicit definitions are that inequality is either a deviation from the perfect state where all incomes are equal, or some function of the proportion of income held by the top 1%, or 10% or even 25% of income receivers. A typical statement is that of Titmuss [70], who, referring to the top end of the income distribution, says that it 'profoundly affects the shape of the whole distribution'. Most authors herald a decline in the proportion of income held by the top 'per cent' as a decline in inequality.[2]

Most of the recent interpretations of U.K. data have used these percentile techniques. This may be a satisfactory manner of judging any given distribution, provided the data are broken down in fine detail. In the U.K. very detailed data have been available, generally, for the upper income groups only. This presumably explains the emphasis put on changes in this sector of the income scale by economists and statisticians.

---

[1] See Brittain [11], Economic Trends [25], Lydall [39], Paish [56], Seers [66], and Titmuss [70]. Nicholson [54] is a recent, somewhat over-simplified study, concluding that since 1959 the trend towards greater equality has been reversed. Titmuss [70], Brittain [11], and Nicholson [54] are the only studies in which the validity of the greater equality conclusion is not accepted.
[2] For examples see Lydall [39], Paish [56], Titmuss [70] and Nicholson [54].

Thus conclusions concerning inequality tend to be drawn from the income characteristics of the rich. Furthermore if, as Titmuss claims, income tax avoidance is predominant amongst the rich, it assumes considerable importance in determining the acceptability of any conclusions drawn from official data.

We argued in chapter 1 that the deficiencies of the Inland Revenue data do not destroy their usefulness, as Titmuss claims to show. Nor do we accept that tax avoidance by less than 5% of the population renders void conclusions on changes in the inequality of the income distribution as a whole. In principle, conclusions about inequality should not be based on the income characteristics of a small section of the population.

A possible technique for the analysis of a complete distribution would be the use of percentiles. Percentiles are calculated either by graphic or by logarithmic linear interpolation. By either method, however, the errors produced in the lower income groups are considerable, if, as is often the case, the first measurable attribute is located somewhere between the 30th and the 50th percentile – surely an extremely important section of any income distribution?

Another factor weighing against an extensive use of percentile techniques is that it is a cumbersome method of analysis when confronted with a large number of distributions, for example, the data from chapter 2. We have in all 22 distributions, four each of Inland Revenue, C.S.O., type 1 by units and type 1 by persons, plus three each of type 2 by units and by persons. We will be adding to this list the 'per adult equivalent' distributions developed later in this chapter.[1]

Alternative measuring techniques employ the use of a single statistic, in an attempt to summarise a given, supposedly paramount, characteristic of the whole distribution. The use of such measures is not unknown in U.K. studies and is particularly common in American and Italian literature.[2]

When measures of this type are used, the basic assumption is invariably that perfect equality entails equal incomes, with inequality as an index of the deviation from this ideal. Assumptions of this nature are clearly open to substantial criticism. Even in the absence of variations in ability, market demands for labour, labour mobility and inheritance, variations in personal needs according to age, and possibly compensation for educational and training investment, would mean that 'perfect' equality is not necessarily the optimum state.[3] These latter factors could to some

---

[1] In chapter 6, where we set out specifically to analyse the complete distribution, we use Lorenz curves, a graphic interpretation of percentile analysis. These curves are sometimes used to infer changes in equality. However, in this respect they have some, though not all, of the theoretical disadvantages of the single statistic measures considered in the next few paragraphs.

[2] See Nicholson [54], Brittain [11], Cartter [14].

[3] For discussion on some of these points see Mincer [43] and J. N. Morgan [51].

extent be dealt with by using a concept of equality based on life-span incomes. Even here we would face difficulties in comparing different life-span patterns, as well as the ethical political problems raised by the first group of factors regarding inheritance, etc. A pragmatic approach rules out such considerations, since we do not have, and could not hope to have, any data on life-span incomes. The main point is that at any given point of time perfect equality is not essential to the attainment of the optimum state.

Concepts of the optimum or ideal state are more the responsibility of the welfare economist or theorist. It is not our intention to add to the considerable literature in this field. To do our approach justice would necessitate a lengthy tract, which would be beyond the scope of our study. We hope it is sufficient to quote in support of our views Little's conclusion that 'with sweeping assumptions, the thesis that economic equalitarianism produces the maximum amount of happiness is more or less true'.[1] Our objection is to the 'sweeping assumptions'. With less sweeping assumptions one could deduce that the above thesis is not more or less true.

Finally, if we were to accept the perfect equality concept, then which of the fifteen most well-known measures would we choose? This question would be unnecessary if they all produced consistent results. However, they do not. Furthermore, some measures involve large errors of grouping.[2] From time to time in the main body of our study we will present some results using the Gini concentration ratio – the most commonly used of the measures – mainly for purposes of comparison with the alternative concepts of inequality which we have tried to develop.

3.2 A NEW MEASURE OF INEQUALITY

Dalton[3] considers that the inequalities of income become relevant when 'the less urgent needs of the rich are satisfied, while the more urgent needs of the poor are left unsatisfied. The rich are more than amply fed, while the poor go hungry'. We believe that a more useful approach to the problem of inequality is to estimate the extent to which needs are satisfied. We are in effect turning the problem the other way round. We are attempting to estimate inequality as an absolute magnitude each year, rather than as a relative deviation from an ideal state. The 'ideal state' is not essential to our purposes. In terms of the Dalton definition the ideal state is reached when urgent needs of the poor are satisfied, presumably at the expense of the less urgent needs of the rich. Absolute equality of incomes

---

[1] Little [37] chapter IV, p. 63; chapter IV is an excellent discussion on the theoretical implications of the concept of perfect equality, which he terms 'equalitarianism'.
[2] Some of these technical criticisms are developed in detail in appendix 3 below.
[3] Dalton [21] p. 10.

is only one of several distributions that may produce this state of affairs. All depends on how more or less urgent needs are defined.

In modern Britain the problems of famine and starvation have largely been superseded by those of malnutrition. The other traditional curses of the poor have also been reduced in gravity, but nevertheless they still exist. The needs of the poorer classes for adequate housing, clothing and education are still unsatisfied. The 'excesses' of the satiated rich are also still with us. They are eagerly reported in the 'society' columns of most leading national daily newspapers.

The idea of what constitutes a 'need' varies over time. It varies even more between people, depending on environment and personal experiences. The traditionally academic and objective economist feels he ought to shy away from such a concept. It is one of the autonomous 'socio-political constraints' economists place in their models without further discussion. However, in a study of inequality we cannot opt for this course of action. Whichever way we look at the problem, a subjective evaluation of the nature and concept of inequality is inevitable. It is even implicit in the traditional measures of inequality, i.e. perfect equality and the optimum state, etc.

The best we can hope to do is to bury our personal concepts of needs and attempt a definition which is acceptable to society. Therefore we bring to bear on our concept of inequality the definitions of poverty and richness embodied in the welfare and taxation systems of the nation. Finally, we must warn that 'need' is an all-embracing term. We are dealing with the pre-tax income distribution in a given year. Income in that year will be our indicator of the ability of the population to satisfy or 'excessively' satisfy needs in that year. No allowance is made for persons who are living off capital, or those whose incomes fluctuate enormously from year to year or for variations in living costs from one part of the country to another. We are in effect quantifying those persons in the economy who *may be* poor and *may be* rich. This number, expressed as a percentage of total population, is our index of inequality.

The resulting index, therefore, does not imply a measure of actual poverty or prosperity. In chapter 1 we stated that our terms of reference would be restricted to an analysis of changes in the 'natural' standard of living of the British population. The 'natural' standard of living of a person or an income unit was defined as the command over resources before taxation and certain types of government expenditure.[1] It is the endogenous standard of living provided by the economy. The poor (or rich) in this context are those with a relatively low (or a generous) command over resources in a given year. They each form a proportion

---

[1] I.e. including the non-taxable benefit incomes in our income definitions. These are the initial and only incomes for their receivers, and hence reflect their 'natural' living standard.

of the population which may or may not be declining – this is what we are trying to measure. In this context we avoid the problems that arise when attempts are made to estimate actual poverty or richness.[1] Because of this we call our index a high/low income index as opposed to a poverty/ richness index.

The high/low income inequality index

A comprehensive definition of high and low incomes is beyond the scope of this analysis. Therefore for low incomes we have adopted, with certain modifications, the definitions prevalent in recent U.K. literature.[2] Since, however, to our knowledge no empirical enquiry has ever been undertaken by economists to define a high income, we have been forced to construct our own definition.

(a) Definition of low incomes

The amount of assistance received by applicants to the National Assistance Board constitutes the basis of our definition. This may, according to some experts, be representative only of the lower levels of the low incomes. Nevertheless these applicants do possess the characteristic of being 'officially' recognised as being in 'need'. Furthermore, the level of national assistance bears a direct relationship to the detailed and renowned definitions of subsistence laid down by Beveridge [6] and Rowntree [64].[3]

We start with the National Assistance Board scales (N.A.B.), including average rent payments, for 1949. To these we add an allowance for rent and a 25% increase to allow for disregarded income and any underestimation of the 'subsistence' level. Applicants are permitted to 'disregard' a certain amount of their resources when applying for assistance.[4] A recent survey conducted by the National Institute of Economic Research (see Hemming [30]) estimated that the national assistance rates, including average rent, in 1949, may have been approximately 15% below the subsistence level of 1949.[5] In view of these factors a 25% increase in the scales did not seem unreasonable (i.e. 15% for underestimation and 10% for disregarded income). There is little doubt that the scales have to be increased. There is, however, considerable discussion as to the extent of the increase. Abel-Smith and Townsend in their study [1] give increases of 20% and 40%. Similar estimates for the present study are reproduced

---

[1] An actual estimate of poverty (or richness) would have to take into account the burden of direct taxation and the differential rates of inflation in the prices of products consumed by each income group, etc. There is considerable evidence that prices have risen at different rates for different income groups: see Seers [66] and Atkinson [4] p. 4 for further references.

[2] For example see Abel-Smith and Townsend [1] and Hemming [30].

[3] See Abel-Smith and Townsend [1] p. 15 and table 2.

[4] See Abel-Smith and Townsend [1] p. 17.

[5] See Hemming [30] p. 52, chart 2.

elsewhere, by Gough and Stark [28], and we see no need for repetition. The 1949 national assistance rates plus the 25% increase were the base year estimates for the definition of low income. For subsequent years the 1949 level was raised by the amount of the increase in income per head between the year in question and 1949 (see table 3.1). In this manner the measure becomes an index of low incomes, at current prices with 1949 weights. The index not only allows for general inflation but also for the average increase in living standards. It provides a low income limit which is a fixed (1949) proportion of average personal income before tax in every year.

The amount of national assistance an applicant receives is also governed by family circumstances. Throughout we have assumed three categories of families, namely single people (S_0), married couples without children (M_0) and married couples with children $(M_i$, where $i = 1, 2 \ldots 6)$. The first category includes the single-person income units in the type 1 and type 2 unit distributions of chapter 2. We assume that the second category contains the two-person units and the third the three or more person units. In other words we are assuming that all income units comprising two or more persons are 'married' units. This is, of course, not strictly true. However, the number of single persons with children is very small indeed. In 1963–4 there were only 388,500 such cases in the Inland Revenue survey data, i.e. 1.88% of all units.[1] At the most this assumption will lead to a very slight exaggeration of the number of low incomes.

Finally, the National Assistance Board provides three rates of assistance for children, depending on their age. Since the data described in chapter 2 do not permit a breakdown of children by age group, we have assumed that all children are between the ages of 5 to 15 years and have accordingly taken the mean of the rates of assistance provided for children between 5 to 9 years and 10 to 15 years.

The limits in table 3.1 are the upper limits for what we consider to be the socially acceptable minimum income levels. The number of income units with this level of income or less, expressed as a proportion of total units, provides our index of low incomes and the first part of our high/ low income index of inequality. These proportions have been estimated for three of the distributions presented in chapter 2: the Inland Revenue distributions, the type 1 and the type 2 unit distributions. The per capita distributions are unsuitable for this type of analysis. At a later stage in our analysis we develop a 'per adult equivalent' distribution to deal with the problems raised by the per capita distribution.

In table 3.2 the actual National Assistance Board scales plus rent are reproduced. These are the 'regressed' trend values for the period 1948 to 1964. We have undertaken the regressions in order to counteract the uneven

---

[1] The percentages for 1959–60, 1954–5 and 1949–50 are respectively 1.88%, 2.0% and 2.05%.

fashion in which the N.A.B. rates have increased since 1948 and so to avoid misleading comparisons between our four years. A comparison between tables 3.1 and 3.2 suggests that the socially acceptable minimum level of income has increased faster than average living standards.

Table 3.1 *Low income limits*[a]

£p.a. (rounded to nearest £5)

Family size[b]	1949	1954	1959	1963
S_0	110	150	195	240
M_0	165	225	295	360
M_1	200	270	355	435
M_2	235	320	420	515
M_3	265	360	475	575
M_4	300	410	535	655
$M_{4\frac{1}{2}}$	315	425	560	685
M_5	330	450	585	720
M_6	365	500	650	795

Source: Hemming [30] tables 11 and 13.
[a] N.A.B. scales including average rent payments for 1949, multiplied by 25% and increased by the average increase in per capita personal income for successive years to 1949.
[b] S = single person, M = married couple; the subscripts indicate the number of dependent children.

Table 3.2 *Low income limits–trend values*
(*1948–64*) (*for the N.A.B. scales plus rent and increased by 25%*)

£p.a. (rounded to nearest £5)

Family size	1949	1954	1959	1963
S_0	110	150	205	270
M_0	165	230	320	410
M_1	200	280	400	520
M_2	235	330	460	600
M_3	265	375	525	680
M_4	300	425	585	760
$M_{4\frac{1}{2}}$	315	445	620	800
M_5	330	470	650	840
M_6	365	510	710	925

Source: N.A.B. Reports (various issues).

The two types of measures or definitions provide different information. The first, i.e. the 'average income' method, shows how the proportion of incomes at the lower end of the scale has changed relative to the base year 1949. The second shows how it has changed relative to the change in the socially acceptable lower income limits. The former indicates the actual change in the lower tail of the income distribution and the latter, in conjunction with the former, the difference between the desired and actual change.

(b)   Definition of high incomes

The definition adopted corresponds broadly to the hypothesis that surtax liability represents the lower limit of a high income level. Though surtax liability is in no manner an accepted or official definition of high income, it is one of the few aspects of social behaviour we can observe on which to base such a valuation. As with the low income index we adopt 1949 as our base year.

Table 3.3   *Lower limits of 'high income' levels*

Family size	($£$p.a.)			
	1949	1954	1959	1963
S_0	2,000	2,695	3,510	4,395
M_0	3,000	4,040	5,265	6,590
M_1	3,640	4,905	6,390	8,000
M_2	4,280	5,765	7,510	9,405
M_3	4,800	6,470	8,426	10,550
M_4	5,460	7,350	9,580	12,000
$M_{4\frac{1}{2}}$	5,720	7,710	10,040	12,570
M_5	6,000	7,985	10,530	13,185
M_6	6,640	8,845	11,655	14,590

In 1949 all incomes above £2,000 p.a. irrespective of family size, were subject to surtax. However, to maintain consistency with our definition of low incomes we must take account of family size. Therefore £2,000 p.a. was adopted as the minimum high income level for a single person only. The minimum levels for other sizes of unit were estimated by assuming that the ratio of the income level of a multi-person unit to a single person unit would be the same as in the low income level estimates. Such a ratio, for each unit size provides a single 'adult equivalence' scale. We were, in effect, using a scale equivalent to that implicit in the 1949 National Assistance Board rates. The levels for the other years were estimated by increasing the 1949 limits by the per capita increase in personal income. The high income part of our inequality index is the proportion of all units at or above the high income limits. The high income levels are given in table 3.3. A valid query is the choice of 1949 as the determinant of the absolute levels. It can also be asked if there was considered an alternative equivalent to the 'trend method' for low incomes for increasing these levels? Since 1949 there has only been one change in the surtax level and this is quite insufficient to derive an equivalent measure to the 'trend' estimates. The absolute level of 1949 was chosen since the 1963 level we considered too high, even in 1949 prices. This is merely a subjective valuation and as such can be contested.

The results of applying the high/low inequality index to the Inland Revenue, type 1 and type 2 distributions are presented in table 3.4. In this table the 'average income' method is used for the low income levels. Estimates using the 'trend' (or actual) N.A.B. scales are given in table 3.5.

Table 3.4 *Percentage proportions of high and low income units ('average income' methods)*

	Inland revenue			Type 1 Units			Type 2 Units		
Year	Low	High	Inequality Index	Low	High	Inequality index	Low	High	Inequality index
1949	4.05	0.59	4.64	18.78	0.46	19.24	—	—	—
1954	3.31	0.44	3.75	22.22	0.35	22.57	22.01	0.35	22.36
1959	4.50	0.37	4.87	16.24	0.30	16.54	16.11	0.30	16.41
1963	2.78	0.32	3.10	16.99	0.25	17.24	16.20	0.26	16.46

Sources: As for tables 3.1, 3.3, 2.2 to 2.10; and A7.1 for the Inland Revenue estimates.

Two obvious conclusions emerge from table 3.4. First, as we may have expected, the inequality index for the Inland Revenue survey data is much lower than for the other distributions. Our objections to the basic Inland Revenue data as a final source (outlined in chapter 1) are substantiated by the misleadingly low inequality indices which emerge. The second main conclusion concerns the relative size of the high and low incomes. The former account for only a very small and steadily declining proportion of total inequality. It may be argued that the 'high income limits' are too high. However, even if they were halved, the proportions would increase only three or fourfold, which would make little impression on the index relative to the low incomes.

The above results indicate that the major area of concern, with respect to inequality, is that of 'low' incomes. This approach, we believe, lends little support to conclusions about inequality based on the income distribution pattern at the top end of the income scale – a method frequently employed in analysis of U.K. data.[1]

The rest of the analysis in this chapter will focus on low incomes. This step is taken for two reasons of convenience. First, in all distributions the proportion of high incomes displays a decreasing trend. Secondly, the changes in the overall index of inequality are clearly determined by changes in the proportion of low incomes. In other words, given the

[1] See Titmuss [70], Paish [56], Brittain [11], Nicholson [53] and several others. Percentile analysis invariably falls into this 'trap'.

constant trend for high incomes, whether there has been a similar movement for general inequality depends on the changes in the proportion of low incomes.

The trend in equality is by no means even over the period. There are not enough observations to enable us to draw any conclusions on the underlying movement, though a slight downward trend is observable. The fluctuation between 1954 and 1959 is, however, large and may reflect some of the data errors in the 1954 Inland Revenue survey.

Table 3.5   *Percentage proportion of high and low income units ('trend' method)*

	Type 1				Type 2	
Year	Low	High[a]	Inequality index	Low	High	Inequality index
1949	18.8	0.46	19.26	—	—	—
1954	22.5	0.35	22.85	23.5	0.35	23.85
1959	18.1	0.30	18.40	17.7	0.30	18.00
1963	21.4	0.25	21.65	20.3	0.26	20.56

Source: As for tables 3.2, 3.3, and 2.2 to 2.10.
[a] Same as for table 3.4. We were unable to devise any suitable 'trend' equivalent for high incomes.

A slightly different pattern emerges when the 'trend' method is used to construct the inequality index (see table 3.5). The rise in the proportion of low incomes from 1959 to 1963 is much larger. Using the 'trend' method the proportion of low incomes is understandingly higher than in table 3.4.

The 'low income unit' concept by itself is not particularly meaningful, particularly as the distribution of family sizes is quite variable from year to year. We are able to overcome this problem by estimating the proportion of total population accounted for by the members of the low-income 'inner' families (see table 3.6). A more definite trend towards greater equality emerges over the period on this basis.

Table 3.6   *Percentage proportion of total population in families with low incomes*

	Type 1		Type 2	
Year	'Average income' method	'Trend' method	'Average income' method	'Trend' method
1949	17.8	17.8	—	—
1954	17.4	18.1	17.5	19.5
1959	12.3	14.4	13.2	14.4
1963	11.9	16.3	12.2	16.3

Source: As for table 3.4.

This trend is especially marked when the 'average income' method is used, indicating that intrinsically the family size/income structure of the community displays a movement towards greater equality. The difference between the estimates by the two methods indicates the divergence between the actual and the desired distribution, the latter being built into the 'trend' method of measurement.

At this point it is interesting to see to what degree changes in the income distribution on the one hand, and in the family size pattern on the other, have contributed towards the movement in the direction of greater equality. Table 3.7 shows the family size pattern for each of the type 1 distributions in each of the years. It is clear that there have been only small changes in this pattern. There is a slight increase in the proportion of single person and five and six person families at the expense of two and three person families.

Table 3.7 *Family size pattern for the type 1 distribution*
(% *of all Units*)

Family size in persons	1949	1954	1959	1963
1	48.2	48.9	48.9	49.8
2	26.0	26.1	24.7	24.3
3	13.5	11.9	12.3	11.2
4	8.0	8.0	8.6	8.8
5	2.8	3.1	3.5	3.7
6 or more	1.5	2.0	2.0	2.2

Source: Tables 2.2 to 2.10.

However, it would be misleading to draw any conclusions about the role of changes in the income structure from the constancy of the overall family size pattern. More relevant for our purposes is the family size pattern of the low income families. This we can look at in two ways. We consider first the number of low income units classified by family size and secondly the proportion of each family size group which comes under the 'low income' definition. For this purpose we use the type 1 distributions with the 'average income' low income limits (see tables 3.8 and 3.9). The results using the other method and the type 2 distributions are virtually identical in structure.

These two tables indicate that the majority of low income units are single persons and that this proportion has increased substantially. The importance of other family size groups has diminished greatly since 1949. The major exception is for the large families, with six or more members. These are still the second largest family size category among the low incomes. The proportion of individuals in the low income group who are members of these large families has risen from 7.69% in 1949 to 10.3%

in 1963 (same definitions and distributions as above). Their importance is more marked by the 'trend' method of estimating low incomes – see table 3.10. The difference between the two sets of data indicates a sizeable bunching of large families between the two low income limits. This bunching is also evident in our other work in this field.[1]

Table 3.8 *Percentage of all low income units classified by family size ('average income' method – type 1 distribution)*

Family size in persons	1949	1954	1959	1963
1	53.3	71.7	72.6	82.6
2	25.6	16.9	16.3	8.0
3	10.7	3.9	4.3	2.9
4	5.6	3.1	3.1	2.6
5	2.5	2.1	1.7	1.7
6 or more	2.3	2.3	1.9	2.3

Source: Tables 2.2 to 2.10, with tables 3.1 and 3.3.

Table 3.9 *Percentage proportion of each family size group consisting of low income units ('average income' method – type 1 distribution)*

Family size in persons	1949	1954	1959	1963
1	20.8	32.6	24.1	28.2
2	18.5	14.4	10.7	5.6
3	14.9	7.3	5.6	4.4
4	13.2	15.0	5.9	5.0
5	16.8	15.0	8.0	7.6
6 or more	27.8	25.0	15.6	17.1

Source: As for table 3.8.

The information in tables 3.9 and 3.10 is not directly relevant to our purpose. Our main use is for table 3.8. We apply the 1949 family size pattern for low income units to the number of low income units in 1963. The difference between the resulting distribution and that in table 3.7 is the change in income equality resulting from changes in the family size structure. We did this for the 'average income' low income estimate for the type 1 distribution. The estimate was that 15.8%, compared to 11.9%, of persons belonged to low income families in 1963. The initial starting ratio was 17.8% for 1949. Thus 61% of the decrease in the low income inequality index from 1949 to 1963 resulted from the change in the family size structure. It would appear therefore that changes in the distribution of income, *per se*, are not the major factor in reducing inequality. The family size structure of society, it might be said, is changing to accom-

[1] See I. P. Gough and T. Stark [28].

modate itself to the structure of incomes, particularly with respect to low incomes. This hypothesis is supported by the differences between the inequality index obtained by using an income units base and that which results from adopting a persons base. The former indicates more or less constancy in equality, the latter a trend towards greater equality. This trend is, however, less in evidence when using the 'trend' method of estimating low incomes (see table 3.6). In this case the 'income unit' base index displays a slight movement towards greater inequality (see table 3.5).

Table 3.10   *Percentage proportion of each family size
group consisting of low income units ('trend' method –
type 1 distribution)*

Family size in persons	1949	1954	1959	1963
1	20.8	32.6	26.2	33.9
2	18.5	14.7	12.0	7.7
3	14.9	7.8	6.7	7.0
4	13.2	9.4	7.7	8.6
5	16.8	16.5	11.2	14.3
6 or more	27.8	28.5	21.7	27.1

Source: As for table 3.9.

A general conclusion at this stage may therefore be that a combination of changes in the family size structure and the distribution of income is reducing the proportion of persons dependent on low incomes ('average' income method), but that this rate of change is insufficient to make much impression on the socially acceptable level of low income. On the latter basis the level of inequality has remained fairly constant from 1949 to 1963 (see table 3.5), with the exception of a large fall in inequality in 1959.

3.3   THE 'PER ADULT EQUIVALENT' DISTRIBUTION

The above analysis has two important disadvantages. First, it is cumbersome. Each time we must work our way through an income and family size distribution, present our results in both units and persons and, in order to achieve some insight, by family size grouping as well. These difficulties can be overcome to a large degree by a 'per adult equivalent' distribution.

Implicit in the definitions of 'high' and 'low' incomes already outlined is the assumption that there are savings in per capita expenditure as family size increases. A family of five does not have one-fifth the standard of living of a single adult with an identical income. An equivalence scale between single person and larger families is embodied in the N.A.B. scales we adopted for the high/low income limits.

Such an equivalence scale is derived from calculations of (a) unit-consumer scales and (b) economies of scale in consumption.[1] A unit-consumer scale shows the income required to maintain persons of different ages (and sometimes sexes) at an equivalent standard of living. The N.A.B. uses such a scale when calculating the needs of a family. They distinguish six age groups, the allowance for an extra person over 21 years of age being about three times that for a child under five. The adult fraction, or children's element, is the most important factor in the savings in per capita expenditure in this category. The economies of scale accounted for in an equivalence scale consist mainly of the 'sharing' of overhead costs, such as rent, fuel and power, household items and consumer durables. Food consumption may also be subject to economies of scale, through cheaper bulk purchase and a reduced wastage factor. The N.A.B. do make an allowance for these economies of scale, but in a most indirect manner. A distinction is made in the basic scales (i.e. excluding rent payments) between single persons and couples. Beyond this there appears to be no allowance – the fifth child of a given age would entitle the family to the same increase in grant as the first child. However, this is offset to some extent when we include rent payments. These, which are based on actual rent payments, do not vary much with the number of children, though they do vary between single persons and larger families. In our estimates of the low income index we permitted only one variation in rent payments, between single persons and units consisting of two or more persons.

The second disadvantage of our analysis in section 3.2 concerns the appropriateness of the equivalence scale implicit in our indexes. Jackson [31] argues convincingly that the implicit equivalence scales in the N.A.B. rates give an incorrect picture: 'the National Assistance scales become progressively less adequate as family size increases'.[2] He reaches this conclusion by comparing the expenditure of the average retired person receiving £4 per week in 1962 with that of larger households, consisting of married couples with and without children. Most of his data is from the Ministry of Labour *Family Expenditure Surveys*. The equivalence scale implicit in Jackson's own estimates is somewhat more dispersed than that of the N.A.B. (see table 3:11). However, he neglects housing costs. If these are included his scale is only slightly more dispersed. (Again see table 3.11.)[3]

It may be argued that the above equivalence scales are relevant mainly to low income families. For instance they correspond closely to the scale implicit in the U.S. Social Security Administration's 'low-cost budget'

[1] For the most detailed analysis of the problems involved here see Nicholson [54].
[2] See [31] p. 242.
[3] I am grateful to Mr I. P. Gough for these points.

limits (see Orshansky [55]). If we wish to construct a 'per adult equivalent' distribution it is essential that we have an equivalence scale based on some average standard for the population as a whole. Nicholson [53] explicitly adopted such a scale for his work on the redistribution of income in the U.K. This scale is applicable to all income levels. It is far more dispersed than previous scales outlined, allowing for a greater cost for a wife and for each additional child (see table 3.11). Much of the dispersion may, however, be attributable to the fact that it is derived solely from data on food expenditure. The economies of scale in housing, etc. are ignored.

The Nicholson scale is clearly an overestimate of equivalence costs, while the Jackson and N.A.B. scales probably underestimate them. The appropriate scale lies somewhere in the middle. Therefore, for want of a better suggestion, we took a geometric average of the three scales – Nicholson, Jackson (excluding rent) and N.A.B. (see table 3.11).[1]

Table 3.11 *Comparison of equivalence scales*

Family size	N.A.B. plus rent (1964)	Jackson excluding rent (1962)	Jackson including rent (1962)	Nicholson	S.S.A. low-cost (1963)	'averaged' scale
S_0	1.00	1.00	1.00	1.00	1.00	1.00
M_0	1.50	1.60	1.55	1.85	1.44	1.60
M_1	1.82	2.10	1.96	2.43	1.68	2.10
M_2	2.14	2.53	2.29	2.87	2.12	2.50
M_3	2.40	2.96	2.61	3.24	2.48	2.80
M_4	2.73	3.38	2.94	3.58	2.79	3.20
$M_{4\frac{1}{2}}$	2.86	3.60	—	3.76^a	—	3.40
M_5	3.00	3.81	3.25^a	3.95^a	—	3.60
M_6	3.32	4.30	3.64^a	4.30^a	3.40^b	4.00

Sources: Hemming [30] table 13; Jackson [31] table 1, p. 239; Nicholson [53] p. vii; Orshansky [55] table E, p. 28.
[a] Extrapolations.
[b] Families of five or more persons.

The estimation of the per adult equivalent distribution, given the equivalence scale, is relatively straightforward. The process is identical to that used in deriving the per capita distribution, with the difference that the actual family sizes are replaced by their adult equivalents. For instance, a four person unit now becomes a '2.5 adult person' unit. If we return to the income/family size matrix of the type 1 and type 2 distributions by income units, as abstracted at the beginning of chapter 2,[2]

[1] The 'more dispersed' Jackson scale was chosen to prevent any bias toward the 'low income' element in the averaging. A geometric average was used in order to prevent bias from extreme values.
[2] See p. 23 above.

Table 3.12   *The per capita distribution of income on a 'per single adult equivalent' basis*

a. Type I distribution

Income range (£)	1949 Adults ('ooos)	1949 Income (£m)	1954 Adults ('ooos)	1954 Income (£m)	1959 Adults ('ooos)	1959 Income (£m)	1963 Adults ('ooos)	1963 Income (£m)
<200	22,718.55	2,912.67	13,491.09	1,921.95	6,000.56	805.56	4,276.25	728.68
200–	9,493.58	2,354.23	11,049.41	2,743.18	9,984.61	2,510.13	6,289.24	1,599.99
300–	3,270.12	1,127.70	7,023.34	2,438.45	9,524.73	3,294.60	8,129.13	2,855.39
400–	1,245.27	553.60	3,641.94	1,621.55	5,589.82	2,500.91	7,014.78	3,153.35
500–	568.83	309.90	1,620.75	883.41	3,357.20	1,833.52	4,841.60	2,672.55
600–	325.08	210.70	809.00	520.78	2,054.68	1,327.53	3,542.12	2,291.84
700–	199.23	148.20	396.05	296.11	1,081.56	807.16	2,206.92	1,651.80
800–	241.09	213.90	397.71	352.67	990.94	879.45	2,306.22	2,065.95
1,000–	273.79	328.80	394.09	475.77	741.15	877.65	1,571.58	1,839.19
1,500–	112.89	192.20	156.97	268.19	236.82	408.93	398.24	671.53
2,000–	83.95	201.70	115.10	274.83	172.99	413.66	251.72	601.20
3,000–	44.06	163.50	61.196	231.25	89.54	334.27	138.59	522.61
5,000–	21.275	141.30	25.729	173.89	37.27	246.01	51.348	342.97
10,000–	5.268	71.70	5.348	74.16	8.265	106.00	9.547	125.50
20,000+	0.727	31.90	0.727	35.81	1.465	52.62	2.155	71.45
Total	38,603.71	8,962.0	29,189.35	12,312.0	39,914.60	16,398.0	41,029.34	21,194.0

Table 3.12 (*contd.*)

b. Type 2 distribution

Income range (£)	1954		1959		1963	
	Adults ('ooos)	Income (£m)	Adults ('ooos)	Income (£m)	Adults ('ooos)	Income (£m)
<200	13,557.73	1,927.18	6,381.83	890.82	4,364.96	733.40
200–	10,729.95	2,689.20	9,351.16	2,370.50	5,996.61	1,525.93
300–	7,113.49	2,469.68	9,531.70	3,303.21	8,048.81	2,827.12
400–	3,667.98	1,632.99	5,597.10	2,507.66	6,995.08	3,145.70
500–	1,627.95	885.02	3,441.59	1,880.58	4,841.94	2,671.90
600–	817.70	528.68	2,015.01	1,304.30	3,547.15	2,295.62
700–	393.37	293.30	1,085.56	811.14	2,212.60	1,653.20
800–	398.89	355.19	998.55	885.58	2,334.42	2,089.86
1,000–	394.19	473.31	738.41	874.33	1,613.57	1,886.64
1,500–	156.97	268.17	244.75	415.08	410.74	691.23
2,000–	115.10	274.88	172.36	413.47	256.36	609.24
3,000–	61.196	231.34	89.54	334.93	139.63	525.40
5,000–	25.279	173.93	37.27	246.71	51.348	341.46
10,000–	5.348	74.16	8.265	106.60	9.547	125.77
20,000+	0.727	35.57	1.465	53.09	2.155	71.53
Total	39,066.32	12,313	39,694.56	16,398	40,824.93	21,194

Sources: As for tables 3.11 and 2.2. to 2.9.

then for each cell, N_{ij}, the per adult equivalent range limits are, for any range i and family size j,

$$\frac{Y_i}{a_i} \cdots \frac{Y_{i+1}}{a_i},$$

where a_i is the adult equivalent of the family size j. Calculations of this nature are performed on each cell. Collation and interpolation, to avoid overlapping, provide us with the per adult equivalent distributions. (See table 3.12.)

The application of the inequality index to these distributions is also a staightforward affair. Since the distribution is expressed in terms of single adult equivalents the degree of inequality will consist of the proportion of such equivalents below the low income limit for single persons and above the high income limit, similarly for single persons. It is clear that, if we were to calculate the degree of inequality similarly for the per capita distribution, the proportion of low incomes would be grossly over-estimated and that of high incomes underestimated.[1]

The inequality indexes for the per adult equivalent distributions in table 3.13 do not display a consistent trend towards either greater or less inequality, though in all cases the highest level of inequality recorded is in 1949. The lowest is in 1959, as is the case in the previous indices calculated in this chapter; this appears to be the most egalitarian year of all. Again the 'trend' measure records a higher level of inequality for the more recent observations. In this instance the rise in inequality since 1959 is quite marked.

The levels of inequality in table 3.13 are very similar to those in section 3.2. They will not, of course, be identical to either the 'units' or 'persons' indices of that section. The difference both in the measurable base, i.e. adult equivalents as opposed to units or persons, and in the equivalence scale used accounts for the divergences between the various indices.

There are, in this chapter, twelve different measures of inequality for the type 1 and type 2 distributions. Of these twelve only two result in a clear movement towards greater equality over the four observations. None, on the other hand, points towards a steady inegalitarian trend. Of the remaining ten, seven display an unevenness, but with the level of inequality less in 1963 than in 1949 or 1954. For the other three we also have unevenness, but the level of inequality is higher in 1963 than in 1954 for two of them, and higher in 1963 than in 1949 for the other.

Our analysis therefore lends little support to the popular belief that there has been a discernible movement toward greater equality and no

---

[1] E.g. for the type 1 per capita distribution, the low income proportions using the 'average income' low income estimates were 50%, 41%, 36%, and 35% for 1949, 1954, 1959 and 1963 respectively.

support to the opposite 'reaction' by som.: academics. Even if we were to adopt some of the more common statistical measures of inequality we would find that the results, with respect to greater or less inequality vary according to the type of measure and type of distribution.[1]

Finally, a few comments are necessary on the exact meaning of our inequality index. In all instances it is dominated by the proportion of low incomes. As previously mentioned, we must caution the reader on drawing any conclusions concerning poverty levels. At the most we only measure potential poverty, that is, the number of persons whose incomes are such

Table 3.13 *Inequality indices for the 'per single adult equivalent' distributions (% of low and high incomes)*

	Type 1			Type 2		
Year	Low	High	Inequality index	Low	High	Inequality index
a. 'Average income' method						
1949	23.36	0.40	23.76	—	—	—
1954	18.36	0.30	18.66	18.51	0.30	18.81
1959	13.92	0.26	14.18	14.88	0.26	15.14
1963	15.82	0.21	16.03	15.85	0.21	16.06
b. 'Trend' method						
1949	23.36	0.40	23.76	—	—	—
1954	18.36	0.30	18.66	18.51	0.30	18.81
1959	16.30	0.26	16.56	17.20	0.26	17.46
1963	20.50	0.21	20.71	20.40	0.21	20.61

Sources: As for tables 3.12, 3.1 and 3.2.

that they could be poor. Whether they are poor or not will depend largely upon the incidence of taxation, the effect of household formation, and other sources of income. Household formation, in this context, means the sharing of certain overhead costs by 'inner families' grouping together. A typical grouping may well be an old person and a married couple with children. The other sources of income we have in mind are fringe benefits, income in kind, capital gains, etc. We shall deal with some of these in chapters 4 and 5.

One may be tempted to argue that a large amount of potential poverty is a necessary condition for substantial actual poverty. One could go further and suggest that welfare policies should be aimed at those who are both poor and potentially poor. The first suggestion, though likely to be true in most instances, does not necessarily hold in all. There are three main

[1] See appendix 3.

areas of divergence between our estimates of low incomes and the 'real' level of poverty. First, the increase of direct taxation in the low income groups could increase the number of actual poor vis-à-vis the potentially poor. Secondly, our low incomes include some part-year single person incomes, which on a whole year basis would not necessarily be classified as low incomes. There are, for example, the incomes of school-leavers (leaving in July or September) and those of single persons dying early in the year. The aggregate total of these and similar items is not large, accounting for approximately 10 to 15% of all low income units, i.e. 2 to 3% of all units.[1] Thirdly, a low income this year may be well balanced by a high income next year. Some sections of the community have highly variable income patterns. Thus conclusions from single year distributions could be quite misleading. Data published by the Inland Revenue indicate that between 1958–9 and 1959–60 2½ million persons out of the 17 million covered by the investigation had incomes that fluctuated by 25% or more.[2] A paper by Professor A. R. Prest and the author has also shown that the degree of dispersion (as measured by Gini's concentration ratio) is substantially reduced when income distributions are based on 'averaged' incomes over two-year periods.[3] This, however, is a fault of all contemporary income distributions and poverty studies in the U.K., including our own.

As far as the second suggestion is concerned, the author considers, in view of the lack of comprehensive and alternative sources of data and the fact that an invariably high proportion of low incomes (potential poverty) is a prerequisite for a high level of actual poverty, that policy suggestions based on the above definitions are acceptable. A number of improvements could be made. The 'spuriously' low part-year incomes could be eliminated. That is a simple task. An extremely difficult, but necessary, task would be a post-taxation analysis, including if possible the whole spectrum of taxation.

---

[1] See Gough and Stark [28] p. 179.   [2] B.I.R. [19] 105, table 137.
[3] Cf. Prest and Stark [60] pp. 231 to 233.

4

CAPITAL GAINS

In this chapter and chapter 5 an attempt is made to quantify the possible distributional effect of a number of elements not included in the definitions of income used in previous chapters. These elements are loosely grouped under two headings: capital gains and fringe benefits (see chapter 5).

Capital gains are defined, for our purposes, as the net increase in the value of personal wealth during a year, irrespective of whether it has been realised or not. Such an increase is part of income when defined as 'an accrual of economic power' or 'command over resources'. The theoretical arguments in favour of this comprehensive definition are outlined in chapter 1.[1] It is an approach to capital gains which has had considerable support from a number of American economists, notably H. Simons [68], as well as the Minority Report of the 1956 U.K. Royal Commission on Taxation [65]. Furthermore, we have pragmatism on our side. There is absolutely no information which could be used to estimate or even hazard a guess at the proportion of 'wealth appreciation' which may have been realised. In this respect at least, two post-war attempts to estimate capital gains were forced to adopt a similar definition.[2]

There is a substantial difference between our concept of capital gains and that embodied in the recent U.K. tax changes. For the purpose of the U.K. capital gains tax, such gains are divided into two categories, long-term and short-term capital gains. The reason is that a different structure of tax rates applies in each case. A short-term gain is defined as a capital gain realised within twelve months. Long-term gains are realised gains where the time between buying and selling exceeds a year. The tax system therefore only recognises realised gains and does not restrict itself to gains occurring in one year only. In other words it is possible under the present system to be taxed on the accumulation of a number of annual capital gains. The lower marginal tax rate on long-term capital gains than on other forms of taxable income could be justified in this manner.

The definition of capital gains in this chapter embodies net appreciation on all forms of *Personalty and Realty*, at least in principle. This is another major difference from the fiscal concept. There are a number of exceptions to the U.K. capital gains tax, such as owner-occupied property, motor cars,

---

[1] Cf. section 1.3.
[2] Cf. Dow [23] pp. 254–65, and Royal Commission on Taxation [65] appendix IV, pp. 465–70.

national savings certificates, bonuses on life insurance policies and certain gains on government securities issued at discount.

It is clear then that any estimate of income from capital gains which used data from tax returns, were it available for our period, would be incomplete both in coverage and in its approximation to income in the pure sense. It is perhaps this less than meaningful concept of income embodied in the capital gains tax that has led to a structure of varying rates and exemptions in order to preserve equity. An alternative scheme might have been to tax the net increase in the value of wealth. This could conceivably be as profitable to the Chancellor, though there is no doubt that the administrative costs incurred by an annual valuation of all estates would be high. However, if the U.K. ever adopts a wealth tax then such costs will be incurred. In this event savings may result if the present system of capital gains tax is abolished and the wealth tax turned into a capital appreciation tax. Again it is merely a simple matter to choose the exemption limits and tax rates which ensure that the net revenue from this tax equals that of a separate capital gains tax plus a wealth tax. A saving in administrative costs would undoubtedly lower the burden of the taxes on the economy and the provisions for equity would become much simpler, if not better. However, all this is, of course, a digression from the main thread of our discussion.

An estimate of aggregate personal wealth, by type of asset, is the essential basis for any calculation of capital gains. The estimation of personal wealth has long been a popular activity among applied economists in the U.K. The 1930s saw most of the pioneering work undertaken by Mallet [42], Campion [12] and G. P. M. Campion and Daniels [13] and Barna [5]. The technique adopted by these writers was the 'estate' multiplier method'. The only other technique – the Giffen 'Income' method, which basically involved the capitalisation of private incomes over a number of years – was rarely used.

The 'estate multiplier method' has been well described in several academic and official works on wealth statistics.[1] Briefly the method uses estate duty statistics, published by age and sex group, from which it is assumed that the total wealth per age and sex group can be estimated by multiplying the capital of the deceased in each category by the reciprocal of the relevant mortality rate. To allow for the fact that the rich, who presumably possess most capital, have a lower mortality rate, the mortality rates used are often those for the higher social classes. The criticisms of this method relate first to the representativeness of estate duty capital with respect to all forms of wealth, and secondly to the degree to which the deceased can be considered as a random sample of wealth holders of each age and sex group – particularly in the younger age groups. These problems will be discussed at a later stage in this chapter.

[1] See particularly Barna [5], Morgan [52], and B.I.R. [19] Reports.

Since 1945, private estimates, along the lines of those by Barna, etc., have been published by Langley [36] (for 1946–7), Cartter [14] and [15] (for 1947–9), Morgan [52] (for 1953, 1954 and 1955 separately), Lydall and Tipping [41] (for 1961) and finally Revell [62] (for 1957 through to 1961). The first two estimates are extrapolations of pre-war data and are averages for the years listed above. As such they are unsuitable for our purposes. We do, however, make use of Morgan's work for 1954, and Lydall and Tipping's projected to 1963. Unfortunately Revell's outstanding piece of work was published after our research was completed, and we regret that we were unable to utilise his data.

The most important development, however, has been that, for 1960 and every year since, the Inland Revenue has produced estimates of personal wealth. The Board uses the 'estate' technique and presents more detailed estimates than were formerly available. Much of this greater detail is essential if capital gains are to be allocated to income groups. This is, of course, our eventual aim. These estimates provide the sole source for our 1959 estimates and the major source for the 1963 estimates, supported by data from Lydall and Tipping [41]. The Inland Revenue estimates also enable us to make comparisons of aggregate capital gains for 1960, 1961 and 1962 and those of 1959 and 1963 data. There are a number of major sources of data for 1954. This is somewhat of a 'hotchpotch' estimate, as will be evident when the estimation procedures and data sources are briefly outlined at a later stage in this chapter. As we shall see, estimates of personal wealth are subject to considerable inaccuracy. Therefore our choice of data sources has been determined largely by comparability. We have attempted to use data which were similarly estimated for all the years concerned. It is for this reason that we make no estimate for 1949.

There are unfortunately numerous sources of error involved in any estimate of capital gains. These errors are in the main attributable to data imperfections. Their importance can best be illustrated by comparison with the ideal method of calculation, entailing perfect data sources, etc.

The capital gains accruing to an individual over a year consist of the net accretion to the value of his or her wealth stock at the beginning of the year plus the 'part-year' net accretion of new additions to that stock less the 'part-year' net accretion that occurred on the items of the original stock sold during the year.

If we consider an individual i, with a homogeneous asset wealth stock W, held at point of time t, which is the beginning of year $\bar{t}$, then his or her capital gains will consist of first: the increase in the value of this stock over the year, i.e.

$$iW(t)P(t+1) - iW(t)P(t), \qquad (1)$$

where P equals price: and secondly the increase in the value of stock acquired during the year

$$\sum_{a\,=\,1,\,2,\,3} i\Delta W_a(\bar{t})\ [P(t+1)-P(pa)],\tag{2}$$

where ΔW_a is each separate addition to the stock over year $(\bar{t})$ and $P(pa)$ the price ruling at the point of time of each purchase: finally a deduction must be made in respect of the stock disposed of during the year:

$$\sum_{d\,=\,1,\,2,\,3} i\triangledown Wd\ (\bar{t})[P(t+1)-P(Sd)],\tag{3}$$

where $\triangledown Wd$ is each separate deduction from the stock and $P(Sd)$ the price at the time of selling. It is irrelevant to this model whether the sales are of stock purchased during the year or not.

If we allow the individual to hold a stock of several types of assets, denoted W_j, then equations (1), (2) and (3) combined become

$$\sum_{j} iW_j(t)\ [P_j(t+1)-P_j(t)]\ +$$
$$+\sum_{j}\sum_{a} i\Delta W_ja(\bar{t})\ [P_j(t+1)-P_j(pa)]\ -\tag{4}$$
$$-\sum_{j}\sum_{d} i\triangledown W_jd(\bar{t})\ [P_j(t+1)-P_j(Sd)].$$

When summing equation (4) for all individuals in order to ascertain aggregate personal capital gains, sales and purchases within the personal sector can be netted out so that the relevant factors are the creation of new personal wealth less any reduction in the personal wealth stock. Thus equation (4) is summed as

$$\sum_{i}\sum_{j} iW_j(t)\ [P_j(t+1)-P_j(t)]\ +$$
$$+\sum_{i}\sum_{j}\sum_{a} i\Delta W_ja(\bar{t})\ [P_j(t+1)-P_j(pa)]\ -\tag{5}$$
$$-\sum_{i}\sum_{j}\sum_{d} i\triangledown W_jd(\bar{t})\ [P_j(t+1)-P_j(Sd)],$$

which can be modified to

$$\sum_{i}\sum_{j} iW_j(t)\ [P_j(t+1)-P_j(t)]\ +$$
$$+\sum_{i}\sum_{j}\sum_{a} iAW_ja(\bar{t})\ [P_j(t+1)-P_j(pa)]\ -\tag{6}$$
$$-\sum_{i}\sum_{j}\sum_{d} iDW_jd(\bar{t})\ [P_j(t+1)-P_j(Sd)],$$

where AW is the increase of wealth in the personal sector and DW the reduction of such wealth.

Equation (6) is the perfect data model. The data actually available deviate considerably from this desired situation. In the first place there are no data on

$$\sum_i \sum_j i W_j(t).$$

The nearest equivalent is

$$\sum_i \sum_j i W_j(\bar{t}),$$

that is average aggregate wealth stock during year $\bar{t}$ as opposed to the stock at the beginning of the year. Furthermore this stock is not evaluated by the use of prices at any point of time in the year, but by an average of prices over the year, which is biased towards prices in the first and fourth quarters because a majority of the deaths from which

$$\sum_j W_j$$

is estimated occur in these quarters.[1]

The solution which we adopted to this initial problem was to assume that the relevant average price of each asset over the year could be approximated by an average of quarterly prices weighted by the proportion of deaths recorded in each quarter. This average was then compared to the beginning- and end-of-year prices of each asset. The percentage change between these two prices and the weighted average was then used to extrapolate the beginning- and end-of-year values of the stock of each asset.

Since the base data are presented in the form of an annual average it is clearly impossible to estimate additions and deductions for each asset over the year, let alone the points of time at which these transactions occurred. One possible solution to this problem is to assume that the value of *net* additions to personal wealth can be estimated by using the difference between the end-of-year approximation and the beginning-of-year approximation for the following year. The actual capital gain involved would consist of this difference measured at end-of-year prices (already given), less the difference measured at purchase-date prices. The implicit assumption here is that the transaction dates of the additions and deductions to personal wealth coincide. A further assumption concerns the purchase prices, for which we have no data. In this case it was assumed that all purchases were made at the unweighted average price over the year.

[1] Cf. B.I.R. [19] 108, para. 27(b), p. 163.

This solution is, however, only possible for the 1954 and 1963 estimates of capital gains. For 1959 we were forced to use a backward extrapolation of the 1960 data, there being no personal wealth data available for that year. The 1959 estimate of capital gains, before the adjustment for additional wealth, will therefore be an overestimate by the amount of the net additions to personal wealth during 1960, deflated to 1959 prices. This is to some extent offset by the inability to make the 'net additions' adjustment for that year. For the other years estimates of capital gains have been made both with and without this particular adjustment.

It is clear that data imperfections have resulted in a considerable deviation from the ideal situation. The position becomes even less favourable when account is taken of the base data errors and the paucity of price indices for some assets.

The Inland Revenue list seven possible sources of error in their wealth statistics. The first concerns the field covered by the estate multiplier technique. They point out that the estates of only about 40% of persons dying in a year are subjected to grants of representation or estate duty. The rest are presumably those where there is no estate or the assets 'are of a kind, such as national savings certificates, where special statutory arrangements exist for transfer without grant in small cases, usually less than £100'.[1]

The fact that not all deaths are covered by the technique reduces to some extent the grounds for believing that estate duty statistics can be held to constitute a representative sample for each age and sex group. The Inland Revenue have partly overcome this by varying the mortality rate used according to the size of the estate. For estates above the £3,000 estate duty exemption limit (now £5,000) the mortality rates for the professional and managerial classes are used (i.e. Social Classes I and II in the Registrar General's Census of Population). For estates below £3,000 a mortality rate mid-way between the above and the national average for each group is adopted.[2] Nevertheless, the Inland Revenue still warns that errors due to unrepresentative sampling can be large, particularly in three cases: the youngest age group, the large estates and the estates of less than £3,000.

There is some overlapping in the above cases. A large number of the estates below £3,000 belong to persons under 25. The number of deaths in the under-25 group is very small and consequently the sample can be very biased by the inclusion of one very large estate, as can the overall distribution for large estates. These errors have been reduced by combining the respective figures for all years for the above-£40,000 estates and under-25 deaths and, after allowing for growth, producing a smoother

---

[1] B.I.R. [19] 108, p. 163, para. 27(a).
[2] For further details see B.I.R. [19] 107, p. 164, para. 11 and B.I.R. [19] 108, p. 162, para. 25.

series for each year. The growth element is determined by reference to other age groups.[1] Since 1963 the sampling fraction for these problematic groups has been increased, giving more information, particularly on the age stratification of the under-25 age segments; as a result, the mortality rates for these persons have subsequently been modified. This, in addition to the provision of further data on the 'age not specified' group, has caused the revision of some earlier estimates,[2] which is why there are variations in the estimates in different B.I.R. [19] *Reports* for the same year.

The other source of error pointed out by the Inland Revenue is the underestimation at death of some items of wealth. The obvious example is cash. On the other hand, items such as life assurance will be overstated, since these are valued in estate duty statistics at the sums assured plus bonus. This is generally more than their market value. It is also likely, however, that the number of life insurances may be too low, since a number of types of life policy are not subject to probate or duty, for example industrial branch death claims, discretionary trust life policies, non-aggregable policies and 'life of another' policies (in the industrial branch).[3] Many of these types of life policies never appear in estate duty statistics or may appear as separate estates.

These categories of life insurance are not the only types of asset that can be omitted from estate duty statistics. Settled property passing when a surviving spouse dies who had no power to dispose of the capital, other forms of discretionary trusts, etc., are examples of items that escape estate duty. In addition to these, annuities and similar assets may disappear altogether at death.

At the other extreme there are errors due to possible double-counting. Gifts *inter vivos* may be counted in both the donor's and the donee's estate. The number of cases may also be overestimated for the technical reason that settled property is usually recorded separately from free estate property in the statistics. This can lead to the number of items, though not the amounts, being reported more than once.

A final source of error is that estate duty statistics do not refer to deaths occurring in a year, but to those estates on which duty was first paid during the year in question. The evaluation of the property may have taken several years and the payment of duty may be spread over a number of years. During the period after the first payment of duty the value of the property may be adjusted. The statistics of the value of property include 'amounts arising from adjustments to estates that first appeared in earlier years and therefore valued at prices then ruling. Similarly, new items of

---

[1] Cf. B.I.R. [19] 105, pp. 272–3.
[2] Cf. B.I.R. [19] 107, p. 164, para. 11, and B.I.R. [19], 108, p. 162, para. 23.
[3] I am grateful to J. R. Revell for this point.

particular types of property are counted whenever they first appear (even if they belong to earlier estates) but adjustments are not.'[1]

These criticisms apply specifically to the Inland Revenue personal wealth statistics, which we use for our 1959 and 1963 calculations. Morgan's data for 1954 are, however, estimated in a similar manner, i.e. from estate duty statistics; therefore the criticisms are also relevant for this source. An additional factor is that Morgan's data do not incorporate some of the adjustments undertaken by the Inland Revenue in order to overcome such deficiencies.

The errors in the basic data, therefore, may be substantial. To these must be added the errors that arise in the approximation of price changes per asset over a year. Table 4.1 lists the items in the Inland Revenue estimates from which a capital gain can be appropriated. The numbers in the third column are the reference numbers of these items as they appear in the Inland Revenue statistics. Those in the second column are our own numerical classifications.

Table 4.1   *Capital gains assets in the Inland Revenue statistics on personal wealth*

Item (1)	Our Ref. Numbers (2)	Inland Revenue Classification Numbers (3)
U.K. government short term securities	1	3
U.K. government medium term securities plus N. Ireland government and British municipal securities	2	8, 7 and 4
U.K. government long term securities	3	5
2½% undated Consols and similar securities	4	6
Foreign government securities (excluding Commonwealth)	5	10
Commonwealth government securities and private shares and debentures	6	9 and 16
U.K. ordinary quoted and unquoted company shares plus all N. Ireland company stock	7	11, 13 and 15
U.K. preference and debenture shares for quoted and unquoted companies	8	12 and 14
Other foreign shares and debentures	9	17
Life insurance	10	24
Landed property	11	45 to 53

Source: B.I.R. [19] 105, table 192.

The reclassification of items is made necessary by the lack of price indices for certain items. These items are therefore grouped with items which we would expect to display a similar movement in prices. The one exception is Inland Revenue item 23 – household goods, pictures, etc. This item we omit. To our knowledge there are no price indices available for second-hand furniture, antiques, pictures, etc.

[1] Cf. B.I.R. [19] 108, p. 164, para. 27(g).

The grouping in our items 2, 7 and 8 should not be open to much dispute. Commonwealth securities and shares (item 6) are combined since data for each item were not readily available. There is of course no reason why share and security prices should move in the same direction. The reverse is, in fact, the case in recent U.K. experience. Therefore the margin of error may be large in this grouping, though the overall effect is not too important, since item 6 accounts for only approximately $2\frac{1}{4}\%$ of the total gross value of 'capital-gain' property. The margin of error for the 1954 data may be larger. Because of the less detailed nature of Morgan's data we were forced to group items 1 to 4 on the one hand and 7 and 8 on the other. A price change for each of these groups was obtained by a weighted average of the price changes of the constituent items. The weights, however, had to be based on 1960 data.

Current year capital gains on life insurance (item 10) are the bonus increases given in the current year by the company on the sum insured.[1] The Inland Revenue data on the life insurance stock includes these bonuses. Thus the estimates for this item are a part of the wealth stock which should be considered as a capital gain. The estimate was arrived at by applying to the life insurance capital value in the Inland Revenue wealth data the average annual percentage increase in the value of the assets of insurance companies over the previous five years.[2] The results will not be accurate because of the errors present in the estate duty estimates of life insurance. In the 1954 estimates we assumed zero bonuses. We estimated that life insurance companies had made a net loss on the value of their portfolios during the years 1949–54.

Item 11, landed property, is not disaggregated as there were no reliable data available on the movements of land prices on the one hand and house prices, excluding land, on the other. However, there were data on house prices plus land and since residential land and buildings amounted to 95% of all landed property it seemed reasonable to group the landed property items.

Monthly or quarterly data were available for all items except item 11, landed property. They were also unobtainable for item 6 in 1954. In these cases half-year or yearly figures were available. Quarterly indices were constructed by linear interpolation.

The major source of error in the indices chosen is in the approximations that were forced upon us. For items 7 and 8, all but the 1963 capital-gain estimates were based on indices for industrial companies only. For years before 1962 the only 'all company' index was for daily prices only. That

---

[1] Cash bonuses given at death or withdrawal are equivalent to a summation of past annual bonus increases in the sum assured.

[2] We are indebted to Messrs Duval and Cochrane, General Manager and Investment Manager respectively of the Co-operative Insurance Company, for the suggestion of estimating bonuses in this manner.

was the Financial Times (F.T.) geometric index.[1] It would have taken too long to convert this information into the quarterly figures necessary for our calculations. For the years after 1962 these indices are published in monthly form. The errors in this approximation should not be too large. A comparison of the post-1962 data indicates that the two sets of indices moved very closely together.

Foreign shares and securities were assumed to be mainly American and their prices were assumed to follow the price pattern of these items in the Wall Street markets. Commonwealth share and securities prices were calculated as a simple average of Australian, Indian, Canadian manufacturing and South African gold mining share prices. Non-government securities, etc. account for approximately 75% of value of assets included in item 6.

Table 4.2 sets out the estimated capital gains per asset for the years 1954 to 1963. This table includes an allowance for the estimated addition of new wealth during each year. Table 4.3 on the other hand presents the same estimates excluding the adjustment for new wealth. Since, as was mentioned earlier there were no data for wealth in 1959, the 1959 estimate is a backward projection of the 1960 wealth stock and cannot be adjusted for the new wealth additions. The price index for the stock of each asset in each year is an annual average price weighted by the quarterly death rate. Capital gains are calculated by the difference between the estimated December prices of two years. New wealth capital gains or losses are the difference between: (a) the following year's asset stock at beginning-of-year prices and the present year's stock at end-of-year prices and (b) this total deflated to the unweighted average for the present year. In all calculations a year is defined on a December to December basis. It was not feasible to use a 1 January to a 31 December definition. Daily prices are not available for all assets and where they are they occasionally show considerable fluctuations. This could cause over- or under-estimation of real capital gains. It was felt that prices calculated on a monthly average basis would give a more stable and realistic result, as well as being easier to compute.

A comparison of the totals for each year in tables 4.2 and 4.3 shows that the adjustment for the addition or deduction of wealth over the year does not have an important influence on the level of aggregate capital gains. The volume of capital gains fluctuates considerably from year to year. The most influential items appear to be first land and buildings, secondly life

---

[1] The new F.T. Actuaries index began in November 1962. It brought together the F.T. Actuaries Financial and Industrial indices. The latter is a survey of the share prices of 500 companies and the former of 94 companies. The Industrial index has for some time been published in the *Monthly Digest of Statistics* in monthly form and is the index we use. The F.T. geometric index of all share prices is available only in daily form and is published in the *Investor's Chronicle*.

Table 4.2 *Personal capital gains by type of asset including the adjustment for new wealth additions (£m)*

Type of asset	Item number	Year 1954	1959	1960	1961	1962	1963
Short term U.K. securities	1	⎫	−2.5	2.4	1.0	11.0	−5.0
Medium term U.K. securities	2	⎬ 287	26.0	−42.2	114.6	104.0	−2.0
Long term U.K. securities	3	⎬	33.0	−46.6	−13.0	61.0	−7.0
Undated U.K. securities	4	⎭	63.0	−103.3	−125.4	120.0	−24.3
Foreign securities	5	3	−3.4	2.3	−0.7	1.0	−1.8
Commonwealth bonds	6	−20	87.0	13.1	39.0	12.0	15.0
U.K. ordinary shares	7	⎫ 2,383	3,190.0	−513.6	−280.0	527.0	1,977.0
U.K. preference and debenture shares	8	⎭	78.0	−125.4	−114.0	119.0	47.0
Foreign shares	9	45	14.5	−0.6	40.0	−35.0	79.0
Life insurance bonuses	10	—	130.0	224.0	325.0	373.0	400.0
Land and buildings	11	−60	439.0	1,276.0	1,013.0	516.0	1,591.0
Total (rounded)		2,648	4,055.0	680.0	999.0	1,809.0	4,069.0

Note: Item number – see table 4.1.

Sources:

A. *Price Indices*

Items 1–4 C.S.O., *Monthly Digest of Statistics*, H.M.S.O.
5 U.S. Department of Commerce, *Survey of Current Business*: U.S. Treasury Bond prices
6 *U.N. International Financial Statistics, 1965/66 Supplement*
7 C.S.O., *Monthly Digest of Statistics* (H.M.S.O.): F.T. Actuaries index of industrial shares. For 1963 the F.T. Actuaries 'all type' share indices were used.
8 C.S.O., *Monthly Digest of Statistics* (H.M.S.O.): F.T. Actuaries index of industrial preference shares. The debentures index was excluded. These we assumed to have a similar price pattern to preference shares, which in fact they did. For 1963 the F.T. Actuaries 'all type' share indices were used.
9 U.S. Department of Commerce, *Survey of Current Business*: Standard Poors (500) Index
10 *Annual Abstract of Statistics* (H.M.S.O.), plus the sources listed for the above items
11 Co-operative Permanent Building Society [20] Occasional Bulletin. Index of second-hand prices derived from the prices of houses for three size groups weighted by sample data from *O.B.* no. 51, table 1 up to 1962 and *O.B.* no. 59, table 1 for 1962 and 1963.

B. *Wealth Stock*

B.I.R. [19] *Report* nos.: 105, table 192; 107, table 144; 108, table 134. Morgan [52] table 29.

Table 4.3   *Personal capital gains by type of asset excluding the adjustment for new wealth additions* (£m)

Item Number	Type of asset	Year					
		1954	1959ᵃ	1960	1961	1962	1963
1	Short term U.K. securities	⎫	−2.5	0.3	1.0	8.0	−5.0
2	Medium term U.K. securities	⎬ 283	26.0	−41.0	115.0	101.0	−2.0
3	Long term U.K. securities	⎬	33.0	−50.0	−12.0	65.0	−6.0
4	Undated U.K. securities	⎭	63.0	−104.0	−126.0	128.0	−24.0
5	Foreign securities	3	−3.4	2.4	−0.8	1.1	−1.1
6	Commonwealth bonds, etc.	−21	87.0	−2.0	42.0	11.0	16.0
7	U.K. ordinary shares	⎫ 2,417	3,190.0	−496.0	−299.0	482.0	1,974.0
8	U.K. preference and debenture shares	⎭	780.0	−132.0	−106.0	120.0	45.0
9	Foreign shares	55	14.5	−6.0	37.0	−33.0	84.0
10ᵇ	Life insurance bonuses	—	30.0	224.0	325.0	373.0	400.0
11	Land and buildings	61	439.0	1,307.0	970.0	490.0	1,509.0
	Total (rounded)	2,676	4,055.0	603.0	946.0	1,746.0	3,990.0

Sources: As for table 4.2.
ᵃ As for table 4.2. No adjustment possible for 1959.
ᵇ As for table 4.2, since we assumed no bonuses on newly acquired policies.

insurance bonuses and thirdly items 7 and 8 – stocks and shares. It is the movements in the prices of the latter that determine whether the value of capital gains is to be moderate or large.

Having estimated the total value of capital gains for 1954, 1959 and 1963 the next step is to attempt to distribute these gains between income units and income groups. In doing this we will rely heavily on a technique outlined by Cartter [15] for cross-classifying estate sizes with income groups.

Given the yields for various sizes of estates, the technique, briefly, is to allocate the estates to various ranges of investment income, which are then cross-classified by total income size, so that a relationship between estate size and income size can be derived. Capital gains can be brought into this relationship if these can be shown to be some function of estate size.

There are numerous snags with this procedure. Estate and income data are derived from independent sources. Furthermore, the latter are presented in the distributions according to income units and the former according to persons. There is also the additional problem that, though our estimates of capital gains have rightly been made by using the totals for gross wealth, data on the distribution of wealth and persons by estate size are based on a definition of net wealth ranges.[1]

Net wealth, i.e. gross wealth less debt and liability deductions, accounted for approximately 93% of total gross wealth. We have made no adjustment to the wealth range limits to allow for the change from a gross to a net wealth definition. Unpublished data made available to us by J. Revell suggest that the ratio of new wealth to gross wealth is fairly constant irrespective of estate size – see table 4.4. This being the case, projection of gross wealth capital gains on to net wealth groups will not produce a substantial error.

Table 4.4, which breaks down broad ranges of estate size into asset composition, was also used to estimate the yields for these ranges of estate sizes (for details see appendix 4). Reversing the yield/estate range relationship, the implicit estate range for each range of investment income was derived for each year. Our data on the size distribution of personal wealth[2] was accordingly interpolated into these new 'implicit' estate size ranges.

---

[1] For example, see B.I.R. [19] 105, table 193.

[2] The sources for the size distribution of personal wealth were for (a) 1963 B.I.R. [19] 109, table 166; (b) 1959 B.I.R. [19] 107, table 145 (i.e. data for 1960 extrapolated backwards by changes in the value of assets); (c) 1954. This was estimated from three sources: first, the control of personal wealth from Morgan [52] table 30; secondly the control of total persons extrapolated backwards from the 1960 to 1964 Inland Revenue data, mentioned above, and finally the distribution within these limits from Lydall and Tipping [41] estimates for estates above £3,000. Estates below £3,000, which comprised the lowest estate range, were estimated as a residual. This latter adjustment was necessary as Morgan's data did not include the large number of very small estates (i.e. below £200 or £300) as did Lydall and Tipping's estimates. Morgan's data, of course, were chosen for their comparability with the 1959 and 1963 estimates.

Table 4.4 Estimate of personal assets and liabilities as a percentage of gross wealth according to net wealth (i.e. estate) size

Item	Net wealth sizes				
	<3,000	£3,000–£10,000	£10,000–£50,000	£50,000–£250,000	£250,000 and over
U.K. government securities	11.70	12.30	10.22	9.47	7.65
Other government securities	0.03	0.25	1.56	2.19	1.78
Unquoted company stocks	1.69	1.83	8.76	11.79	31.63
Other company stocks	1.42	2.52	18.23	36.51	21.33
Money on mortgages	0.13	1.02	1.72	1.20	1.47
Money on municipal bonds	2.22	9.94	9.45	4.01	1.32
Other debts	3.83	1.44	1.71	1.72	2.53
Household goods	6.41	3.11	2.20	1.64	1.41
Insurance policies	20.41	13.69	5.74	2.21	1.78
Cash	17.29	17.73	10.39	6.91	5.95
Trade assets	3.16	2.25	4.55	1.59	1.21
Miscellaneous personalty	14.53	4.89	8.00	8.70	8.57
Land	0.24	0.70	2.37	4.19	5.84
Buildings	14.16	28.30	14.78	6.77	4.69
Other realty	0.01	0.20	0.32	1.10	2.85
Gross wealth	100.00	100.00	100.00	100.00	100.00
Deductions	10.35	5.08	5.49	4.59	4.95
Net wealth	89.65	94.92	94.51	95.41	95.05

Source: Unpublished data from J. Revell.
Note: Data for the <£3,000 range refers to 1960. That for the other ranges is an average for 1957 and 1958 for England and Wales only.

Graphic techniques were adopted; the 'Pareto' technique having proved itself unsuitable for wealth data.

The next step was to find some relationship between estate size and the extent of capital gains. Table 4.4. was used to calculate the amount of capital gains by estate size in each of our years. Implicitly we were assuming that no significant change had occurred in the structure of capital gain assets over the data period. In all years the ratio of capital gains to total wealth with respect to estate range size increased in a similar but nonlinear manner. The volume of capital gains per estate size range and net investment income range was therefore derivable by graphic interpolation.

The remaining factor was the link between capital gains and total income size. In 1959 the Inland Revenue published a detailed analysis cross-classifying net investment income size by total net income size.[1] This type of analysis had never appeared previously and has only appeared on one occasion since, in the 1964–5 survey.[2] There are, however, similar cross-classifications for most years, for surtax income units. Unfortunately, surtax incomes do not constitute the major proportion of investment income. It is therefore an incomplete source. We overcame this for 1963 by adopting the 1964–5 pattern for incomes up to £2,000 p.a. and the surtax pattern thereafter. In 1954 the surtax data was our only source. It was extended to cover non-surtax incomes, using a procedure outlined by Cartter [14] and used in his studies.

For each of the three years there now emerged a detailed cross-classification between net investment income and total net income by income ranges. The estimated volume of capital gains per net investment range we already have. If we accept the assumption that the structural pattern between net investment and total net income is identical to that between wealth and total income, then we can allocate capital gains to each income range. For example it may well be that a net investment range of £10,000 to £12,000 implies an estate (wealth) range of £310,000 to £375,000. In this estate range we may have 800 persons, a total personal wealth of £283m and capital gains of £50m. It may be that 93.9% of the total net investment in this range falls into the £10,000 to £20,000 income range and 6.1% into the £20,000 plus range. Thus following our assumption, we place 93.9% of the 800 persons, the £283m wealth and the £50m capital gains in the former income range, and so on. This type of adjustment was carried out for each net investment income range. A cross-classification between capital gains, wealth holders and total taxable (i.e. net) income ranges was drawn up along these lines. The resulting cross-classifications are reproduced in appendix 7.

---

[1] B.I.R. [19] 105, table 106.
[2] This survey unfortunately came out when we had nearly finished preparation for this book. This explains why our data do not extend up to 1964.

These cross-classifications provide us with estimates of the amount of capital gains and the number of capital gain recipients in each income range. If we assume that none of the adjustments caused by the elimination of double-countings and the addition of non-taxable income significantly affects the income status of units with investment income between the Inland Revenue and type 1 (units) distributions, then the number of capital gain recipients mentioned above can be readily linked to the number of persons in the type 1 distribution (see table 4.5).

The above assumptions are not too outrageous. The bulk of non-taxable income added to the Inland Revenue distributions is *not* investment income, except in the cases of incomes below the exemption limit, in which instance the income range location of the recipient is unaffected because they are excluded from the Inland Revenue distributions. The double-counting elimination techniques for the type 1 distribution (see appendix 1 below) could only be carried out on the earned income relationship, thereby reducing the possibility of significant effects on incomes with a substantial investment income factor.

The last column in table 4.5 gives the proportion of total persons in each income range receiving capital gains.[1] The movement of persons and their income can be traced when the adjustments were undertaken to derive a per capita distribution from the type 1 distribution by units. If we assume that, for each such movement of persons, the proportion of persons receiving capital gains is the same as that for the whole range in which they were placed in the type 1 units distribution, then the movements of capital gain receivers can also be traced. The per capita distribution can be adjusted to allow for capital gains by adding the average value of the capital gains received in each income range of the type 1 distribution by income units to the average income of the relevant per capita income range, thus linking the movements of capital gains receivers and capital gains, and moving income receivers to higher per capita income ranges where appropriate (see table 4.6).

A preferable technique would have been to marry off the capital gains and income by the addition of income and capital gains ranges, in the same

[1] Some readers may wonder why we did not use, for 1959 at any rate, a cross-classification between investment income units and capital gains. Such a relationship could have been derived from B.I.R. [19] 105, table 106. However, the main snag here would be that approximately half of all income units with investment income are recorded as having zero net investment income and are therefore excluded from the cross-classification of net investment income and taxable income. This would have meant an underestimation of the number of units receiving capital gains. The reason is that capital gains are derived from gross wealth figures, and via a fairly constant ratio to net wealth can be classified by range of net wealth, which in turn via gross yields is related to gross investment income. The relationship between net investment income and taxable income is assumed to reflect that between gross investment income and taxable income. Given these assumptions and manipulations, capital gains are apportioned to income groups, as are the receivers of capital gains. Table 106 is therefore used to extract a pattern, as opposed to an absolute relationship, between investment income and taxable income.

Table 4.5 *Capital gains, and persons receiving capital gains[a], per income range of the type 1 distribution by units*

Income range (£)	1954 Capital gains (£m)	1954 Persons receiving capital gains ('000s)	1954 Proportion of persons receiving capital gains per range (%)	1959 Capital gains (£m)	1959 Persons receiving capital gains ('000s)	1959 Proportion of persons receiving capital gains per range (%)	1963 Capital gains (£m)	1963 Persons receiving capital gains ('000s)	1963 Proportion of persons receiving capital gains per range (%)
50–	498	8,572	80.22	153	3,222.9	48.5	154	1,457	33.4
250–	63	822	35.88	55	865	43.5	65	572	
300–	133	1,364	22.95	141	1,712	49.3	244	2,036	70.33
400–	185	1,307	17.28	171	1,647	38.5	206	1,418	45.88
500–	162	1,143	15.24	162	1,560	27.7	214	1,320	36.95
600–	111	886	14.88	155	1,446	22.4	207	1,233	28.19
700–	80	652.5	15.53	158	1,298	20.72	174	1,073	22.18
800–	143	837.7	23.06	235	2,098	23.9	361	2,212	21.59
1,000–	192.5	870.8	43.94	429	2,712	42.5	596	3,871	29.30
1,500–	129	370.4	61.47	311	898	73.5	355	1,493	42.39
2,000–	243.5	337.2	81.9	498	594	75.5	404	1,099.5	86.31
3,000–	255	170.5	65.49	492	262	62.2	376	541	93.95
5,000–	286.4	58.5	52.0	529	69	42.25	352	158	55.72
10,000–	155.5	7.2	27.69	256	7.4	23.9	205	11.8	23.45
20,000–	39.1	1.2	27.91	310	1.7	25.4	77	1.7	19.54
Total	2,676	17,400	34.00	4,055	18,393	35.12	3,990	18,497	34.24

Sources: As for tables 2.3, 2.4, 2.5 and 4.3. Also B.I.R. *Reports* [19] nos.: 109, tables 96 for incomes up to £2,000; 108, table 82 for 1963 Surtax incomes; 105, table 106; 101, table 98.
[a] Excluding any adjustment for the net accumulation of wealth during the year.

Table 4.6   Distribution of per capita income including capital gains (type 1 per capita distribution)

Income range (£)	1954 Number of persons ('000s)	1954 Amount of income (£m)	1959 Number of persons ('000s)	1959 Amount of income (£m)	1963 Number of persons ('000s)	1963 Amount of income (£m)
<200	21,313	2,738	14,927	2,234	9,113	1,457
200—	15,875	3,853	14,697	3,630	11,115	2,805
300—	6,385	2,210	8,781	3,062	10,912	3,748
400—	3,683	1,647	5,334	2,375	7,508	3,387
500—	979	536	3,324	1,829	4,821	2,655
600—	1,035	665	1,481	958	2,940	1,893
700—	433	324	1,058	786	2,639	1,963
800—	424	375	926	816.3	2,079	1,827
1,000—	441	532	837	1,021	1,904	2,317
1,500—	232	405	455	781.9	379	655
2,000—	197	472	230.8	560	279	671
3,000—	86	327	200.5	724.6	219	831
5,000—	68	450	56.6	374.1	70	418
10,000—	7	89	56.1	634.5	15	193
20,000+	9	365	10	666.6	13	364
Total	51,167	14,988	52,356	20,453	54,006	25,184

Source: As for tables 4.5 and 2.6.

way as was done for marriages, scholarships, etc. in chapter 2. However, to work out the matrices which would result from using this technique involves interpolation and, as stated earlier, data derived from the wealth statistics are not suitable for the 'Pareto' interpolation technique. To our knowledge there is no other interpolation technique which could cope with the combination of two widely differing distributions in this manner.

If we compare the per capita distributions before and after the inclusion of capital gains (see tables 4.6 and 2.6), there is little doubt that the shape of the distributions is changed substantially. The degree of dispersion is greater, particularly in the 1954 and 1959 distributions. We can illustrate this in two ways. The first is by a comparison of the Gini concentration ratios (see table 4.7). This measure records an increase in inequality due to the inclusion of capital gains. Though the volume of capital gains in all our years is very large, their inclusion in the type 1 distribution is significantly more even in 1963 than for the two earlier years. In the 1954 and 1959 type 1 units distributions the bulk of the capital gain recipients were in the lower income ranges. This was not the case in 1963. The modal income range of recipients in 1954 and 1959 was the lowest range, i.e. £50–£250. In 1963 it was the £1,000–£1,500 range. The greater dispersion of capital gains in 1963 amongst income units, we believe, accounts for the smaller effect on the inequality (dispersion) index of the per capita distribution.

Table 4.7 *Gini concentration ratios, type 1 person distributions*

Year	Without capital gains	With capital gains
1954	34.78	38.99
1959	35.35	41.03
1963	35.40	36.80

Source: As for tables 2.6 and 4.6.

We have stated elsewhere that we put little confidence in conclusions about inequality derived from measures of dispersion.[1] An alternative is the low/high income index. In table 4.8 we present a comparison of these indices when applied to per capita distributions. We have used the 'average' income method,[2] which in effect gives the proportion of all persons above or below certain limits (as the case may be). The limits change in the same proportion as average income.

It is clear from table 4.8 that the inclusion of capital gains severely distorts the number of incomes at the upper and lower ends of the distribution. There is a sharp reduction in the number of low incomes, and the proportion of high incomes is trebled, though it is still a minor factor in the overall index. This shift into the higher income ranges is even more

[1] Cf. chapter 3, section 1.   [2] Cf. chapter 3, section 2.

marked in the range immediately below the high income limit. For instance, the increase in the number of persons with incomes of £2,000 p.a. and over after the introduction of capital gains is 117% in 1954, 123% in 1959 and 65% in 1963. These are quite dramatic shifts into the upper echelons of the income scale.

Table 4.8 *Proportion of high and low incomes per capita ('average income' method) (% of high and low incomes)*

	Without capital gains			With capital gains		
Year	Low	High	Total	Low	High	Total
1954	41.46	0.29	41.85	27.07	0.62	27.69
1959	35.77	0.13	35.90	27.43	0.55	27.98
1963	35.55	0.25	35.80	23.20	0.57	23.77

Source: As for tables 2.6, 4.6 and 3.1.

It would be misleading to use the index values in table 4.8 as a guide to the absolute level of inequality. The high/low income index is, of course, totally unsuitable for a straightforward per capita distribution. However, the sharp reduction in inequality caused by the inclusion of capital gains suggests that a similar index movement might be expected if we were able to construct a 'per adult equivalent' distribution which incorporated capital gains. Since we have no data at all on the family classification of wealth holders, this is quite impossible. It is also impossible to draw any conclusions about the effect of capital gains on the trend movements in inequality. This again would require per adult equivalent distributions. A comparison of the results in tables 4.8 and 3.13 indicates that we should not expect any similarity in the changes in inequality over time between the per capita and the per adult equivalent distributions.

An overall conclusion to this chapter then is that capital gains are a significant factor in the distribution pattern and would appear to reduce considerably the number of low incomes and increase the number of high incomes. Data imperfections make it impossible to draw more detailed conclusions. There is a glaringly obvious need for an improvement of data sources in this area. In fact it could be justifiably argued that the results of this chapter are rendered useless by virtue of the data imperfections. Nevertheless we feel that two worthwhile achievements have been made. First, we can conclude categorically that capital gains are very important, and secondly we have developed a technique for incorporating the gains into our income distributions. This also has the advantage that it enables suggestions to be made on the form that future data improvements ought to take.

5

FRINGE BENEFITS
AND OTHER MISCELLANEOUS ITEMS
OF PERSONAL INCOME

In the final part of our analysis, an attempt is made to complete the estimates, given our broad definition of income. We use the word 'attempt' literally and advise the reader to treat the results of this chapter, as those of the previous chapter, with some degree of caution.

Broadly speaking, two groups of income have been excluded from our estimates up to this point. The first are fringe benefits, which are the pecuniary and non-pecuniary benefits provided by an employer on behalf of an employee which are not included as a part of taxable income or included in the estimates of personal income made by the C.S.O. This definition must not be confused with the more usual definitions of fringe benefits used in some studies on labour costs.[1] In these cases 'fringe benefits' generally means overtime and bonus payments, national insurance contributions and so on. These are already included in our estimates. The second category is 'unallocated' income. This is that portion of the C.S.O. estimate of total personal income which is not allocated to income ranges.

As in previous chapters we continue with our adopted definition of income. This definition is basically that personal income is consumption plus savings plus net capital gains or losses.[2] With this conceptual definition there was little difficulty in justifying the incorporation of capital gains in the distribution of incomes (see chapter 4). However, if we wish to include some of the items to be discussed in this chapter in personal income, then the above definition cannot be strictly adhered to in every case.

Let us put the problem formally. The saving (or dissaving) part of the Simons definitions conceptually requires that all additions to personal wealth be included and deductions subtracted. Thus incomes, such as pensions, which are solely the result of dissaving, should be netted out in the income distribution statistics and presented as non-existent, symptomatic of a zero command over resources.

If we were to follow this procedure to the letter, a number of practical

---

[1] See Reid and Robertson [61]
[2] Cf. Simons [68]. Simons defined income (p. 49) as the algebraic sum of (1) the market value of rights exercised in consumption and (2) the change in the value of the store of property rights between the beginning and end of the period.

79

problems would arise, quite apart from the question whether it is meaningful, for any given year, to represent pensions as zero incomes. The practical problems are embodied in the presentation of official statistics. Their pattern is generally in opposition to the dictates of the Simons definition – savings tend to be excluded and dissavings included. The best example of this procedure is provided by private pensions, which are included in the Inland Revenue and C.S.O. data, whilst personal (employee) contributions to private pension schemes are deducted. Except for 1963,[1] we have the same situation with state pensions and national insurance contributions. In 1963 both the saving and dissaving portions are included. In that year we have a double-counting. The same can be said for other years with respect to transfer incomes which are financed out of taxation, e.g. national assistance.

The solution to this problem is first to draw a fine distinction between property rights and forced or compulsory savings, secondly to be consistent in our measures and thirdly to modify our income definition to obtain a meaningul measure of income within the restrictions enforced by the data.

It can be argued that 'forced' saving, be it tax or national insurance contributions, produces no increase in personal property rights and hence no decrease, as the 'saver' has no withdrawal rights. The same can be claimed for contributions by employers on behalf of employees. Therefore all national insurance contributions should be treated as a tax and, as no other taxes are deducted from our definition of income, to be consistent these too should be included. We can argue along similar lines with respect to employer contributions to private (superannuation) schemes. In this case the employee has no withdrawal rights. These are savings by the corporate sector on behalf of the personal sector, thus dissaving at a later stage implies no capital (property right) loss by the personal sector. The government sector can be likened to the corporate sector in the case of state schemes. The problematic item is employee contributions to private schemes.

In most cases, employees can recover their superannuation contributions to private schemes if they opt out before the date of retirement. In this sense these savings are additions to personal property rights. However, in other senses they are not. First profits made by the funds cannot in some cases[2] be recouped; secondly, although the personal contribution element of pension payments during retirement may exceed or fall short of actual contributions, the difference at death is not treated as a part of personal wealth. These two points define the fine difference between this form of saving and other types of personal contractual saving.

---

[1] Since 1961 employee national insurance contributions have been included in the income definition.   [2] Especially in uninsured schemes.

We decided to include employee (and employer) contributions in our distributions. The reasons are, in the first place, that they are a part of the income of the contributors. Pilch and Wood argue that 'at the executive level, the cost of providing pension benefits must be seen as an integral part of the company's overall policy on remuneration, incentives and rewards'.[1] We see no reason why this argument should not be extended to all levels of employment. Secondly the inclusion is justified on the grounds of consistency with the treatment of other contractual savings in the official statistics on income distribution. For example, life insurance premiums are not deducted from as here defined.[2] Some critics may claim that official statistics themselves are inconsistent in their treatment of contractual savings – for example mortgage debt repayments are excluded from the income definition. This is not, however, an inconsistency. The repayment of a debt is the reverse of asset accumulation (or saving), but cannot, on the other hand, be equated with the running down of assets, which is dissaving.

A final justification lies in the misleading comparisons that arise when contractual savings (in particular pension contributions) are omitted. If two income units, A, and B, with identical initial monetary incomes, are compared and A is able to deduct contractual savings from his income whilst B is not, then the statistics will record B as having the higher level of income. This is clearly a misrepresentation. A undoubtedly derives benefit, in the form of security, etc., from his saving. In conceptual terms A and B have flows of income, during the period in question, which give them the same current command over resources.[3]

Having decided to include contractual savings, i.e. in particular, employee contributions to private schemes, we are faced with the problem of deducting the proportion which these form of pension incomes, in order to avoid double-counting. There are, unfortunately, no data with which we could possibly make an adjustment of this nature. Therefore no adjustment is made.

A double-counting of this nature may not be such an error as one might suppose. Consider the case where an adjustment is made, reducing the value of some pension incomes. This clearly under-states the standard of living, or the consumption possibilities, of pensioners in comparison to other income units. If we could adjust past or future income distributions to eliminate this double-counting, by a consistent treatment over a lifetime for each individual unit (or person), we would be able to avoid the problem of misinterpretation in any given year.[4] This is, of course, impossible.

---

[1] [59] p. 71.

[2] Life insurance premiums are permitted a two-fifths allowance, however.

[3] A, in fact, has a higher current 'command' if we include employer contributions.

[4] A further conceptual point arises here in connection with the Simons definition. If savings are included and dissavings excluded, the fact that the individual is deriving a benefit, or

Therefore, on the grounds that we have two different sets of individuals as income receivers for any particular year, we include the double-counting. This means that we have in effect partially redefined our concept of income. The consumption element is now defined to include all current payments that do not add to the stock of personal property rights. Property rights, in turn, are defined to exclude assets not considered in fiscal law as part of personal wealth.[1] In this manner we are able to avoid the problem of the transfer within the personal sector of pension incomes and contributions and to permit some double-counting.

There are also a number of difficulties that arise from the incorporation of fringe benefits and income in kind into the income distributions. The problems are, first, which items should be included, and, second, at what monetary value should they be considered as income equivalents.

There is little doubt that fully convertible incomes in kind, which are part of the contract of employment, should be considered as income. To our knowledge only one item of the fringe benefit and 'unallocated' income comes into this category, that is free coal to coal-miners, for which the market value of the coal can be substituted if the employee wishes. Other incomes in kind are not of this nature. Free or factory-cost products in other industries, subsidised meals, transport and travel, etc., are all on a take-it-or-leave-it basis. Few of these items could be sold by the employee on his own initiative at their current market value. Travel, transport costs and factory meals are clearly unmarketable. It is unlikely that free or cheap factory-cost products or luncheon vouchers could be resold by employees at their market values. The question arises, with respect to imperfect convertibility, whether these items should be considered as income or not?

There is no clear-cut answer. Some may argue that by presenting income receivers with such opportunities one is adding to their 'economic' power by induced savings in consumer expenditure. To the extent that any given employee does not take advantage of these subsidised products, on the above line of reasoning, he or she is therefore being remunerated at a lower rate. This is the view taken by the Majority Report of the Royal Commission on Taxation [65] and strongly supported by Titmuss [70].[2] The Royal Commission stated: 'Theoretically all benefits in kind ought to be brought under charge' (to income tax).[3] In general we are in sym-

---

'economic power' at both points of time is denied. In the savings period he is able to satisfy a current desire, which is to save for the future, whilst in the dissaving period he is satisfying his consumption needs at that time. An ideal concept should accept that an income spread over several periods will bring a similar spread of 'economic power'. How to spread these factors is, of course, an insurmountable practical problem.

[1] These items are listed in B.I.R. [19] 109, table 158.

[2] Titmuss [70] chapter 8.

[3] See Royal Commission on Taxation [65] pp. 67–72, and quote from para. 215, p. 69.

pathy with this view. However, taking this argument to its logical conclusion results in an absurdity. Are the expenditure savings accruing to
persons who live in low-price areas or who follow highly rational shopping
plans or who have useful 'trade' contacts also to be considered as additions
to income?

The intuitive answer is obviously, no. The reason for the distinction is,
however, not clear. It may be that one form of expenditure saving results
from employment and the other from a person's ability or good luck as a
consumer. This may be a tenuous reason. However if we are to include all
consumer expenditure savings, etc., logic would require that taxation and
the whole array of the post-tax redistribution distributions of income be
analysed. As stated in chapter 1, this is beyond the scope of this study.
Therefore this distinction must be accepted and will be used as a guideline
in determining which fringe benefits, etc. are to be included as income.

The second problem is the evaluation of 'income in kind'. Theoretically
we should take the market value plus an allowance for the tax which would
be incurred if the same amount of disposable income was received. Where
possible we use market values (in some cases factory cost – see appendix 5),
but make no adjustment for the tax factor. The reasons for not making an
adjustment are: the difficulties of choosing the appropriate tax rates; the
fact that hardly any of these types of income are taxed by the Inland
Revenue, and lastly the fact that fully convertible incomes, included in the
B.I.R. and C.S.O. distributions, do not include a tax avoidance adjustment.
Therefore in order to be consistent and avoid considerable complication
the adjustment is not made.

The final point concerns the treatment of expenses incurred by the
employee in the course of employment and deducted from his or her own
taxable income. It is unlikely that there is much avoidance in this field.
The Inland Revenue are very strict on these matters. The abuse is more
probably in the realm of company taxation and to some extent in schedule
D self-employment and professional income, where entertainment and
company cars can be obtained free of tax. Legislation in 1965 has made
a number of these avoidance techniques impossible. The only one of these
items on which we shall comment is cars, although we shall also have
something to say on tax evasion as distinct from tax avoidance. There is a
complete dearth of data on the other items.

Table 5.1 lists and estimates the items considered in this chapter.

Items 1 to 9 are those components of personal income normally left
'unallocated' by the C.S.O.[1] Our only omissions were grants to universities
and schools and the depreciation allowances of self-employed persons.
The former were not considered as part of personal income and for the
latter there were not enough data, though part of this item is included in

[1] [16] pp. 14 and 123.

Table 5.1   *'Unallocated' income by type of income* ($£m$)

Type of income	Year		
	1954	1959	1963
1. Some income in kind	122	152	171
2. Non-taxable grants	84	90	113
3. Schedule A excess	139	251	541[a]
4. National savings certificates	22	3	41
5. Post-war credits	23	62	30
6. Incomes below £50 p.a.	66	66	85
7. National insurance contributions	532	897	611[b]
8. Superannuation contributions	763	1,235	1,690
9. Investment income of private, non-profit making bodies	244	394	627
10. Labour cost benefits	50	52	66
11. Car subsidy benefits	40	79	108
12. Self-employed persons' expenses and depreciation allowances	38	86	126
Total	2,123	3,397	4,209

Sources: C.S.O. Blue Books [16], and appendix 5 below.
[a] All imputed rent.
[b] Employers' contributions only.

item 12. Data inadequacies also prevented estimates being undertaken for 1949.

The C.S.O. do not normally publish estimates for each of the separate components of 'unallocated' income, but only for the grand total. Table 5.1 is based on a combination of data obtained from the C.S.O. and our own estimates – see appendix 3. Adding on the depreciation element of item 12, we were able to account for 81.1% of unallocated income in 1954, 80.4% in 1959 and 75.2% in 1963.[1] In other words, the proportion of omitted and residual items has risen by 6% over the nine years.

Items 10, 11 and 12 are the fringe benefits group, conventionally excluded from estimates of personal income. The first group, i.e. item 10, includes the provision of housing and recreational facilities, some free or cheap products, creches and subsidised transport by firms for their employees. These we call labour cost fringe benefits. The second group comprises the value of cars which are owned by firms but are at the complete disposal of employees, or personal cars for which a company finances part or all of the running costs. This we call the car subsidy

[1] The C.S.O. Blue Books [16] estimate for the three years: 1954, £2,065m; 1959, £3,351m; 1963, £4,308m. The first nine items in table 5.1 plus the depreciation element in item 12 totalled £2,015m, £3,196m and £3,971m respectively. However, our coverage is not as large as may at first appear. In order to get an accurate idea of the amount of unallocated income covered we must deduct from our total the income of private pensions and annuities. These items are included in the classification by ranges but the contributions for such schemes are not. Since these are merely a form of transfer income within the private sector, if both contributions and pensions are included the value of total personal income will be overestimated. These deductions come to £341m for 1954, £500m for 1959 and £773m for 1963.

fringe benefit. There may be some double-counting between this group and the last item in group 10. However, group 10 is derived from data for manual workers in the main and includes subsidised travel to and from work only in company vehicles, mainly buses.[1] The third group is an estimate of the value of depreciation and expenses claimed by self-employed persons with respect to cars. The car running cost expenses claimed by self-employed persons were estimated on the basis of complete tax evasion. No adjustment was made for the allowance for personal use of a vehicle, which of course cannot be claimed. An adjustment of this nature was made when we were estimating the value of depreciation allowances. In this context we considered evasion less likely.

The twelve types of income enumerated in table 5.1. were reduced to nine groups and each of these nine groups separately allocated to income units classified by income ranges. As we had no data for 1949 it seemed sensible to attempt to bring the above categories of income into the type 2 income distributions. However, in seven out of the nine groups the initial allocation was to income groups of units classified by taxable income size. Therefore two step-by-step adjustments were undertaken in these cases. The first was to allow for the addition of non-taxable income in the C.S.O. distributions and the second to allow for changes in the distribution of income resulting from the elimination of all the double-countings discussed in chapter 2.[2]

Of the remaining two groups, one, non-taxable grants, required only the latter adjustment, as the basic relationship to income groups was expressed in terms of the C.S.O. definition of income, and the other, income below £50 p.a., was brought in directly to the type 2 distributions and thus all adjustments were unnecessary.

Details of the adjustment are not set out in this book (see Stark [69] appendix 6.3). Broadly they amount to a mirror image of the net effect of the adjustments, described in chapter 2 and appendix 1, made to the original Inland Revenue and C.S.O. distributions. A brief outline of the estimation of the initial or original distribution of the above nine categories is set out in appendix 6 and in table 1 of that appendix (i.e. table A6.1).

The final type 2 distribution including these categories of income, after adjustment is made for those income units which would move to a higher income range, is given in tables 5.2, 3 and 4. This adjustment involved a minor but unimportant deviation from the techniques used in chapter 2 and appendix 1 for bringing in new income to the distribution. Details of the adjustment and the problems involved are explained in appendix 6. Tables 5.5 and 5.6 are the per capita, and the 'per adult equivalent',

[1] See Reid and Robertson [61] p. 91 and appendix.
[2] See Stark [69] appendix 6.3, pp. 333–8.

Table 5.2 *Type 2 distribution of income, by income units, including 'unallocated' personal income and some fringe benefits, 1954*

Income range (£)	Number of units ('000s)	Amount of income (£m)	Average income (£)	Persons per unit						
				1 person ('000s)	2 persons ('000s)	3 persons ('000s)	4 persons ('000s)	5 persons ('000s)	6½ persons[a] ('000s)	7 persons ('000s)
50—	7,228.9	1,324.58	183.2	5,911.5	796.4	340.2	91.4	54.1	21.7	13.6
250—	1,024.2	279.7	273.1	837.6	112.8	48.2	12.9	7.7	3.1	1.9
300—	2,775.7	979.0	352.7	1,888.9	535.0	182.9	93.1	43.8	31.9	0.1
400—	2,812.0	1,263.92	449.5	1,472.3	726.9	311.3	176.1	74.9	50.1	0.4
500—	2,930.2	1,619.45	552.67	1,035.3	914.7	483.1	301.5	116.9	77.9	0.8
600—	2,414.2	1,565.78	648.57	444.8	885.6	526.8	344.2	125.3	86.8	0.7
700—	2,124.3	1,590.61	748.8	315.1	801.7	473.7	326.1	129.7	77.3	0.7
800—	2,279.2	2,019.78	886.2	204.8	927.7	521.4	391.5	145.3	87.2	1.3
1,000—	1,355.1	1,582.92	1,168.1	151.7	588.8	277.3	219.5	77.1	39.7	1.0
1,500—	330.6	567.02	1,715.1	56.2	137.1	59.1	52.4	18.3	7.2	0.3
2,000—	202.9	489.88	2,414.4	40.5	82.2	21.2	32.2	11.2	5.2	0.3
3,000—	127.0	477.27	3,758.0	23.3	51.9	19.6	20.2	8.5	3.3	0.2
5,000—	58.8	384.79	6,544.0	11.3	25.4	8.3	8.3	4.1	1.4	—
10,000—	13.2	171.63	13,000.2	2.5	6.9	1.3	1.3	1.2	—	—
20,000+	2.7	94.67	35,063.0	0.6	1.3	0.5	0.3		—	—
Total	25,679	14,411	561.2							

Sources: As for tables 2.7 and A6.1.

[a] 6½ = Six or more.

Table 5.3 *Type 2 distribution of income, by income units, including 'unallocated' personal income and some fringe benefits, 1959*

Income range (£)	Number of units ('000s)	Amount of income (£m)	Average income (£)	Persons per unit							
				1 person ('000s)	2 persons ('000s)	3 persons ('000s)	4 persons ('000s)	5 persons ('000s)	6 persons ('000s)	7 persons ('000s)	8 persons ('000s)
50–	4,502.3	780.96	173.45	3,942.4	295.5	159.1	51.3	33.0	21.0	—	—
250–	1,882.3	513.85	273.0	1,670.45	131.65	41.7	17.6	11.2	7.5	2.2	—
300–	1,017.1	357.11	351.1	845.45	113.05	23.7	11.8	6.5	3.8	1.2	0.6
400–	2,577.6	1,173.10	455.1	1,968.85	414.75	104.2	49.1	23.2	10.8	3.4	3.5
500–	2,093.1	1,146.30	547.1	1,306.5	484.5	167.0	78.8	30.8	12.8	7.9	4.8
600–	2,120.6	1,375.56	648.7	970.0	643.6	327.0	184.5	63.9	21.6	6.2	3.8
700–	2,189.6	1,632.84	746.6	601.4	840.1	369.8	204.0	113.6	39.2	18.0	3.5
800–	3,439.8	3,059.54	889.4	671.75	1,024.95	794.8	595.5	230.5	84.8	26.4	11.1
1,000–	4,213.7	4,939.39	1,172.2	475.6	1,557.0	955.8	754.3	300.5	118.0	42.9	27.9
1,500–	929.9	1,562.59	1,680.4	97.0	381.7	196.2	158.8	62.6	21.5	7.1	5.0
2,000–	493.1	1,167.93	2,368.5	75.1	184.3	90.6	89.6	40.4	9.5	2.2	1.4
3,000–	232.0	858.99	3,702.5	38.9	88.5	39.2	40.8	17.8	5.3	1.1	0.4
5,000–	119.1	757.97	6,364.1	22.1	49.9	16.9	18.2	8.2	3.4	0.4	—
10,000–	21.7	278.79	12,847.5	4.6	11.3	2.0	2.1	1.5	0.2	—	—
20,000–	4.1	153.08	37,336.5	0.9	1.9	0.7	0.5	0.1	—	—	—
Total	25,836	19,760	764.8								

Sources: As for tables 2.8 and A6.1.

Table 5.4 *Type 2 distribution of income, by income units, including 'unallocated' personal income and some fringe benefits, 1963*

Income range (£)	Number of units ('000s)	Amount of income (£m)	Average income (£)	Persons per unit					
				1 person ('000s)	2 persons ('000s)	3 persons ('000s)	4 persons ('000s)	5 persons ('000s)	6½ persons[a] ('000s)
50-	3,083.0	675.82	213.4	2,765.6	194.9	85.1	18.4	14.6	4.4
250-	1,611.3	443.02	274.9	1,401.7	135.2	40.0	18.6	8.8	7.0
300-	2,370.0	831.37	350.8	1,990.4	256.7	53.2	36.2	17.4	16.1
400-	1,239.4	561.20	452.8	972.5	188.9	37.9	19.5	9.5	11.1
500-	1,782.2	988.55	554.7	1,292.2	336.5	74.5	41.4	18.4	19.2
600-	1,681.7	1,089.74	648.0	1,015.7	423.4	112.3	76.0	30.6	23.7
700-	1,787.0	1,343.13	751.6	814.6	509.2	235.2	143.8	58.0	26.2
800-	3,303.3	2,971.91	899.7	1,085.2	1,014.8	555.8	383.0	169.4	95.1
1,000-	5,912.7	7,275.17	1,230.4	945.1	2,124.6	1,183.2	984.9	412.8	262.1
1,500-	2,060.4	3,566.37	1,730.9	214.8	825.7	414.0	365.2	149.5	91.2
2,000-	1,068.5	2,457.71	2,300.1	115.3	449.0	207.5	183.8	76.3	36.6
3,000-	420.0	1,526.28	3,634.0	59.3	160.0	75.8	75.4	35.1	14.4
5,000-	163.8	1,072.82	6,549.6	26.1	66.5	25.3	25.1	14.1	6.7
10,000-	30.4	397.86	13,087.5	5.5	13.1	4.3	4.3	2.7	0.5
20,000+	5.3	177.35	33,462.2	1.3	2.3	0.8	0.8	0.1	—
Total	26,519	25,360.3	956.3						

Sources: As for tables 2.9 and A6.1.

[a] 6½ = Six or more.

Table 5.5 *Type 2 distribution of income, by persons, including 'unallocated' personal income and some fringe benefits*

Income range (£)	1954			1959			1963		
	Number of units ('000s)	Amount of income (£m)	Average income (£)	Number of units ('000s)	Amount of income (£m)	Average income (£)	Number of units ('000s)	Amount of income (£m)	Average income (£)
<200	24,362	3,380	138.7	13,274	1,848	139.2	9,018	1,361	150.9
200–	11,336	2,791	246.2	14,733	3,650	247.7	12,562	3,184	253.5
300–	6,826	2,365	346.5	8,107	2,796	344.9	9,765	3,438	352.1
400–	3,843	1,712	445.5	5,634	2,522	447.6	5,978	2,702	452.0
500–	1,991	1,090	547.5	4,034	2,187	542.1	5,123	2,847	555.7
600–	1,005	653	649.7	2,095	1,356	647.3	3,228	2,108	653.0
700–	490	367	749.0	1,328	991	746.1	2,299	1,728	751.6
800–	509	453	890.0	1,406	1,243	884.1	2,627	2,342	891.5
1,000–	423	505	1,193.8	1,057	1,243	1,176.0	2,290	2,723	1,189.1
1,500–	162	277	1,709.9	293	494	1,686.0	540	917	1,698.1
2,000–	124	295	2,379.0	228	537	2,355.3	350	830	2,371.4
3,000–	61.5	227	3,691.0	107	387	3,616.8	152.5	567	3,718.0
5,000–	28.5	184	6,524.8	50	322	6,440.0	61	397	6,508.2
10,000–	5.2	69	13,269.2	8.4	113	13,452.3	10.2	134	13,137.2
20,000+	1.1	43	39,090.9	1.6	71	44,375.0	2.3	82	35,652.1
Total	51,167	14,411	281.6	52,356	19,760	377.4	54,006	52,360	469.6

Sources: As for tables 5.2, 5.3, and 5.4.

Table 5.6   *Type 2 distribution of income, by 'per single adult equivalence', including 'unallocated' personal income and some fringe benefits*

Income range (£)	1954			1959			1963		
	Number of equivalent adults ('000s)	Amount of income (£m)	Average income (£)	Number of equivalent adults ('000s)	Amount of income (£m)	Average income (£)	Number of equivalent adults ('000s)	Amount of income (£m)	Average income (£)
200	10,867.19	1,684.94	155.04	5,069.6	629.24	124.10	3,033.01	513.07	168.88
200–	8,563.56	2,163.25	253.31	6,457.75	1,671.33	258.81	5,290.85	1,352.45	255.62
300–	8,078.35	2,816.66	348.66	7,044.83	2,462.38	349.53	6,067.82	2,157.85	355.09
400–	5,011.73	2,237.94	446.54	7,574.36	3,396.11	448.37	6,036.85	2,741.45	454.11
500–	2,836.60	1,550.15	546.48	4,438.09	2,416.68	544.53	5,281.45	2,939.17	556.50
600–	1,321.90	853.06	645.32	3,130.58	2,031.82	649.02	4,157.59	2,718.83	653.75
700–	754.69	563.59	746.78	1,831.11	1,412.07	744.97	2,862.35	2,156.06	753.24
800–	643.22	564.53	877.66	1,854.61	1,644.55	886.73	3,438.33	3,131.82	899.11
1,000–	524.49	623.69	1,189.13	1,413.69	1,953.39	1,169.50	3,044.50	3,707.49	1,217.83
1,500–	193.70	331.01	1,708.87	379.17	633.12	1,669.75	769.96	1,263.91	1,641.52
2,000–	147.81	352.04	2,381.70	277.50	648.68	2,337.58	471.30	1,090.57	2,313.96
3,000–	81.43	298.12	3,661.05	151.602	550.35	3,630.10	222.884	824.51	3,699.20
5,000–	33.752	227.73	6,747.10	58.619	383.47	6,541.70	79.935	495.12	6,520.30
10,000–	6.676	89.27	13,371.70	10.742	138.56	12,898.90	14.086	174.47	12,385.00
20,000+	1.222	49.08	40,163.60	2.307	88.25	38,253.10	3.015	94.61	31,379.70
Total	39,066.32	14,411	368.80	39,694.56	19,760	498.30	40,824.93	25,360.3	621.20

Sources: As for tables 5.2, 5.3, and 5.4 and 3.11.

distributions respectively, which emerge from the adjusted and expanded type 2 distribution of income units. These were derived in the same way as the other per capita and per adult equivalent distributions presented in this book.

The effect of the new income on the proportion of 'high' and 'low' incomes is shown in table 5.7. If this table is compared with tables 3.4, 3.5 and 3.13, it will be observed that in each year the new income has reduced the inequality index by 3 to 4 percentage points. In all cases except one, this reduction has been sufficiently uniform to leave the relative position of the inequality index between the years unaffected. The exception is for the per adult equivalent distribution in 1963, where, using the 'trend' method, the inequality index is now less than that of the 1954 distribution. Formerly it was slightly larger.

Table 5.7 *Proportion of high and low income units for the type 2 distributions plus 'unallocated' income and some fringe benefit income*

	Type 2 units			Per adult equivalent		
Year	Low	High	Inequality index	Low	High	Inequality index
		a. 'Average income' method				
1954	20.40	0.35	20.75	16.80	0.39	17.19
1959	13.38	0.36	13.74	11.98	0.34	12.32
1963	12.65	0.27	12.92	12.61	0.33	12.94
		b. 'Trend' method				
1954	20.59	0.35	20.94	16.80	0.39	17.19
1959	14.60	0.36	14.96	13.64	0.34	13.98
1963	17.44	0.27	17.71	16.50	0.33	16.83

Sources: As for tables 3.2, 3.3, and 5.2 to 5.6.

Table 5.8 *Proportion of total population in families with low incomes for the type 2 distribution plus 'unallocated' income and some fringe benefit income*

Year	'Average income' method (%)		'Trend' method (%)	
1954	15.40	(17.50)	15.81	(19.50)
1959	10.03	(13.20)	10.86	(14.40)
1963	9.67	(12.20)	13.11	(16.30)

Sources: As for table 5.7.
Note: Table 3.6 percentages in brackets.

The changes in the inequality indexes result entirely from the reductions in the number of low income units. The proportion of high incomes in all years is only insignificantly influenced by the additional income. The direction of this small influence is to increase the proportion. Finally, for readers who wish to have a comparison of results with table 3.6, we present table 5.8. Here again we observe a reduction in the proportion of the population in families with low incomes in the order of 3 to 4 percentage points each year.

6

SUMMARY

We set out in this study to achieve two specific ends. The first was to derive distributions of income which as far as possible would meet the requirements of social commentators. The second was to provide a technique of analysis for social commentators. These aims of course were very much interdependent and both covered a very large area of study. For this reason we restricted our analysis to an intertemporal comparison of the distribution of income before taxation but after the provision of direct transfer incomes, such as pensions and scholarships. This we defined as the 'original' or 'natural' distribution of income. In the earlier chapters it corresponded more or less exactly to personal income, as defined in the National Income Accounts and as allocated to income ranges in the official C.S.O. estimates of the distribution of income. In chapters 4 and 5 the scope of the income definition was broadened to include capital gains, fringe benefits and some items of personal income considered unallocatable to income ranges by the C.S.O.

The years chosen for the intertemporal comparison were 1949, 1954, 1959 and 1963. These were determined by the timing of the Inland Revenue surveys of the distribution of taxable income. These have been the base data for the distributions published by the C.S.O. We used these surveys to develop the data published by the C.S.O. for the years under scrutiny. The outcome of these developments was a distribution of income for each year, where each recipient unit was defined as either a single person income unit or a married person unit; both types were cross-classified according to the number of dependent children. There were in fact, for the years 1954, 1959 and 1963, two such distributions for each year, one which included only a partial adjustment for the large number of double-countings encountered in our developments and one which was wholly adjusted. These two categories were named the type 1 and type 2 distributions respectively. The distinction was made because it was felt that the additional adjustments involved in the type 2 distributions were subject to greater error than those for type 1. Further we wished to preserve comparability with the estimates for 1949, where data availability restricted us to a type 1 estimate.

The differences between the type 1 and type 2 distributions were, however, very small indeed. If, for any year, we were to compare both distributions by any of the well-known graphic techniques, such as Pareto,

93

Gini or Lorenz curves, the distinction would hardly be perceptible to the human eye. This closeness is also shown by a comparison of the single statistic measures we made for each of the distributions (see table 6.1 below).

Table 6.1   *Measures of dispersion and skewness for the type 1 and type 2 distributions by income units*

| | Measure | |
Distribution	R	$\alpha3$
1954 Type 1	39.21	22.182
1954 Type 2	38.99	22.145
1959 Type 1	38.99	16.152
1959 Type 2	38.62	16.136
1963 Type 1	38.31	12.949
1963 Type 2	37.98	12.849

Source: As for table A3.4.
Notes: R is the Gini concentration ratio and $\alpha3$ is a measure of skewness (see appendix 3).

This similarity in the structure of the two types is further demonstrated by the measure of inequality we devised in chapter 3. This was the attempt to achieve our second aim. Essentially we defined inequality in a very normative manner, as comprising the proportion of low and high income units. This is a definition which we felt had its origin in the early works of Chiozza-Money [18] and would find support from Dalton [21]. Our definition of low incomes was that used first by Beveridge and later by Abel-Smith and Townsend [1], namely a definition derived from the National Assistance Board scales, which were supposed to reflect subsistence living. For high incomes we devised a measure based on the surtax limits. In both instances we were able to take into account the differences in the 'inner' family size of each income recipient unit.

Though our inequality index was quite insensitive to the differences between the type 1 and type 2 distributions, it was sensitive to the two methods we adopted to allow for inflation and the fact that low income is a relative concept. The first method was to increase the 1948 N.A.B. scales by the average increase in income per unit between each of the years. This method enabled us to conclude that the level of inequality fell from 19.24% in 1949 to 17.24% in 1963 (for the type 1 distributions), though the fall was not a steady decline. In 1954 it was 22.57% and in 1959, 16.24%. The second measure, however, was derived from a regression of actual N.A.B. scales, which had risen faster than average income per unit, and this led to the conclusion that the level of inequality was a couple of percentage points higher in 1963 than in 1949 (see table 3.5). What this meant in effect was that the change in the distribution of income, though leading to a proportionate fall in the number of low and high incomes, was not keeping pace with the desired rate of improvement, as reflected in poverty legislation. This is particularly relevant because our index of inequality is very much biased toward the proportion of low income units.

This bias, we feel, is justified in the context in which we use our index of inequality. If, however, we wish to move away from the problem of inequality and its meaning and to analyse the structural significance of the distribution of income, then we cannot ignore the majority 'middle' incomes. This is important, because it permits us to consider the effects of our developments on the total distribution of income. This of course, was not specifically relevant to our discussion in chapter 3.

There are two ways in which we can look at the distribution of income *in toto*. The first is by the use of percentiles and the second by a number of graphic methods, particularly the Lorenz diagram. We have opted for the second. The obvious approach would be to present a Lorenz diagram[1] for each year displaying the Inland Revenue distributions, the C.S.O., the type 1 and the type 2. As mentioned previously, the types 1 and 2 would be visually indistinguishable. The C.S.O. distribution would also suffer in this way. Since the aim is to show the importance of developing a distribution of income directly related to family size and the total population, we decided to compare for each year the Inland Revenue, the C.S.O., the per capita, and the 'per adult equivalent', distributions.

The per capita distributions we derived in chapter 2 for type 1 and type 2; and the per adult equivalent (p.a.e.) distributions, again categorised according to type, were derived in similar manner in chapter 3. The latter differed in that there was scaling for the cost of supporting each size of family, compared with the cost of living of a single adult person. The p.a.e. distributions were used in chapter 3 to support the inequality conclusions derived from the units/family-size distributions, which, with the exception of the higher inequality index values for 1949, they did. In charts 6.1 to 6.4 we present the Lorenz Curve for each of the type 2 per capita and p.a.e. distributions (type 1 for 1949), along with the Inland Revenue and C.S.O. distributions.

We can derive a number of valuable conclusions from the Lorenz curves in charts 6.1 to 6.4. The first is that the difference between the Inland Revenue and C.S.O. distributions is much the same in every year, the gap being particularly pronounced for the lowest 80% of incomes. This is what we would expect. Most of the manipulations and additions made by the Inland Revenue for the C.S.O. distributions have their effect on the lower and middle income groups, as do our adjustments for

[1] For a description of the Lorenz Curve see Morgan [51].

the type 1 and type 2 distributions, with little or no effect on the top 5% of income recipients. The second interesting feature is that, except for 1949, the per capita distributions are closer to the line of Perfect Equality than the C.S.O. distributions, for the lowest 80 to 85% of incomes. This is because of the higher concentration in the lower income groups that results from conversion to a per capita definition. The year 1949 is an exception because the C.S.O. distribution for that year initially has sufficient bunching in the lower income groups to outweigh the 'concentration' effect that results from conversion.

Chart 6.1   Lorenz Curves: 1949 income distributions.

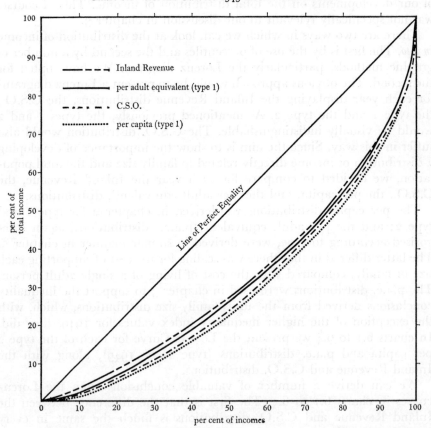

A significant feature, however, is the closeness in all years, but especially in 1959 and 1963, of the p.a.e. and Inland Revenue distributions. This we must attribute to pure coincidence. There is no *a priori* reason why this should be the case. A final feature is that differences in structure between the top 5% of the distributions do not show up in these Lorenz diagrams. They would emerge if we were to 'blow up' the top 5%, but they would be very small indeed; for example see chart 6.5, where we make such a 'blow up' for 1963.

Chart 6.2 Lorenz Curves: 1954 income distributions.

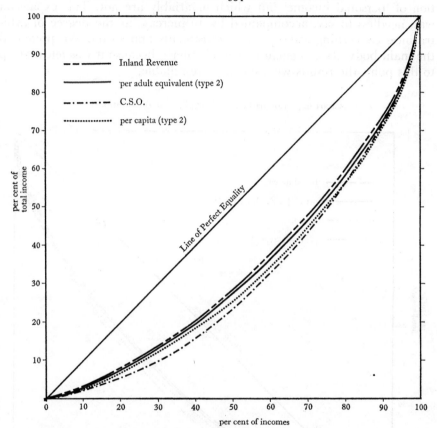

The p.a.e. distributions provide a more comprehensive summary of the income distribution than do the others. They incorporate and display the importance of the family size factor. It is for this reason that for the remainder of this chapter we limit our analysis to the p.a.e. distributions where possible. Thus we compare the intertemporal pattern of the distribution of income in chart 6.6 by the Lorenz curves for the type 2 p.a.e. distributions for 1954, 1959 and 1963 and for the type 1 for 1949. From this chart we observe a steady movement towards the line of Perfect Equality. In chapter 3 we refused to interpret this as a movement toward greater equality. It may represent a trend to greater egalitarianism, which need not necessarily reflect the society's concept of inequality. This is certainly the case in the high/low income index of inequality when we adopt the 'trend' method of measurement (see table 6.2.).

Up to this point we have summarised and analysed the topics covered in the first three chapters of this book. In chapters 4 and 5 we broadened our scope to include items which we felt should be included in the definition of 'personal income' but which invariably are not. This expansion was, needless to say, accompanied by an increase in the degree of arbitrariness concerning assumptions, adjustments and so on. We presented the main body of our conclusions in chapter 3 because it was felt that up to this point the results were much more reliable.

Chart 6.3   Lorenz Curves: 1959 income distributions.

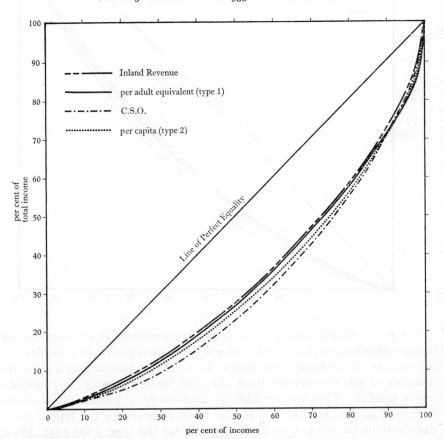

In chapter 4 we introduced 'capital gains', defined as the annual appreciation in the money value of the 'personal wealth' stock. In chapter 5 we included the following categories of income:

Chart 6.4   Lorenz Curves: 1963 income distributions.

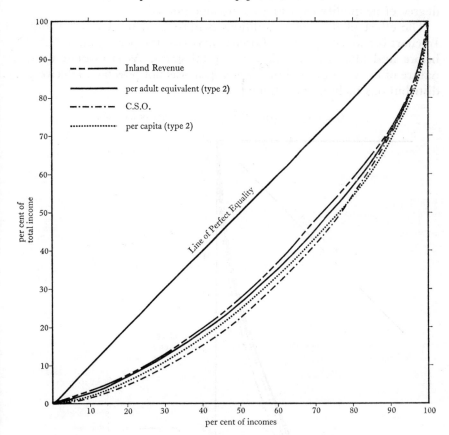

(a) National insurance contributions,
(b) Some income in kind,
(c) Superannuation contributions and the investment income of such funds,
(d) Schedule A excess,
(e) Self-employed expenses and depreciation,
(f) National savings certificates and post-war credits,
(g) Non-taxable grants,
(h) Employer provided car services,
(j) Incomes below £50 p.a.

These categories of income come under one of two groups, either fringe benefit incomes such as (e) and (h), which are considered as 'intermediate' products in the national income accounts, or items of personal income not normally allocated to income ranges in the C.S.O. distributions. In all cases, as far as it was possible to ascertain, these additions reduced the degree of inequality by 2 to 4 percentage points.

The effect of the above additions is illustrated in charts 6.7 and 6.8. In chart 6.7 we compare the Lorenz curves for the per capita distributions before and after the addition of capital gains. As is evident from the nature of the data utilised in chapter 4, it was not possible to derive p.a.e. distributions including capital gains.

Chart 6.5   Lorenz Curves: 1963, top 5% of incomes.

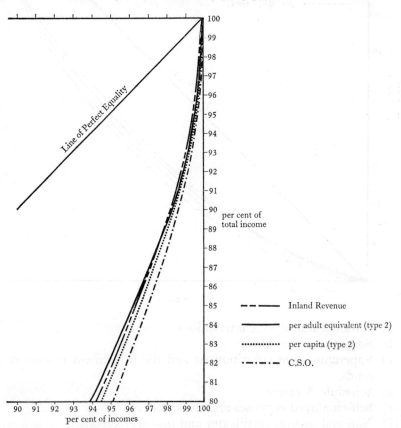

No clear conclusions can be drawn from chart 6.7. For the 1959 distribution there is a substantial increase in the proportion of income held by the higher income groups, particularly by the top 20%, but this time clearly at the expense of other incomes in the top half of the Lorenz curve, since the proportion of income going to the lowest 45% actually rises quite significantly. This is indicative of a relatively large number of low 'unearned' incomes compared to 1959 (see table 4.5). It could also be a result of the poverty of the data that were available for 1954. Interestingly though, the phenomenon of the increase in the proportion of income received by the lowest 45% of recipients is reflected in the 1963 data. The data and conclusions reached for 1954 do not therefore seem implausible. The major difference between 1954 and 1963 is that capital gains do not bring about such a large increase in the proportion of income held by the top 50% of incomes. This difference is also significant between the 1959 and 1963 distributions. As far as egalitarianism is concerned, the Lorenz curves allow us to conclude only that the introduction of capital gains clearly increases the disparity amongst incomes. Since the curves intersect for most of the years, we have to resort to the Gini concentration ratio (see table 6.3).

Chart 6.6   Lorenz Curves: 'per adult equivalent' distributions.

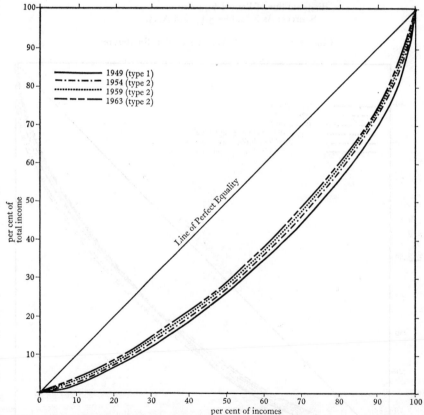

It is evident from table 6.3 that the *increase* in income going to the low income percentiles does not *compensate* for the effect of the *increase* in the upper percentiles. The overall effect of capital gains is then an increase

Table 6.2   *Measures of concentration and inequality for 1949 (p.a.e. type 1 distribution) and for 1954, 1959 and 1963 (p.a.e. type 2 distributions)*

| | | High/low index of inequality | |
| | | 'Average income' | 'Trend' |
Year	R^a (%)	method (%)	method (%)
1949	34.36	23.76	23.76
1954	34.04	18.81	18.85
1959	33.33	15.14	17.46
1963	32.99	16.06	20.61

a R represents the area between the line of Perfect Equality and the distribution curve expressed as a percentage of the area under the diagonal line of Perfect Equality.
Sources: As for tables 3.13 and A3.5.

Chart 6.7   Lorenz Curves: per capita distributions.

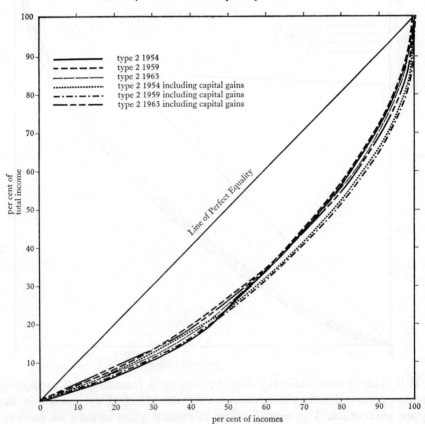

type 2 1954
type 2 1959
type 2 1963
type 2 1954 including capital gains
type 2 1959 including capital gains
type 2 1963 including capital gains

per cent of total income

per cent of incomes

Line of Perfect Equality

in the disparity of incomes, largely due to the substantial increases in the income of the very high income groups.

The effect of adding fringe benefits and other items of personal income to the p.a.e. distributions generally shows up much less clearly in the Lorenz diagrams than did the addition of capital gains. In 1954 the distinction is only barely perceptible in the diagrams. The effect in 1959 is a slight decrease in the proportion of income held by incomes between the third and ninth deciles, at the expense of the groups outside this range. In that year the curves intersect twice, at the points mentioned above. Since both the 1954 and 1959 cases indicated no substantial effects, we decided not to include them in chart 6.8. That chart includes only the effect for 1963, where we again observe intersecting Lorenz curves. The lowest 75% of incomes show a fall in the proportion of income held and the top 25% a rise. The overall effect is a rise in disparity in terms of the concentration ratio (see table 6.4).

Chart 6.8   Per adult equivalent distributions, type 2, 1963.

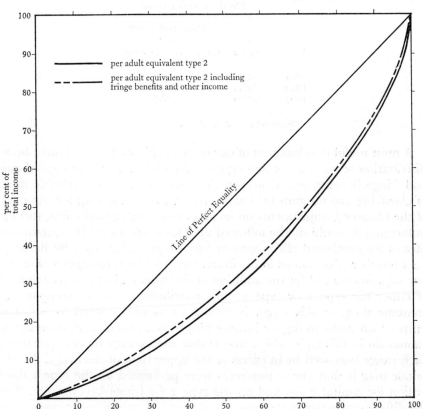

per cent of total income

per cent of incomes

per adult equivalent type 2

per adult equivalent type 2 including fringe benefits and other income

Line of Perfect Equality

We note that our conclusion on the effect of fringe benefits and 'unallocated' income is not dissimilar from that reached by Lydall [39] though the two estimates are difficult to compare. The main snag in comparison is that Lydall made his adjustments on after-tax income.

Table 6.3   *Gini concentration ratios*

Year	Per capita distributions of income (type 1)	
	Without capital gains	With capital gains
1954	34.78	38.93
1959	35.35	41.03
1963	35.40	36.78

Sources: Table 4.7 and A3.5.

Table 6.4   *Gini concentration ratios*

Year	Distribution of income	
	P.a.e. type 2	P.a.e. plus fringe benefits and 'unallocated' personal income
1954	34.04	33.98
1959	33.33	34.78
1963	32.99	34.87

Sources: As for table 5.6.

A most useful development of our work at this stage would have been a distribution of income combining the effects of adding both capital gains and fringe benefits, etc. However, since we had no really reliable means of clarifying capital gain by family size and then allowing for the effects of the chapter 5 adjustments on incomes receiving capital gains, this idea unfortunately could not be followed up. However, if we wish to gain some idea of the combined effect, we can adopt a procedure used by Barna [5] on a number of occasions in his study. Since for both categories of income our adjustments call for the addition of the imputed income to each range of either the type 1 or type 2 units distribution, we can compare and combine them at this stage. Normally we would proceed to adjust for units which move to higher income ranges as a result. This, however, we cannot do in this case, which means that the average income per unit in each range may well be in excess of the upper limit of the range. Another minor snag is that our adjustments were performed on the type 1 distribution for capital gains and on the type 2 for fringe benefits, etc. Since the differences between the type 1 and type 2 distributions are very small,

Table 6.5   *Type 1 distribution of income including capital gains, fringe benefits and 'unallocated' income per range (units distribution unadjusted)*

Income range (£)	Number of units ('000s)	Amount of income (£m)	Capital gains (£m)	'Other'*a* income (£m)	Total income (£m)
			1954		
50–	8,449.1	1,392.98	498	223.9	2,114.88
200–	1,655.9	453.02	63	102.6	618.62
300–	3,352.5	1,175.76	133	228.3	1,537.06
400–	3,371.0	1,515.14	185	297.0	1,997.14
500–	2,837.9	1,556.04	162	279.7	1,997.74
600–	2,174.0	1,403.03	111	231.3	1,745.33
700–	1,465.3	1,093.80	80	182.3	1,356.10
800–	1,301.1	1,142.88	143	189.2	1,475.08
1,000–	764.6	907.82	192.5	146.7	1,247.02
1,500–	234.6	401.67	129	53.7	584.37
2,000–	162.0	392.37	243.5	60.8	696.67
3,000–	98.0	365.72	255	51.5	672.22
5,000–	45.0	294.63	286.4	26.9	607.93
10,000–	11.0	143.49	155.5	18.8	317.79
20,000+	2.0	73.65	39.1	6.3	119.05
Total	25,924	12,312.0	2,676	2,099	17,087

Income range (£)	Number of units ('000s)	Amount of income (£m)	Capital gains (£m)	'Other'*a* income (£m)	Total income (£m)
			1959		
50–	5,456.0	911.56	153	70.9	1,135.46
200–	1,691.6	463.39	55	23.5	541.89
300–	2,657.2	925.65	141	223.8	1,290.45
400–	2,616.2	1,177.24	171	224.6	1,572.84
500–	2,701.0	1,483.46	162	301.4	1,946.86
600–	2,550.5	1,650.44	155	334.5	2,139.94
700–	2,253.2	1,684.90	158	345.5	2,188.40
800–	3,000.6	2,668.60	235	569.6	3,473.20
1,000–	2,275.7	2,670.33	429	611.7	3,711.03
1,500–	445.5	759.65	311	199.5	1,270.15
2,000–	289.3	692.96	498	173.6	1,364.56
3,000–	157.0	592.83	492	147.0	1,231.83
5,000–	65.2	434.60	529	93.5	1,057.10
10,000–	14.0	182.25	256	31.9	470.15
20,000+	3.0	100.14	310	10.0	420.14
Total	26,176.0	16,398.0	4,055	3,362	23,815

Table 6.5 (*continued*)

			1963		
Income range (£)	Number of units ('000s)	Amount of income (£m)	Capital gains (£m)	'Other'[a] income (£m)	Total income (£m)
50–	4,174.8	819.01	154	87.3	1,060.31
200–	1,373.7	376.78	65	23.5	465.28
300–	2,286.2	805.83	244	33.6	1,083.43
400–	2,258.8	1,012.67	206	151.1	1,369.77
500–	2,130.0	1,170.96	214	177.9	1,562.86
600–	2,180.7	1,416.55	207	243.7	1,867.25
700	2,104.2	1,575.43	174	292.4	2,041.83
800–	3,815.2	3,418.45	361	666.7	4,446.15
1,000–	4,573.9	5,483.71	596	1,283.2	7,362.91
1,500–	1,263.1	2,122.35	355	510.6	2,987.95
2,000–	463.6	1,100.2	404	328.6	1,832.80
3,000–	212.4	798.31	376	185.5	1,359.81
5,000–	105.1	698.88	352	127.7	1,178.58
10,000–	20.0	265.09	205	35.1	505.19
20,000+	4.0	130.08	77	19.1	226.18
Total	26,996.0	21,194.3	3,990	4,166.0	29,350.3

Sources: Tables 2.3, 2.4, 2.5, 4.3, and A6.1.
[a] Fringe benefits, and 'unallocated' income.

we decided to ignore this problem and simply add the appropriate capital gains and fringe benefits, etc. income to each range of the type 1 units distribution (see table 6.5). We can now consider the effects by contrasting the Lorenz curves for each year of the type 1 units distributions, before and after this addition (see charts 6.9, 6.10 and 6.11).

We see from the Lorenz curves that for 1963 and 1959 the expansion of the income boundary increases the disparity amongst incomes, particularly in 1959. The greater effect in 1959 probably results from the greater relative importance of capital gains in that year, accounting for 54.7% of the additional income, as opposed to 48.9% in 1963. Furthermore, as a proportion of all income, capital gains were of greater relative importance in 1959, accounting for 17% as against 13.5% in 1963. Without the adjustment to a per capita or similar basis the introduction of capital gains will lead to a bias in the proportion of income held by the top income groups.

In 1954 we witness an increase in the proportion of income held by both the high and low income groups. This is similar to the effect which we saw that capital gains had on the per capita distribution for that year. There is no doubt that the large amount of capital gains falling in the £50–250 income range compared to other years has much to do with the 1954 effects. Since this 'allocation' of capital gains income is derived from an extrapolation from surtax data there could well be errors in it. As men-

Chart 6.9 Distribution of income by income units, 1954.

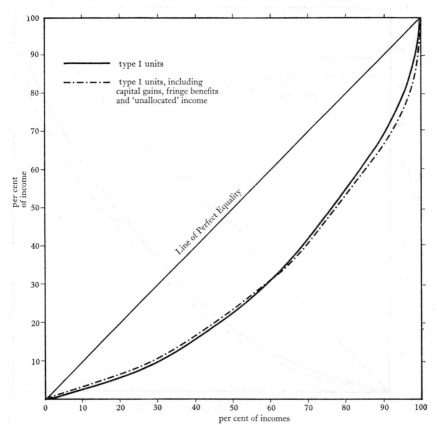

tioned previously, we would not advocate total acceptance of the estimates for 1954.

There can be little doubt, however, that the structure of the size distribution of incomes is substantially altered by the introduction of capital gains, fringe benefits, and 'unallocated' income. Insofar as these are excluded from official data, the point, made by Titmuss [70], that official data could be misleading in its conclusions, is to some extent justified. On the other hand, if we bear in mind the areas where we had insufficient data in making these estimates, it is difficult to criticise the authorities for limiting themselves to the more reliable estimates that they do publish. Hopefully, the procedures needed to make the required data more readily available in the future are now being set up.

We have now analysed the size distribution of income, before taxation, with respect to inequality and structure, for the period 1949 to 1963. A

Chart 6.10   Distribution of income by income units, 1959.

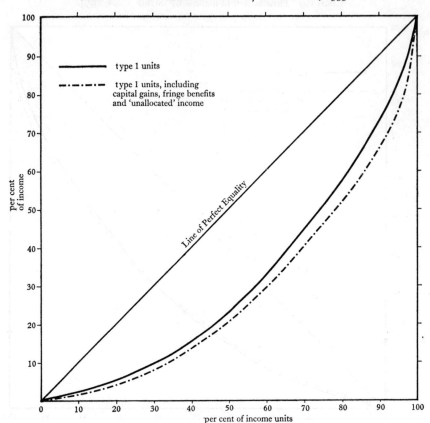

final topic for consideration is a comparison of our distributions with pre-war data. There are two possibilities for comparison in this field. The first is to trace out the Inland Revenue distributions since the first one for 1918–19. This is occasionally done in the Inland Revenue reports and little is gained by repeating the exercise here. The Board's distributions indicate a steady reduction in the disparity between taxable incomes. The second possibility is to see if we can find a link between our distributions and those of Barna [5] for 1937.

Though Barna constructed an income distribution with persons, as opposed to units, as recipients, he was unable to take into account the family size factor and hence could not readjust his distribution to produce per capita income ranges. His distributions classified the per capita distribution with respect to income ranges based on the range of income per income unit. The number of persons in each such range was estimated as the number of units multiplied by 2.57, the average persons/unit ratio,

Chart 6.11   Distribution of income by income units, 1963.

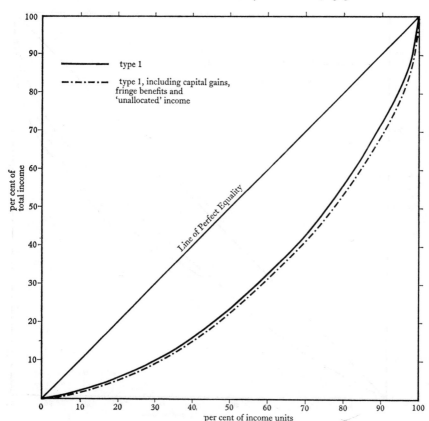

save for the lowest income range, where the number of persons was estimated as the residual with respect to total population. There were no allowances made for double-countings, and since Barna does not describe how he estimated the total population control total we must have doubts on this factor. A further problem is that Barna had his own specific definitions of income, designed to cope with the redistribution analysis which, of course, was the aim of his study.

In spite of these problems we can find some scope for comparability. Barna's nominal unadjusted producers' income in table 6.6. is approximately the same concept of income used in our distributions in chapter 2. In addition, if we draw up a distribution between the income of units in each range in one column and the number of persons forming these units in another, we have essentially the same concept as used by Barna. In Chart 6.12 we make such a comparison between the 1949 distribution and Barna's data. Since the first measurement point for the 1937 distribution

Chart 6.12   Distribution of income 1937 and 1949.

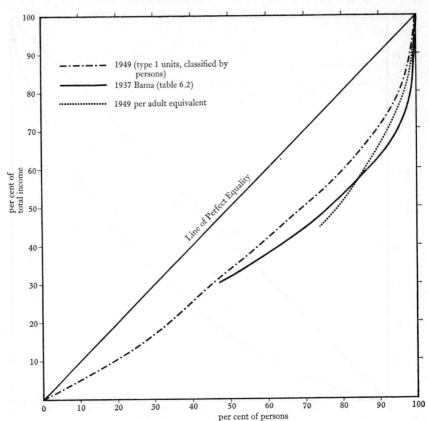

does not occur till the fourth decile, it would be pure guesswork to complete the distribution below that point. For the area above that decile, however, the disparity or spread of incomes is much larger in 1937 than in 1949. This probably means that the high/low inequality index for 1937 would be larger. There is in Barna's data a substantial degree of concentration of persons in the lowest, i.e. <£125 p.a., income range. We can guess at approximately the proportion of population with low incomes in 1937. In 1949 the single person low income limit we used was £110. This is reduced to £61.5 for 1937, to allow for the difference between the average income per head in the two years. Assuming all the persons in the less than £125 range were single persons, we have a minimum low income proportion of 16.9% of the population. On the other hand, if we assume they were all two-person families, then, making the approximate scaling for this family size, a low income proportion of 29.5% results. They are unlikely to be all two-person families. On the other hand they are not likely to be all single persons and we must remember that no account has been taken of families in higher ranges, which would fall within the low income limits. Therefore it can be predicted that a full-scale analysis for 1937, were it possible, would result in a low income proportion of at least 20% of the population. This compares to 17.8% for 1949. A proportion of 20% would also be higher than for any of the other years. I think we can safely conclude that the degree of inequality and probably dispersion was much less in 1963 than 1937.

Table 6.6 *Distribution of incomes, 1937*

Range of incomes (£)	Persons per range ('000s)	Nominal unadjusted producers income (£m)	Number of income units ('000s)
<125	21,800	1,407	n.a.
125 –	14,750	969.2	5,780
200 –	6,090	599.7	2,390
300 –	1,890	263.7	740
400 –	836	154.1	328
500 –	471	109.3	185
600 –	486	143.3	190.6
800 –	252	98.3	98.9
1,000 –	309	166.2	121.2
1,500 –	142	110.8	57.7
2,000 –	124.5	139.3	48.8
3,000 –	85.2	151.5	33.4
5,000 –	48.7	156.3	19.1
10,000 –	16.0	102.9	6.3
20,000+	5.9	120.2	2.3
Total	47,300.0	4,692.0	10,000.0

Source: Barna [5] tables 13 and 62.

A DETAILED ANALYSIS OF THE PROCEDURES FOR DERIVING A PER CAPITA DISTRIBUTION OF INCOME

In chapter 2 we listed two broad categories of double-countings which were the main obstacles in the path of deriving a per capita income distribution (or meaningful family size distribution) from the C.S.O. published statistics on income distribution. The listed double-countings were:

A. Direct double-countings, which arise from:
   (i) marriages during the year,
   (ii) divorces during the year,
   (iii) deaths of husbands during the year.

B. Indirect double-countings which comprised:
   (i) Dependent relatives receiving incomes below the maximum permitted before the dependent relative allowance is rendered unclaimable,
   (ii) adults in receipt of covenants below the effective exemption limit,
   (iii) scholarship incomes and grants to young persons,
   (iv) children under 15 in receipt of L.E.A. maintenance awards,
   (v) children under 15 in receipt of covenants,
   (vi) young persons, in full-time study, in receipt of unearned and/or vacation earned income below the effective exemption limit and also minors under 15 in receipt of unearned income other than covenants, etc.

We pointed out in chapter 2 that a formal attempt has been made to eliminate all these types of double-countings except items A (iii) and B (vi). In this appendix we analyse in greater detail the techniques used in the elimination procedures and the steps taken after the eliminations. We start first with the procedures adopted for the type 1 or partially adjusted distributions.

I THE TYPE I OR PARTIALLY ADJUSTED DISTRIBUTIONS

The dependent relative double-counting was very easily eliminated. Dependent relatives were simply extracted from the Inland Revenue survey family classification tables. The family classification pattern, so adjusted for each year, is reproduced in appendix 7. Marriages and divorces, however, presented greater problems. These two cases we shall examine in greater detail.

I A   THE ELIMINATION OF DOUBLE-COUNTING DUE TO NEW
MARRIAGES

The number of marriages each year can be readily obtained from the *Annual Abstract of Statistics*. Not all marriages, though, will cause double-counting. Those where the female unit had an income of less than £50, whilst single during the year of marriage, will not be incorporated in the C.S.O. distributions and hence will not be double-counted. Such units are generally estimated by the Inland Revenue to constitute 17% of the total of newly married units. This is a rule of thumb used by the Inland Revenue, devised from experience in handling this type of data. For want of greater precision we allow this rule to stand.

The elimination technique involved the construction of a matrix cross-classifying the levels of income of brides whilst single (during the year of marriage) over £50 p.a., with those of newly married income units, similarly grouped by income level. This process requires three sets of information:

(a) the income level of newly married income units,
(b) the income level of single females who married during the year and who received more than £50 p.a. whilst single during that year,
(c) the matrix relationship of the above categories (a) and (b), which are the aggregate column and row of our postulated matrix.

In addition to the above adjustments the income of those brides who received less than £50 p.a. whilst single will be brought into our distribution. This manipulation will be described below.

I A I   INCOME DISTRIBUTION OF NEWLY MARRIED INCOME
UNITS

The income distribution of newly married persons in each of our years is presented in table A1.1. There were no direct data on the income levels of such couples. It was, therefore, assumed that their income distribution is, in all probability, closest to that of married couples without children. This is readily obtainable from the Inland Revenue income surveys. Furthermore, it was implicitly assumed that all newly married couples would have an annual income in excess of the exemption limits. As most single female incomes are in the £50 to £300 p.a. range (for all years), it is unlikely that many newly married incomes, which are combined incomes, will be below the £200 to £300 p.a. level. This assumption is further strengthened by, first, the general tendency for women to marry men who earn at least as much as they do themselves, and secondly, the fact that a substantial proportion of wives continue to earn after marriage. Moreover, these assumptions are useful in that they permit the main burden of elimination to be carried out on 'taxable' income units, incorporating data from the Inland Revenue surveys. The adjustments for non-taxable income were made after the double-counting adjustments.

Table A1.1   *Distribution by income of newly married income units*

Income range (£)	1949 Numbers ('000s)	1949 Income (£m)	1954 Numbers ('000s)	1954 Income (£m)	1959 Numbers ('000s)	1959 Income (£m)	1963 Numbers ('000s)	1963 Income (£m)
Exemption limit	67	13.7	13	2.7	4	1	—[a]	—
250–	55	15.2	13	3.6	5	1.4	2	0.58
300–	96	33	44	15.6	18	6.3	12	4.25
400–	57	25.4	57	25.7	35	15	18	8.12
500–	31	16.9	64	35.1	40	22	28	15.5
600–	15	9.7	39	25.2	50	32.5	32	20.85
700–	8	6.0	34	25.4	44	33	33	24.75
800–	8	7.1	33	29	62	55	67	60.3
1,000–	8	9.6	17	20	50	58.5	100	120.1
1,500–	3	5.0	5	8.5	7	11.3	24	40.6
2,000+	7	29.0	7	27.5	11	40	18[b]	68.6
Total	355	170.6	326	218.3	324	276	344	363.65

Sources: Inland Revenue [19] *Reports* nos.: 94, tables 93, 11; 99, tables 58, 82; 105, tables 80, 92 and 93; 108, tables 65, 68 and 69.
[a] Range begins at £275 for 1963.
[b] For 1963 the family classification data extended up to £5,000 and the extension was:

	Numbers	Income
£2,000–	10	23.8
£3,000–	5	18.9
£5,000+	5	25.9

Income per range estimated from the average income for all married couples given in the tables in each Inland Revenue survey on income by type, source and marital status.

IA 2   INCOME DISTRIBUTION OF BRIDES WHILST SINGLE

The Inland Revenue provided us with data on the distribution of the earned incomes of single females who married during the year 1962–3. This was the only year for which they had such information, which was taken as representative for 1963. Similar figures were estimated for 1959 by extrapolating the 1962–3 figures. The procedure was to decrease the income range limits by the (negative) difference in average single female income between 1963 and 1959. This, of course, left us with some odd income range limits. By interpolation the newly estimated range limits were reconverted to those conventionally used by the Inland Revenue. The average income per range for 1959 was estimated by reference to the shape of the distribution. This technique is outlined in appendix 2 on the Pareto interpolation method.

It would not be justified to assume that the 1962–3 relative structure of single female incomes held good for 1954 and 1949. For those years we adopted an entirely different approach.

Let us assume that we had the following sets of data, as in fact we did, namely:

(i) Income distribution by age, represented by matrix A, where

$$A = \begin{bmatrix} (a_{11} & \cdots & a_{1n})\mathcal{N}_1 \\ \cdot & & \cdot \\ \cdot & & \cdot \\ \cdot & & \cdot \\ (a_{j1} & \cdots & a_{jn})\mathcal{N}_j \end{bmatrix}$$

and 'a_{jn}' is the proportion of income units ($\mathcal{N}$) in range j in a certain age bracket n.

(ii) Income distribution by sex and marital status, given by matrix B, where

$$B = \begin{bmatrix} (b_{1f} + b_{1m} + b_{1mf} + b_{1fm})\mathcal{N}_1 \\ \cdot \\ \cdot \\ \cdot \\ (b_{jf} + b_{jm} + b_{jmf} + b_{jfm})\mathcal{N}_j \end{bmatrix}$$

and b_j is the proportion in each income range j, of $\mathcal{N}_j$ which is either:

	single female	b_{jf},
	single male	b_{jm}
	married male	b_{jmf}
or	married female	b_{jfm}.

Given that A and B refer to the same year and population, we can assume that the income distribution of single females by age can be approximated, though not precisely identified, by a combination of the two sets of data. The combined distribution would be

$$C = \begin{bmatrix} (a_{11} & \cdots & a_{1n})b_{1f}\mathcal{N}_1 \\ \cdot & & \cdot \\ \cdot & & \cdot \\ \cdot & & \cdot \\ (a_{j1} & \cdots & a_{jn})b_{jf}\mathcal{N}_j \end{bmatrix}$$

Finally, let us assume that we know the age distribution of newly married females for the year in question. Then, by expressing the unit composition of the age/income cells in C as a proportion of the total number of single female units,

$$\sum_{=1, 2 \cdots j}^{j} b_{jf} N_j$$

which in turn we subject to the age structure of newly married females, we are able to proximate an income distribution for such females. That is algebraically:

$$M = \begin{bmatrix} (x_{11} \cdot \quad \cdot \quad \cdot x_{j1}) M_1 \\ \cdot \qquad\qquad \cdot \\ \cdot \qquad\qquad \cdot \\ \cdot \qquad\qquad \cdot \\ (x_{1n} \cdot \quad \cdot \quad \cdot x_{jn}) M_n \end{bmatrix}$$

where x_{jn} is $a_{jn} b_{jf} N_j / b_{jf} N_j$ (where j is a column and n a row) and M_n is the number of newly married females in each age group n.

By summing up each column in the matrix M, we obtain the desired income distribution.

We were able to obtain all the above sources of data in one form or another. That for matrixes A and B we obtained from Lydall's survey of U.K. incomes and savings.[1] From this we derived matrix C. However, before we proceeded further a number of adjustments were made to Lydall's data, to make them more suitable for our purposes. First the data referred to 1951–2. Therefore we extrapolated to 1954. This was again achieved by changing the income ranges with respect to the percentage change in average total personal income per unit from 1951–2 to 1954. This now gave us a C type distribution for 1954.

Our second adjustment was to allow for the difference in income definition between that which we used for 1963 and 1959 and that used by Lydall. The latter includes many forms of non-taxable income and unearned income. The income range limits were therefore reduced by the proportion of earned taxable income to total personal income. We used the increase in average total income in our first adjustment as opposed to that of single family earned income,[2] because total personal income corresponds closely to Lydall's definition.

The final adjustment was to adopt a 'cut-off' upper income range. The 1963 data indicated that incomes in excess of £600 p.a. were improbable for newly married females whilst single. This is not unreasonable, as the majority of women have only single person incomes for part of the year. Therefore in deriving the C distribution we omitted all income above £600 p.a. in the A and B distributions. (This approximates to a £450 to £500 taxable income upper limit for 1954.)

The age structure of newly married females for 1954, obtained from the *Annual Abstract of Statistics*, is combined with the C matrix and the 1954 distri-

---

[1] H. F. Lydall [38] appendix 2, tables 1 and 2.
[2] See Lydall [38] appendix 3, for a comparison between his definition of income and that of the C.S.O. Blue Books [16] for total personal income.

Table A1.2 *Income of newly married females, while single*

Income range (£)	1949 Numbers ('000s)	1949 Income (£m)	1954 Numbers ('000s)	1954 Income (£m)	1959 Numbers ('000s)	1959 Income (£m)	1963 Numbers ('000s)	1963 Income (£m)
50–	210	17.3	199	20.0	227	27.0	190	20.36
180–[a]	116	20.0	69	14.5	60	13.0	88	18.8
250–	15	4.1	23	6.0	22	6.0	24	6.75
300–	14	4.8	22	7.5	15	4.0	28	9.27
400+	—	—	13	6.0	—	—	4	1.88
Total	355	46.2	326	54.00	324	51.0	334	57.06

Sources: Inland revenue: Lydall [38] appendix 2, tables 1 and 2; *Annual Abstract of Statistics*.
[a] £135 for 1949.

bution of brides' income whilst single is derived. A similar procedure was undertaken for 1949, using 1949 income range limits.[1] The final results are given in table A1.2. In both 1954 and 1949 the income totals were estimated at the last stage of manipulation, again by reference to the shape of the distribution, from which we are able to derive the average income per range (cf. appendix 2).

A comparison of these distributions for the four years revealed that the income of newly married females whilst single was distinctly higher in 1954 than in 1959. This, however, should not be entirely unexpected. Data on the age distribution of newly married females indicate a sizeable increase in the proportion of marriages where the wife is under 24, particularly between 1954 and 1959.[2] This could well have offset the trend increase in the general level of money incomes.

IA 3   THE INCOME CROSS-CLASSIFICATION MATRIX BETWEEN
SINGLE FEMALES WHO MARRIED AND NEWLY MARRIED
INCOME UNITS

From sections IA1 and IA2 of this appendix we now have the summary column and row data for our final matrix. As it stands the number of matrix structures is almost infinite. Thus a number of restrictive assumptions are necessary in order that a unique structure can be derived.

The basic assumption made is that a woman will only marry a man whose annual income exceeds her own. The annual income of women who cease to earn after marriage is already given by their part-year 'single' income. The annual income of those who become 'working wives' can be approximated if we know the dates of marriage and assume no change in the earnings rate after marriage. For example, consider a woman who earned £200 during the year up to the date of marriage and continued earning at the same rate after marriage. If she married during the first quarter of the year, her annual income would lie in the £800 to £2,400 range, if she married in the second quarter it would be £400–£800, in the third quarter £267–£400 and, finally in the last quarter £200–£267. The upper range limit assumes that the marriage took place on the first day of the quarter and the lower limit assumes that it took place on the last day.

If we extend the above example, it can be deduced from our basic assumption that the minimum possible annual incomes for the husband are £800, £400, £267 and £200 respectively. This being so, the minimum possible amounts

---

[1] The actual estimation procedure differed slightly in order from the one described above. Readers who are interested, and who wish to consult the data, are referred to the author's Ph.D. thesis [69] pp. 115–21.

[2] Consider the age distributions of newly married females in percentages:

Age group	1949	1954	1959
24 and less	60	65	72
25 –	27	23	18
35 –	8	6	5
45 –	3	3	3
55+	2	3	2

of income for them after marriage, as it would appear in the Inland Revenue surveys, are £1,400, £600, £334 and £200 respectively.

In other words we are able to introduce a minimum income level for the newly married income units, depending on the date of marriage, with respect to each level of the earnings of women whilst single. This greatly restricts the potential number of matrix structures.

Information on the number of marriages per quarter is available in the *Monthly Digest of Statistics* and on the earning status of wives in the Inland Revenue surveys. With the aid of these two sources we constructed five separate distributions, for each year, for the income of females whilst single. The distributions were:

    (i) wives not earning after marriage[1]
   (ii) wives earning after marriage – first quarter marriage,
  (iii) wives earning after marriage – second quarter marriage,
  (iv) wives earning after marriage – third quarter marriage,
   (v) wives earning after marriage – fourth quarter marriage.

We assumed that the pattern of these single female income distributions would be the same in each of the five cases, and that only the numbers of units varied.

These distributions we used as the aggregate row of five corresponding sub-matrices. The aggregate column was provided by the relevant distributions of newly married income units. In the case of distribution (i) we used the relevant distribution from the Inland Revenue surveys. For the others, each quarter was given a different minimum possible income level. Our basic assumption was slightly modified so as to provide greater restriction. We assumed that the lowest possible annual income of the husband would correspond either to the upper limit possible for his wife or to the lower limit of the next highest income range. The higher of the two was chosen. The minimum 'cut-off' income levels for each 'quarter' matrix were then derived for newly married income units. The distribution above these lower limits followed, as closely as possible, the pattern of the aggregate distribution above these income levels, limited, of course, to the control totals per range when the five distributions were summed.

The five sub-matrices were then 'filled in' subject to two constraints:

  (a) the assumption, mentioned above, of a 'higher' income for the husband with respect to each 'single' female income level, and
  (b) that, given the above constraint, the distribution of new marriages per column should follow, where possible, that of the aggregate distribution per sub-matrix.

The five sub-matrices for each year were then combined. Up to this stage all manipulations had taken place with respect to the number of units only. The income totals for each of the aggregate columns and rows were estimated. The income totals per cell now consisted of the incomes of the newly married

---

[1] As the data were not available the number in this group was approximated by the proportion relevant to married couples without children for 1963 to 1959, and by that relevant to all married couples for 1949 and 1954.

income units plus those of the wives whilst single. These income cells were then grouped into new income ranges. For example, if the single female income lay in the £250–£300 income range and that of her husband (plus her own after marriage) was in the £700–£800 range, then their 'combined' income would be in the £950–£1,100 range. Operations of this nature were performed on each cell. The cells were then gathered into their new ranges, with interpolation being used where there were overlaps.

We now had at our disposal the relevant information for the double-counting adjustment (i.e. elimination) on the taxable income distributions and the family classification tables. The units and incomes of the two separate distributions, i.e. those of the newly married females whilst single and of the newly married persons, were extracted from these tables. The former were extracted as 'one person' units and the latter as 'two person' units. They were replaced, as two person units, by the income units from the cells of the final 'combined' matrix. The 'marriage' double-countings were thereby eliminated.

IB   INCOME OF BRIDES WHO RECEIVED LESS THAN £50 P.A. WHILST SINGLE

As mentioned previously, the income of those brides who received less than £50 while still single were also incorporated into our distribution. These form part of 'unallocated' personal income as defined by the C.S.O., and hence no double-counting is involved. The adjustment required simply adding on the appropriate amount of income to the relevant married income unit and adjusting for the movement into a higher income range, if any.

The appropriate amount of income we assumed in all cases to be the average income in the less than £50 p.a. range. This was estimated from the shape of the distribution.[1] The relevant married units, however, could not be deduced. Did women who earned less than £50 marry men who quite comfortably compensated for their poor earning power, or did they marry men whose income status was not much higher? Put another way, were they the non-working daughters of the rich, the unemployed daughters of the poor, or simply women who were married after only a few weeks of their working year, either just after leaving school or after the beginning of the year?

We opted for the assumption that they were likely to be a mixed bunch and that the income range pattern of these females after marriage followed the aggregate distribution of other newly married income units.

IC   THE ELIMINATION OF DOUBLE-COUNTING DUE TO DIVORCES

Divorces are defined to include nullities and separations. Only those women who earned *more* than £50 p.a. after their divorce will cause double-counting. As in the case of marriages, we reduced the number of divorces by 17% – a 'guestimate' at the number of cases with incomes less than £50 p.a. after divorce.

To recall, the principle in this particular instance is to create two unmarried

---

[1] See appendix 2.

person incomes, where formerly we had a married unit and one unmarried person unit. Throughout we have assumed, as previously mentioned,[1] that an unmarried unit is a single person unit and a married unit a two person unit. No allowance is made for the placement of children after the break-up of the marriage. This unsatisfactory procedure is forced on us by the total lack of detailed 'socio-economic' statistics on divorces. We do not even have any information about the earnings of divorced females. Therefore for all aspects of this problem we had to devise 'proxy' estimates.

Since the number of divorces is, however, very small, we avoided elaborate 'proxy' variables and estimates. The proportion of all 'divorced' units in a given income group was assumed to be the same as the proportion of all married income units in that group. Implicit here is the assumption that the probability of divorce is a linear function of the number of marriages, irrespective of income size, etc. This assumption, in fact, located a sizeable proportion of the divorces in the higher income brackets, mainly because these brackets contain a sizeable proportion of all marriages. This characteristic of the distribution of divorces is accepted by some writers as a social phenomenon.[2]

With the above estimated income distribution of divorced couples, we also needed information about the distribution of income of the females before and after divorce. The first step was to divide the 'divorced' marriages into those where the wife earned during marriage and those where she did not. In the case of the former the double-counting elimination simply involved changing a two-person unit into a one-person unit. The earnings of the wife as a single woman after the divorce were irrelevant in this case. We assumed that 'divorced' marriages followed an identical pattern with respect to the working status and earning capacity of wives, before the divorce, as did all other marriages. Data on these factors are readily obtainable from the Inland Revenue surveys (see B.I.R. [19] *Reports*).

With respect to divorced females who earned before and after marriage three steps were necessary in the adjustment process. First the married unit was changed into a single person unit; secondly the income of the wife, whilst married, was deducted from the 'converted' single person (i.e. husband) unit, which in turn was moved to a lower income range if necessary; and finally, the wife's deducted income was added to her post-divorce income as a single woman, with appropriate changes in the income range placing. The income of a divorced wife, in each income range, was determined by taking half the average earnings of wives for that particular range. This in turn was further assumed to equal her post-divorce earnings. The implicit assumption here is that all divorces occurred at mid-year, another heroic assumption made necessary by the absence of data.

By using these 'unsophisticated' measures, we were able to eliminate the double-counting resulting from divorces. We should again emphasise that the numbers involved are so small that any errors resulting from the rough approximations will be of zero significance, as far as the shape and structure of the overall distribution of incomes is concerned.

---

[1] Cf. p. 28.　　　　　　　　　[2] Titmuss [70] p. 51.

We now have at our disposal the necessary data for the type 1 distributions. The adjustments outlined in this section were incorporated into our estimates of taxable income units classified by family size.[1] That is, the family classification tables were readjusted for the omission of dependent relatives and changes in the number of one and two person units, etc. Our adjustments for single female incomes affected non-taxable income units below the effective exemption limits. These were taken into account when we added on non-taxable income and units. As previously mentioned, non-taxable units above the exemption limits were assumed to have the same family size pattern as taxable income units in the same income range. The family size patterns were further adjusted by taxable income units which in addition received non-taxable income which moved them to a higher income range. Data from the Inland Revenue enabled us to trace the income range movements of the latter group of units. They were accredited with the family size pattern of their 'origin' income range.

There remained now the family size classification of units below the effective exemption limit. Due to the double-counting elimination we now had substantially fewer units than persons.

Subject to the 'residual' control totals, a family size pattern for these incomes was estimated with reference to some unpublished sample data supplied by the Inland Revenue. The correlation between the actual family size patterns devised and the 'sample' patterns was very high.[2] This completed the type 1 income distribution by income units, with a family size pattern for each income range (see tables 2.2 to 2.5). The per capita distribution in table 2.6 was derived in the manner outlined at the beginning of chapter 2.[3] To recall, we stated that in any given cell N_{ij}, the per capita income would lie between the limits y_i/j and y_{i+1}/j. The total amount of income in each cell we approximated by $N_{ij} \times Y_1/N_1$ i.e. the number of units in the cell multiplied by the average income for the whole income range. There is no evidence to indicate that there is any appreciable divergence between the average income per unit according to family size within one range.[4] Given the per capita range limits per cell, the number of units and the amount of income per cell, the derivation of the per capita distribution was a relatively straightforward procedure. The cells were grouped into the new income ranges with interpolation overcoming the inevitable problem of overlapping ranges (cf. table 2.6).

II   THE TYPE 2 OR FULLY ADJUSTED DISTRIBUTION

The type 2 distribution extends the type 1 to allow for double-counting arising out of scholarship incomes and minors' covenants. These are cases where the

---

[1] A minor problem arose because the Inland Revenue survey family classification tables lumped all incomes above £2,000 p.a. (£5,000 in 1963) in one open-end income range. For 1959 the Inland Revenue provided us with a more detailed break down of the family sizes of these high income groups. For the other years we extrapolated the family sizes with reference to the 1959 patterns.

[2] The correlation coefficients were all 0.99 and highly significant at the 1% level.

[3] Cf. pp. 23 to 40.

[4] The interpolation technique we used was particularly insensitive with respect to average income estimates. Inland Revenue experience in this type of estimate substantiated this conclusion.

young person is in all probability receiving a non-taxable income above £50 p.a., and is therefore included in the C.S.O. distributions, whilst simultaneously included as a dependent child in the Inland Revenue family classification tables.

The techniques adopted for these problems were similar in principle to those used for the marriage double-counting. By cross-classification the single person units are 'married off' to the family units. Appropriate adjustments are, of course, made to the family income units which as a result move to higher income ranges.

The primary difference in this section is that the 'inner family' units can no longer be assumed to be two person units. These units will include at least three persons and, in many cases, four, five, or more. The sizes of the family units were approximated, by assuming they had a similar size/income distribution to all other units. For example, if in a given income range there were n family units who had claimed scholars' and minors' covenants for dependents, then some proportion of these n were three-person units, some four, and so on. The exact proportions were determined by the proportion of units accounted for by each family size (say three-person units) in relation to all units in that range with three or more persons. If all the above n units in our example were moved to a higher income range, as a result of the addition of the dependents' non-taxable income, then they retained this family size pattern.

In all our adjustments for the type 2 distribution we assumed that no family claimed more than one double-counted dependent child. We had no data which permitted any adjustments to overcome this deficiency. A further implicit assumption was that all the family units concerned were either married units or single-person units with two or more dependent children, i.e. the assumption of three or more persons per unit. This meant that no allowance was made for single persons with one dependent child, who might be double-counted. The Inland Revenue surveys indicate that this type of family structure is very rare indeed.[1]

A further criticism might be that not all scholarship holders should be regarded as part of the 'inner' family, particularly university students. The British system of university scholarships is, however, designed to encourage some financial participation by parents, especially at the undergraduate level. Few postgraduate awards permit complete financial independence of the students, and wives (husbands) can claim tax relief for such students. This, we believe, is a good enough justification for their inclusion in the 'inner' family.

No type 2 distribution was estimated for 1949. The precise number of scholarships for dependent children was difficult to extract from published data on scholarships, which were considerably increased as the result of Forces Educational Training awards. The numbers of scholarships and minors' covenants for other years are given in table 2.1. The totals refer only to incomes of £50 p.a. or above. In respect of those below £50 p.a., it was simply assumed that the only scholarships in this category were given in partial payment of fees to non-state owned schools by the Local Education Authorities. These scholarships

[1] For example for 1963, 1.1% of all units enter this category in the Inland Revenue surveys: see B.I.R. [19] 108, tables 68–71.

were excluded from our data. In all years minors' covenants were taken to be greater than £50 p.a.

The data for scholarships in table 2.1, for 1959, were provided by the Inland Revenue. They also provided a detailed breakdown by type of award, thereby supplying us with the technique for making similar estimates for the other years. The data on minors' covenants for all years were also supplied by the Inland Revenue.

IIA. THE ELIMINATION OF DOUBLE-COUNTING DUE TO SCHOLARSHIPS

As in the marriage problem, we required three sets of data, namely:

(a) the income distribution of scholarship holders,
(b) the income distribution of the families on whom scholarship holders are 'fiscally' dependent, and
(c) the matrix relationship between (a) and (b) above.

IIA.1   THE INCOME DISTRIBUTION OF SCHOLARSHIP HOLDERS

In order to ascertain this and the probable matrix relationship with family incomes, it was necessary to break down scholarships by type of award. There were six types of award, which were:

(i) University awards given by the Local Education Authority (L.E.A.).
(ii) L.E.A. awards to pupils at non-state owned or direct grant schools.
(iii) L.E.A. awards to pupils at Special Schools.
(iv) Teacher Training College awards.
(v) Ministry of Education state scholarships.
(vi) D.S.I.R., Ministry of Education state studentships, and other miscellaneous groups.

The numbers in each of these categories for the three years are presented in table A1.3.

The techniques used for grouping each of these items by income size of award varied for each year, according to the extent of our detailed information.

IIA.1(a)   THE YEAR 1963

The awards were subdivided into two broad groups: secondary education awards (items (ii) and (iii)) and further education awards (all other items). The former awards we assumed to be all in the £50–£250 income range. The distributions for the latter were derived from various types of data collated in the Robbins Report (Robbins [63]).

As is invariably the case, a major source of information like Robbins [63] contains data in every form except that required by the researcher. However, it was possible to manipulate their data for our purpose. One table[1] presented a

---

[1] Robbins [63] appendix 2(A), part VI, table 9, p. 224.

percentage distribution by income size, for various types of income sources for undergraduate and pre-diploma students.

This set of data we assumed to be representative of items (i) and (iv) of table A1.3. The sources of income listed in the table were: the L.E.A.s, the Scottish Education Department, vacation earnings, state scholarships, and aid from parents and employers. All that had to be done was to weight each source and then combine each source to produce an overall percentage distribution, which was applied to the number of awards contained in items (i) and (iv).

Table A1.3   *Numbers of scholarships by type of award[a] – incomes of, or above, £50 p.a. only ('ooos)*

	Type of awards	Year		
		1954	1959	1963
(i)	L.E.A. university	57	91	154
(ii)	L.E.A. direct grant and independent schools[b]	51	84	82
(iii)	L.E.A. special schools[b]	61	64	73
(iv)	Teacher training	33	40	64
(v)	State scholarships	11	8	9
(vi)	Other	4	13	5
	Total	225	300	387
	Total amount of income (£m)[c]	24	40	74

Sources: Information from Inland Revenue; Ministry of Education, *Education in 1955*, Cmnd. 9785; *Statistics of Education*, *1963*, Part I, and Part II, tables 20, 22 and 29, and tables 28 and 34; *Robbins* [63] part VI, appendix 2(A), various tables; *Annual Abstract of Statistics*, *1955*, tables 105, 106, 99, 107, 110 and 116.

[a] All data include Scotland and N. Ireland.

[b] Items (ii) and (iii) correspond to item 16 in table 1.4, less those over 15 years of age.

[c] Same sources as above. Only 1963 includes an estimate for vacation earnings.

The weights were estimated from the sample returns in Robbins [63].[1] The relative weighting was adjusted to allow for the fact that not all the sources of income were relevant to our calculations. First, aid from parents had to be omitted, as it was already included in the family income in the Inland Revenue surveys. Second, aid from employers, were it included, appeared to distort the data substantially. It would have produced a very high proportion of large scholarships, since it included all those students who were paid salaries or wages by companies. These, of course, would render impossible, in most cases, any dependency claim by the parents. The omission of this item would be much less serious than its inclusion. Employer-aided students were only 3% of all full-time further education students in continuous courses and 25% of all full-time students plus sandwich course students. The vast bulk of sandwich course students are financed by wage payments.[2]

Finally, state scholarships were omitted. In Robbins's table these were combined with grants from the Scottish Education Department. Our omission

[1] Robbins [63] appendix 2(A), part VI, separate tables on each source of income.
[2] Robbins [63] appendix 2(A), part VI, table 10, p. 225.

took the form of scaling down the weight for this item by the ratio of state scholars to students financed by the Scottish authorities.

All other sources of income, including vacation earnings, were retained.[1] The final distribution that resulted (cf. table A1.4) was further adjusted to bring in fees. Throughout the Robbins Report, the data were relevant only to the maintenance aspects of awards. A standard £50 was added in all cases, to cover fees. Finally, though the Robbins data were for the academic year 1961–2, we undertook no adjustment with respect to our time period, which was the calendar year 1963 – a difference of six months from end to beginning.

Table A1.4   *Income distribution of scholarship incomes, 1963 (table A1.3 Items i, iv)*

Income range (£)	Undergraduate and teacher training ('000s)	Postgraduate and state scholars ('000s)	Secondary school awards ('000s)	Total ('000s)	Income (£m)
50–	110	1.3	155	226.3	36.35
250–	65	1.9	—	66.9	18.11
300–	37	6	—	43	14.5
400–	6	3	—	9	3.95
500–	—	0.8	—	0.8	0.44
600–700	—	1	—	1	0.65
Total	218	14	155	387	74.00

Sources: Robbins [63] appendix 2(A), part vi.
Notes: The income totals per range were estimated via the Pareto interpolation method, subject to the control restriction of £74m.
Fees are included.

So far we had derived income distributions for all but 14,000 students in 1963. The remainder consisted of:

(i) 9,000 state scholars,
(ii) 5,000 students with postgraduate awards.

For the latter group is was also possible to derive a distribution directly from the Robbins Report.[2] For state scholarships there was much less information available. The main type of state scholarship was the G.C.E. supplementary award. This award had an average value of £374[3] in 1962/63, including fees. We assumed a minimum possible value of £200 and a maximum of £600, then, by way of the Pareto interpolation technique,[4] we interpolated for sub-ranges between these two limits. This procedure produced a distribution giving an average of £374.

[1] Only for 1963 did we include an estimate for vacation earnings in our estimates of income from scholarships (cf. table 2.13). From the Robbins [63] appendix 2(A), part vi, table 7, p. 222, we estimated that vacation earnings were on average £65 and that approximately 23% of students worked during their vacations. This produced a total of £3.12m.
[2] Robbins [63] appendix 2(A), part vi, table 39, p. 248.
[3] Robbins [63] appendix 2(A), part vi, table 6, p. 221, and table 2, p. 218.
[4] See appendix 2 below. The method was to derive a Pareto α for the range £200 to £600 which gave an average income of £374.

IIA.I(b)   THE YEAR 1959

For both 1959 and 1954 there were no data available permitting such detailed calculations as were undertaken for 1963. Data supplied by the Inland Revenue indicated that the £50–£250 range had 225,000 scholarships valued at £17m. This left 75,000 and £23m for other ranges. This we assumed to be entirely further education scholarships. Their average value was £300, so, by assuming the maximum scholarship to be £400, and using the same technique as was used for the 1963 state scholarships, we were able to estimate the numbers in the £250–£300 and £300–£400 ranges. The complete distribution is presented in table A1.5.

Table A1.5   *Income distribution of scholarship incomes, 1959*

Range (£)	Numbers ('ooos)	Income (£m)
50–	225	17
250–	38	10.4
300–400	37	12.6
Total	300	40

Source: Information from the Inland Revenue.

IIA.I(c)   THE YEAR 1954

For this year we had very little information on which to base our calculations. All we knew were the total numbers and amounts of income. A cursory glance through university calendars suggested that the maximum value of a scholarship was likely to be £300. We then experimented with combinations of numbers and incomes between the £50–£250 and £250–£300 ranges, trying to find a combination which gave a realistic distribution. Following the 1959 data we expected over 70% of the units to be in the lower range with a very low average. The final combination, arbitrarily chosen, is shown in table A1.6.

Table A1.6   *Income distribution of scholarships, 1954*

Range (£)	Numbers ('ooos)	Income (£m)
50–	175	10.5
250–300	50	13.5

Source: Table A1.3.

IIA.2   THE INCOME DISTRIBUTION OF THE FAMILIES OF SCHOLARSHIP HOLDERS AND THE MATRIX RELATIONSHIP TO THE SIZE OF SCHOLARSHIP

The techniques of estimation in this section were such that the matrix relationship evolved from the computation of the family income distribution.

Again we made the broad division between further education and secondary education scholars. For the latter group, we assumed that the proportion of families per income range would be the same as the proportion of dependent children per range. For 1959 we were actually able to make our estimates more accurately. The Inland Revenue provided us with data from which we were able to estimate the proportion of children between 11 and 16 years of age who were 'claimed' by income units in each income range. Since the majority of the secondary education scholars were in this category, we took the opportunity of using this more exact distribution for 1959.[1] In the other two years we followed the method first outlined, with a special modification for 1954.

The initial estimates for 1954 indicated a considerable bias in the distribution of low income families. This we distrusted for two reasons. First, it was not evident in the other two years and, secondly, a substantial proportion of these awards were for children at direct grant and grammar schools, which led us to expect that the mode of the distribution would be in the 'middle' income ranges. Therefore the number of families with an annual income below £400 p.a. and with children receiving secondary education awards was limited to 5% of the total. The distribution of the remaining 95% above this £400 limit was made according to the proportion of children per range, from and including the range £400 to £500 up to the range £1,000 to £1,500. £1,500 was selected as an upper limit. It was assumed that in 1954 Local Education Authorities did not give such awards to what would then have been relatively high income families. The upper and lower cut-off limits were not chosen randomly. They are based on information relevant mainly to further education awards. However, since to a large extent the two types of awards mainly affect the same socioeconomic group, an income pattern for one may not be too far different from that of the other. We admit, though, that our estimates for 1954 are far from satisfactory.

The matrix relationship for these secondary education awards presented no problems. Since in section 11A.1 we had put all the scholarships in this group into one income range, namely the £50–£250 range, we simply had a 1 × 1 matrix.

For the family income distribution of further education scholars, changes in the methods of finance necessitated a different estimating technique for 1963

---

[1] The difference between the income distribution of children aged 11 to 16 and of all children is illustrated below. As can be seen, it is not large.

Income range (£)	Children (11 to 16) (%)	All children (%)
50–	1	2
250–	1	1
300–	3	3
400–	5	6
500–	10	12
600–	15	16
700–	16	17
800–	25	24
1,000–	20	16
1,500–2,000	4	3
Total	100	100

from that for the two earlier surveys. Since 1961 the relationship between parental income and the size of L.E.A. and Teacher Training awards has been standardised over the country, according to regulations laid down by the Ministry of Education [44]. Basically the system is that, after allowances for insurance fees, ground rent and dependents, an assessed parental income of £700 p.a. or less entitles a student to the maximum maintenance award of £250, exclusive of fees. For parental incomes between £700 and £1,400, 8% of the parents' income is deducted from the value of the scholarship. For incomes between £1,400 and £2,000 the deduction is 10% of the assessed income, reaching a minimum of zero for the students of wealthier families. Since all local authorities pay a student's fees, irrespective of the parent's income, then by our definition of scholarship income, the minimum value will be £50 and the maximum £300.

We used the above structural relationship to estimate for the 218,000 L.E.A. university and Teacher Training awards: first, the income distribution of parents (i.e. families) and secondly, the matrix between the two sets of data. In general we derived an inverse matrix, that is, the higher was the scholarship income, the lower the parental income. The only adjustment was a slight widening of the parental income ranges resulting from the scholarship income ranges, to allow for the special allowances granted by the authorities. The income distributions of parents with incomes below £700 and above £3,000 (the adjusted upper limit) were determined in the same manner as for secondary education awards, i.e. by the proportion of dependent children per range.

The distribution of the family incomes for the remaining 14,000 further education awards was assumed to be the same as that for the above further education awards. These were mainly postgraduate and other university awards. It seemed reasonable to assume that these students were likely to come from the same income/social structure as the remainder of the student body. The major difference between these and the other awards is that they are not tied to parental income. Therefore there is no possibility of the 'inverse' set-up. The awards vary in size with academic ability in many cases and with the prosperity of the university in others. We opted for a cross-classification matrix based on a neutral relationship. That was that the probability of the family income size pattern was identical for each group of scholarship income sizes, in which case each would display an identical pattern to that for the aggregate distribution, which we have just described above (table A1.7).

The 1960s have witnessed rapid changes in the further education structure in the U.K. From 1959 to 1963 the annual rate of increase in the number of L.E.A. further education awards was twice that in the 1954 to 1959 period. 1961 saw the introduction of standardisation by region and type of further education among L.E.A. awards and by 1963 state scholarships had almost disappeared. For these reasons it did not seem appropriate to use the 1963 technique for either 1959 or 1954.

Vaizey [71] has stated that by the mid-1950s university scholarships (in which we include other further education awards) were most common in families earning between £500 to £1,500 p.a., and improbable in those earning more than £2,000 p.a. This is a large difference from 1963. In that year 95%

of the further education awards went to families with incomes between £800 to £5,000. If the 1963 limits were reduced by 25% (the money income increase per unit between 1959 and 1963) the limits would be £600–£3,750. Thus not only has the number and value of scholarships increased rapidly since the 1950s, but so have the numbers given to wealthier families. This extension of awards to wealthier families can also be gauged by the decline in the proportion of unaided students at universities, namely, 27.6% in 1954, 15.2% in 1959–60 and 3.2% in 1962–3.[1] Klein [35] has estimated that 79% of the students at school and universities in 1953 who came from families with incomes above £1,000 p.a. were unaided. Thus the bulk of unaided students probably came from upper-income families.

Table A1.7 *Income distribution of the families of scholarship holders*[a]

Income range (£)	1954 Numbers ('000s)	1959 Numbers ('000s)	1963 Numbers ('000s)
300	4	3	0.4
300–	7	5	2.8
400–	47.5	10	3.6
500–	58	29	8.5
600–	38	41	13.5
700–	32	43	17.0
800–	26	76	48.4
1,000–	12.5	83	88.8
1,500–	—	10	78.8
2,000–	—	—	90.2
3,000–	—	—	22.7
5,000+	—	—	12.3
Total	225	300	387

Sources: B.I.R. *Reports* [19] nos.: 108, tables 68–71 and 65; 99, table 82. Information from the Inland Revenue. Table A1.3 and Ministry of Education [44].
[a] The income totals used, per range, can be readily estimated from the average income for married units by ranges, in the respective Inland Revenue surveys published in B.I.R. *Reports* [19].

Vaizey's conclusions apply broadly to the 1955 to 1957 period. The figures in the Robbins Report, our source for 1963, relate to the 1962 calendar year. Therefore we decided to adopt for 1959 the Vaizey limits and the Robbins parameters. This is to say, we assumed that 95% of the further education awards went to families in the £500 to £1,500 range, with a further 2% to the £1,500 to £2,000 range and 3% to those below £500 p.a. The allocation to each range within these limits was determined by the distribution of children over 16 by ranges: see table A1.7.

For 1954, the Vaizey limits were arbitrarily changed. The lower limit was

[1] Robbins [63] appendix 2(A), part vi.

altered to £400 and the two upper limits of £1,500 and £2,000 were replaced by one of £1,500. Thus 95% of further education awards went to families in the £400–£1,500 range and the other 5% to those with incomes below £400 p.a. The allocation per range within these limits was determined by the distribution of all children by ranges.

At this stage we feel compelled to emphasise again that the 1954 estimates are rather rough and ready. The lack of information and the number of arbitrary assumptions we have had to make can only give rise to scepticism. The estimates have been included mainly because of desire for comprehensiveness.

The cross-classification matrix was filled in by broadly assuming an inverse relationship between scholarship income size and dependent family income size.

The final procedure was to collate for each an overall cross-classification matrix and then to follow the same technique as outlined for the marriage double-countings. This is to combine the incomes in each cell and to estimate the deductions and additions of income and units per range and the consequent adjustments to the family size classifications. These manipulations were carried out on the type 1 distributions.

IIB   THE ELIMINATION OF DOUBLE-COUNTING DUE TO MINORS'
     COVENANTS

All our data on minors' covenants are from estimates provided by the Inland Revenue (see table A1.8).

Table A1.8 *Numbers and value of minors' covenants*

Year	Number (ooo's)	Value (£m)	Average value (£)
1954	20	2	100
1959	40	5	125
1963	60	9	150

Source: Information from the Inland Revenue.

All the income units in table A1.8 are located in the £50–£250 income range. However, they will not all be double-counted. It is only since 1964 that the sliding-scale arrangements have been in operation which permit parents to claim some child allowance, even though the child's income may exceed the statutory limit below which the full allowance can be claimed.[1]

Before 1964 any income above these limits made the child allowances inadmissible. The family classification tables only include children for whom allowances are claimed and due. Therefore double-counting between minors' covenants and the family classification tables will only exist for those minors' covenants below the statutory limits. These limits for our years were: 1954, £85; 1959, £100; 1963, £115.

The statutory limits therefore required us to split the £50–£250 income range

[1] For details on the sliding scale see any of the recent B.I.R. *Reports* [19].

into sub-ranges with respect to minors' covenants. This was achieved by using the average incomes given in table A1.8 and the Paretian interpolation technique. The range was in fact subdivided into four smaller ranges. This gave the added advantage of a more detailed cross-classification with parental income.

The minors' covenants not subject to double-counting were combined with the income units of their dependent families. In doing this we were adhering strictly to the concept of the 'inner family' which we have adopted.

There was no information to hand on the income distribution of families containing children receiving covenants. We assumed that these families were predominantly from the higher income groups. Therefore for each year an income limit was arbitrarily chosen to define the lowest income level of the so-called higher income ranges. Above these limits the distribution per income range was determined by the distribution of children per range. The limits selected were for 1954, £800; for 1959, £1,000; and for 1963 £1,500.

The estimated distributions are presented in table A1.9. Tables A1.8 (subdivided) and A1.9 provide the aggregate columns and rows for the construction of a cross-classification matrix between the two types of income units. We assumed a positive relationship, that is that the highest covenants belong to the families with the highest incomes.

Table A1.9   *Distribution of income of families with children receiving minors' covenants*

Income range (£)	1954		1959		1963	
	Numbers ('000s)	Income (£m)	Numbers ('000s)	Income (£m)	Numbers ('000s)	Income (£m)
800–	10.8	9.5	—	—	—	—
1,000–	5.3	6.3	29	34	—	—
1,500–	1.7	2.9	5	8.5	33	55.8
2,000–						
3,000–	2.2	8.8	6	22.7	7	26.4
5,000+					4	34.6
Total	20	27.5	40	65.2	60	155

Sources: B.I.R. *Reports* [19] nos.: 99, table 82; 105, tables 92–5; 108, tables 68–71.

Finally we had to make the same type of adjustments to the type 1 distribution and its family classification tables as was undertaken for the scholarship incomes. The minors' covenants where there was no double-counting required a slightly different adjustment. In these instances we had to increase the family size of the dependent family unit by one person. For example, a three person unit became a four person family and so on. Furthermore, for this item we made allowances for the fact that some families with no 'fiscally' dependent children, i.e. two person units, would be affected. Basically the procedure was to take the family size distribution per range estimated for the double-counted minors' covenants[1] and to reduce the family size pattern by one person. In other words, if we started within range y_i to y_{i+1} with n per cent of three-person

---

[1] This was estimated in the same way as for the families of scholarship holders.

units, m per cent of four-person and so on, these now became n per cent for two-person units, m per cent for three-person units, etc. Implicit in this manipulation is the assumption that the family size classification is identical for all families with minors' covenants per range, irrespective of the state of fiscal dependency.

The above double-counting eliminations were performed on the type 1 distributions. As a result we had, of course, to readjust the family size distribution of the £50–£250 range, since the 'residually' derived control totals of units and persons had changed. Again we attempted to follow the sample distributions provided by the Inland Revenue and were able to achieve an equally high degree of correlation.

CONCLUSION

This appendix is, we hope, as much an exercise in techniques as in actual measurement. The distributions are by no means accurate. They cannot be and there is no method by which we can evaluate the extent of their errors. Even the base data, i.e. the C.S.O. distributions, are subject to continual improvement and revision for past years.

The whole area of income distribution statistics is one where extreme caution is essential in interpreting the results. It would be foolish to attempt any qualification of the extent of our errors. If we could use perfect data for comparison and thereby discover a substantial margin of error, then we could hypothesise that a good proportion of error would derive from the base data. Our manipulations do have some influence on the shape of the distribution, but they are insufficient in total to bring about any substantial errors. We do not believe that there is any reason to suppose that the Inland Revenue statisticians have not succeeded in producing statistics as reliable as any other government or academic body.

There does remain the possibility of small errors. These will result from wrong assumptions and adjustments made by us. This is inevitable in the construction of proxy variables and the like. Their effect on the shape of the distribution is small; their importance with respect to policy and social comment negligible. For example, our data could be used, as is done in chapter 3, to estimate the number of 'low incomes units'. Our calculations may show that 22% of persons have low incomes. The actual figure may be 19% or 25%. We have no means, however, of ascertaining the actual figure or the precise error of our estimate. The point is that about 20% of the population are 'poor' – a sufficiently sound conclusion on which to base comment or decisions.

Errors of the above magnitude do make inter-year comparisons difficult, if we are unable to conclude that the 'directional' effects are not the same in all years. Nevertheless, much of this type of error can be eliminated in future years, as new data become available and improvements are made to our techniques. This, however, does not detract from our results. Official statistics are now presented in a form meaningful for economic analysis. The method of adjustment, we hope, will be useful to future researchers in this field.

THE PARETO INTERPOLATION

This is an interpolation not widely known in academic literature. It was brought to our notice by the Inland Revenue who not only use it but were largely responsible for its development.

The technique is derived from Pareto's Law of Income Distribution. The Pareto formula is normally written as:

$$\varUpsilon_x = A_x^{-\alpha} \tag{1}$$

where $\varUpsilon_x$ is the aggregate number of incomes above income level x,

$\quad x$ a given level of income,

$\quad A$ a location parameter, and

$\quad \alpha$ a parameter describing the shape of the distribution.

The integral form of equation (1) for values of x from x to ∞ is:

$$\varUpsilon = \int_x^\infty Ax^{-\alpha}\ \mathrm{d}x = \left| \frac{Ax^{1-\alpha}}{1-\alpha} \right|_x^\infty. \tag{2}$$

From equation (2) it can be derived that the number of incomes from x_1 to x_2 is:

$$\int_{x_1}^{x_2} \varUpsilon_x \mathrm{d}x = A(1/x_1^\alpha - 1/x_2^\alpha). \tag{3}$$

If the range is extended from x_1 to x_3, then the proportion of incomes from x_1 to x_2 in the x_1 to x_3 range is:

$$\int_{x_1}^{x_2} \varUpsilon_x \mathrm{d}x \Big/ \int_{x_1}^{x_3} \varUpsilon_x \mathrm{d}x = \frac{1/x_1^\alpha - 1/x_2^\alpha}{1/x_1^\alpha - 1/x_3^\alpha} = k, \tag{4}$$

where k is a proportion. k is clearly a function of α, such that if α is known k can be calculated.

α can be approximated for a relative frequency graph drawn on a double log scale by:

$$\alpha = \frac{\log_e \varUpsilon_1 - \log_e \varUpsilon_3}{\log_e x_3 - \log_e x_1}. \tag{5}$$

In drawing a graph of this nature it must be remembered that the essence is relative frequency, thus the numbers of income units for each income range must be adjusted for variations in the width of these ranges. The Inland Revenue provided us with considerable graph material which made the calculation a very simple matter indeed.

If we postulate from equation (5) that α is constant over the x_1 to x_3 income range, equation (4) can then be solved in terms of equation (5).

When α is positive we will have:[1]

$$k = \frac{1 - (x_1/x_2)\alpha}{1 - (x_1/x_3)\alpha} \tag{6}$$

and for negative values of α:

$$k = \frac{x_1^\alpha - x_2^\alpha}{x_1^\alpha - x_3^\alpha} . \tag{7}$$

Likewise if $\alpha = 0$, equation (4) becomes

$$k = \frac{\log_e x_1 - \log_e x_2}{\log_e x_1 - \log_e x_3} . \tag{8}$$

and finally if $\alpha = 1$, then

$$k = \frac{x_3}{x_2} \frac{x_2 - x_1}{x_3 - x_1} . \tag{9}$$

The amount of income in a given income range can also be derived from equation (2).

$$\int_{x_1}^{x_2} Ix.x dx = \frac{A\alpha}{1 - \alpha} (1/x_1^\alpha - 1/x_2^{\alpha-1}), \tag{10}$$

where $Ix = A\alpha \,/\, x^{\alpha+1}$, i.e. aggregate income above income level x. From equation (10) the average income in the x_1 to x_2 range is

$$\bar{x} = \frac{\alpha x_1}{\alpha - 1} \frac{(1/x_1^{\alpha-1} - 1/x_2^{\alpha-1})}{(1/x_1^\alpha - 1/x_2^\alpha)} , \tag{11}$$

which reduces to

$$\bar{x} = \frac{\alpha}{\alpha - 1} \bigg/ \frac{1 - (x_1/x_2)^{\alpha-1}}{1 - (x_1/x_2)^\alpha} \tag{12}$$

when α is positive and

$$\bar{x} = \frac{\alpha}{\alpha + 1} \bigg/ \frac{x_2^{\alpha+1} - x_1^{\alpha+1}}{x_2^\alpha - x_1^\alpha} \tag{13}$$

when α is negative.

The average income equivalent of equations (8) and (9) are:

$$\bar{x} = x_2 - x_1 / \log_e \frac{x_2}{x_1} , \tag{14}$$

when $\alpha = 0$,

---

[1] The following equations follow closely Bowley's manipulations of the Pareto law of income distribution. See Bowley [8] pp. 346–8.

$$\bar{x} = \frac{\log_e (x_2/x_1)}{(1/x_1) - (1/x_2)},$$ (15)

when $\alpha = 1$.

For further references on this technique of interpolation see House of Commons Committee on Income Tax (House of Commons no. 365 of 1906, pp. 220–30, 240–1 and 245–6).

A DIGRESSION ON THE STATISTICAL
MEASURES OF INEQUALITY

I

We have argued in chapter 3 that the traditional statistical measures often adopted in treatises on income distribution do not produce a meaningful measure of inequality. However, even if we accept the perfect equality concept, upon which all such measures are founded, there is still a major technical criticism that can be levied against these measures, namely, that they produce inconsistent results and that no measure really commends itself over and above the others. Furthermore some measures also have large errors of grouping.

There are fifteen well-known statistical measures of income inequality.[1] These can be broadly divided into three groups. (A) Measures of variation (or dispersion); (B) Measures of skewness and (C) Measures derived from the empirical laws of income distribution. We shall discuss each of these groups in turn.

A. MEASURES OF VARIATION[2]

In this category we have six measures which sum the deviations of each magnitude (or attribute) in the distribution from a central value, in most cases the mean. The measures are all relative, permitting inter-year comparisons.

The measures are:

(a) the relative mean difference (M),
(b) the concentration ratio (R),
(c) the coefficient of variation (V),
(d) the mean deviation of the logarithmic values of the attributes in the distribution over the logarithm of the geometric mean $(M \log)$,
(e) the standard deviation of the logarithmic values of the attributes in the distribution $(\sigma \log)$,
(f) the coefficient of variation referred to the standard attribute $V(S)$.

There is a brief algebraic summary of each measure in section II of this appendix.

Of these measures the concentration ratio is the most common, having gained almost universal support.[3] It is generally described as the ratio of the area

---

[1] See Yntema [72], Bowman [9], Dalton [21], and Andic [3].
[2] This section owes much to Yntema's [72] fine article on the measurement of income inequality.
[3] See Morgan [51].

between the Lorenz curve and the diagonal to half the area of the box, or half the Gini coefficient, which in turn is the mean difference without repetitions divided by twice the arithmetic mean.[1] Yule and Kendall [73] have shown that there is a strong link between the standard deviation and the mean difference without repetitions. This being the case, the concentration ratio will suffer from the disadvantage of any measure employing the standard deviation, i.e. measures (c), (e) and (f). The standard deviation, by virtue of the 'squaring' process, will exaggerate large deviations from the mean and as a consequence be biased towards the dispersion at the upper end of a distribution. This bias is partially overcome by using a logarithmic version of the standard deviation, which expresses absolute differences as ratios, and the two mean deviation measures, i.e. (a) and (d).

Table A3.1   *Concentration ratios of three hypothetical income distributions*

Income range (£)	Case A		Case B		Case C	
	Numbers ('000s)	Income (£m)	Numbers ('000s)	Income (£m)	Numbers ('000s)	Income (£m)
0–	70	3.5	60	3	60	3
100–	20	3	20	3	20	3
200–	5	1.2	15	3.7	15	3.7
300–	3	1.1	3	1.1	3	1.1
400+	2	1.2	2	2.2	2	1.2
Total	100	10	100	13	100	12
Concentration ratio	38.3		46.1		41.1	

The concentration ratio is also very much biased, particularly in highly positively skewed distributions, where the concentration is considerable in the lowest income range. Examples of this sensitivity are given in table A3.1 above. Here three highly skewed distributions are presented and their concentration ratios compared. It will be noted that the concentration ratios of distributions B and C are appreciably higher than that of A. This is a particularly disturbing result since it could be strongly argued that distributions B and C are more egalitarian. They have fewer persons in the lowest income range, compensated for by increases in a higher income group (i.e. the £200–300 range). We have a reduction in the numbers of low incomes and increase in the 'middle' income groups indicating less inequality. In case C the two top income groups are left unchanged. In comparison to A, B and C are surely preferable states of affairs. The comparison between B and C is an example where a substantial

---

[1] A detailed account of the relationship between the concentration ratios, the Gini coefficient of concentration and the mean difference is given in Kendall [33] vol 1, pp. 43ff. and Yule and Kendall [73] pp. 146–7.

increase in the amount of income held by the top income group has a considerable influence on the concentration ratio; in effect a change of almost 5%.[1]

In table A3.1 we have, of course, picked our examples. The concentration ratio is the worst offender in this respect. Of the other dispersion measures, only the coefficient of variation and σ log give greater inequality in either distributions B or C (actually only in case C). However, this phenomenon does occur in the measurement of the per capita distribution of income in chapter 2 (see table A3.5) with respect to R and σ log.

Table A3.2 presents the limit values of each measure. The limits are the perfect equality state and the perfect inequality situation, that is where one income unit or person is in possession of all income. In the logarithmic measures perfect inequality was defined so that all save one person or unit held one unit of currency with the one person receiving the remainder of total income. It is clear from table A3.2 that, for all measures, the larger the statistic value the greater the inequality, though, in the limiting case of perfect inequality, a comparison between two distributions of unequal attribute size will reflect the difference in attribute size and not greater inequality. At all levels of inequality some aspect of this factor will be present in the statistic value. This criticism does not apply to the concentration ratio. It is presumably this invariability to the attribute size of a distribution which has commended the concentration ratio to income distribution statisticians.

Table A3.2 *Limit values of the statistics of variation*

Coefficient	Perfect equality	Perfect inequality
(a) M	o	$2(\Upsilon-1)/\Upsilon$
(b) R	o	I
(c) V	o	$1+\sqrt{(\Upsilon-1)}$
(d) M log	o	$2(\Upsilon-1)/\Upsilon.\{\log x\}$
(e) σ log	o	$\Upsilon-1/\{\log x\}$
(f) $V(S)$	o	$1+\sqrt{(\Upsilon-1/\Upsilon)}$

Note: Υ is the number of units or persons in a distribution. $\{\log x\}$ is the logarithm of the geometric mean.

B. MEASURES OF SKEWNESS

A distribution of income where all persons are in the same income group also has the property of being perfectly symmetrical. Thus a distribution showing perfect equality can be equated with perfect symmetry, with the obvious corollary that inequality is synonymous with anti-symmetry, i.e. skewness.

There are three well-known measures of skewness:

---

[1] The larger income totals in distributions B and C of table A3.1, in comparison to A, are inevitable, since some units are moved to a higher income range. Only in case B does this seem to cause a higher value for the concentration ratio and this is because some of the increase falls in the top income range. Generally though, the larger concentration ratio is a result of greater dispersion.

(g) Bowley's index (Q),
(h) Pearson's coefficient (Sk),
(i) cubed deviations (α_3).

These measures are described in section II of this appendix.

The Bowley index has been widely used in income distribution studies and, to a lesser extent, so has the Pearson coefficient.[1] α_3 is a recent measure of skewness, introduced after the period during which measures of skewness were 'fashionable' in this field.

These measures have the advantage that they equal o under conditions of perfect equality (see table A3.3). Bowley's index has the further advantage that perfect inequality in a positively skewed distribution gives a value of 1. The assumption of positive skewness is empirically justified for income distributions.

The main criticism of the skewness measures is that the concept of perfect equality is ambiguous. Perfect symmetry does not necessarily entail perfect equality of incomes. A normal distribution of incomes would produce a perfectly symmetrical pattern. At one time it was held that a normal distribution of incomes should be the 'natural' state of affairs.[2] This view is no longer accepted and, even if it were, little is achieved when one is able to conclude only that inequality may or may not exist, although we have a normal distribution of incomes. The degree of variation (i.e. dispersion) and inequality under our proposed definition could be substantial in a normal distribution. These measures, like the measures of variation, are also incapable of throwing much light on the nature or classification of inequality.

Table A3.3 *Limit values of the measures of skewness*

Coefficient	Perfect equality	Perfect inequality
(g) Q	0	1
(h) Sk	0	$^3/1 + \sqrt{(\Upsilon - 1)}$
(i) α_3	0	$(\Upsilon - 1)^3 - \Upsilon - 1/\Upsilon[(1 + \sqrt{(\Upsilon - 1)}]_3$

C. MEASURES DERIVED FROM THE 'LAWS' OF INCOME DISTRIBUTION

There are six measures in this group. At this stage we shall simply enumerate the measures and their origin. In section III we shall deal at length with the theories which can be empirically tested. The validity of these indices of inequality, from a statistical viewpoint, will depend largely on the goodness of fit, etc. of the theory from which they are derived. In most cases the models fail to pass the autocorrelation test.

The measures are:

(j) the Gini coefficient, δ,
(k) the Pareto coefficient, α,
(l) the Lydall coefficient, λ,

[1] See Mincer [43].   [2] See Mincer [43] on this point.

(m) the Dalton–Bernoulli coefficient, g, which is the arithmetic mean referred to the geometric mean,
(n) the Dalton coefficient, h, which is the harmonic mean referred to the arithmetic mean,
(o) the Gibrat coefficient, C, or the log-normal coefficient,

The Gibrat measure is a multiple of σ log from section (A),

$$C = 100 \cdot \sqrt{(2.\sigma \log.)}$$

The limit values of the 'theory' measures are given in Table A3.4. In the case of the Pareto coefficient, α, generally the greater the slope of the Pareto line, the greater the inequality. However, in some cases, the upper tail of a distribution may be prolonged and large in which case the reverse assumptions on the slope of the line may hold.[1] It is an unstable measure of inequality.

Summarising the discussion so far, we can conclude:

(1) The measures of variation, in general, are biased to dispersion in the upper income groups. The concentration ratio and σ log are sensitive to concentration in highly positively skewed distributions.

Table A3.4 *Limit values of the 'theory' measures*

Coefficient		Perfect equality	Perfect inequality
(j)	δ	1	∞
(k)	α	∞	0
(l)	λ	0	∞
(m)	g [a]	1	$Y/I \cdot {}^{Y}\!\sqrt{I-1}$
(n)	h [a]	1	$1/I \cdot Y$
(o)	C	0	$141.42\ Y - 1/\{\log x\}$

[a] Perfect inequality was defined in these cases as previously for the logarithmic measures of variation (cf. p. 139). I is the aggregate amount of income.

(2) The measures of skewness are ambiguous.
(3) The theory measures are dependent on other statistical judgements before they can be accepted as valid. In most instances these are not forthcoming.
(4) In only five of the measures is the statistic value independent of the attribute size. These five measures are unacceptable for the reasons mentioned in (1), (2) and (3).

In the above analysis little is said concerning the standard errors of the measures. Since the number of income units or persons is large, these will be small. However, in the case of sample surveys, as conducted by the Ministry of Labour for its family expenditure publications, the number of attributes is much lower, in the order of three or four thousand cases. In this context standard errors may assume greater importance.

For the regression coefficients, α, δ, λ and C, the standard error is implicit in the significance tests on the parameter. In practically all regressions these tests have been satisfied. For the other measures it was difficult to find any expressions of the standard errors. Nicholson [53] has estimated the standard

[1] See Bowman [9].

error of R to be approximated by $1/4\sqrt{\varUpsilon}$, where $\varUpsilon$ is the total number of units. Yule and Kendall [73][1] express that of the coefficient of variation as $V/\sqrt{(2\varUpsilon)}$ and that of the arithmetic mean as $\sigma/\varUpsilon$. The standard error of the coefficient of the variation, however, is not applicable to strongly leptokurtic distributions (i.e. those with long tails), which are frequent in our data. Nevertheless the above examples give some indication of the probable magnitude of the standard errors. In our data they will be small, but this is not to say that they are universally insignificant.

In a nutshell, no measure commends itself as significantly preferable to the others.

The next stage of our analysis is to test the measures for consistency in ranking. We also conducted tests with respect to the grouping errors.[2] Consistency was tested by estimating the coefficient of concordance for the 15 measures with respect to their ranking of 22 distributions of income. These 22 distributions are made up of the 14 distributions presented in chapter 2 plus the Inland Revenue and C.S.O. distributions for 1949, 1954, 1959 and 1963.[3] We made no allowance for the different characteristics of the types of distribution used. If all the measures purport to measure inequality, these characteristics should not enter as significant factors determining differences in ranking.

The coefficient of concordance[4] is no more than an approximation of the average correlation coefficient between n by $n-1$ rankings of the same group of items. If it is zero in value, then there is no consistency between rankings and, conversely, if it is 1 there is complete consistency. The statistic measures for each of the 22 distributions by the 15 measures are given in table A3.5. The consequent rankings for each statistic measure are presented in table A3.6. The coefficient of concordance for this table is 0.19 and is highly significant at the 1% level.[5] This is a low value, indicating roughly that there is only, on average, a 20% agreement between the measures. What agreement there is results from consistency within subsets of measures. We were able to distinguish five subgroups of measures where there was a good level of agreement. These were:

(1) $M, R, g,$

(2) $V, V(S),$

(3) σ log, M log, $C, h,$

(4) $Q, Sk,$ and

(5) $\delta, \lambda.$

[1] Yule and Kendall [73] pp. 434 and 457.

[2] In testing the grouping error no adjustment was made by using correction formulae. The best known is Sheppard's Correction for the standard deviation of grouped data. This is, however, not applicable to skewed distributions – see Yule and Kendall [73] p. 133. These authors also point out that it would be most difficult to correct for grouping errors in the mean deviation. We came across no mention of corrections for the other measures. In general most statisticians seem to take the line that the greater the number of equal width ranges the less likely error in grouped data.

[3] These are presented in table A7.1.

[4] The coefficient of concordance is $W = 12S/m^2(n^3 - n)$ where S is the sum of the squares of the deviations of the sum of each set of rankings from the mean sum for the ranking set. The mean sum of each ranking is estimated as $m^2(n-1)/2$, where m is the number of ranking sets (15 in our case) and n is the number of rankings (i.e. 22). See Kendall [34] ch. 6 for details.

[5] See Kendall [34] pp. 99–100.

Table A.3.5 *Values of the statistical measures of inequality*

Type of distribution	Year	(a) M	(b) R	(c) V	(d) M log	(e) σ log	(f) V(S)	(g) Q	(h) Sk	(i) a_3	(j) δ	(k) α	(l) λ	(m) g	(n) h	(o) C
B.I.R.	1949	0.514	35.31	1.497	0.404	0.541	0.831	0.189	0.488	24.868	1.966	1.902	2.574	1.037	0.718	76.508
	1954	0.470	33.89	1.194	0.430	0.562	0.767	0.099	0.435	21.581	1.840	2.018	2.397	1.032	0.712	79.478
	1959	0.470	33.66	1.044	0.451	0.579	0.722	0.086	0.455	16.157	1.760	2.014	1.879	1.031	0.704	81.882
	1963	0.451	32.24	0.951	0.437	0.556	0.689	0.150	0.487	13.477	1.697	2.072	1.652	1.027	0.724	78.629
C.S.O.	1949	0.560	38.72	1.590	0.499	0.607	0.846	0.098	0.454	26.609	1.968	1.736	2.522	1.046	0.667	85.842
	1954	0.570	39.26	1.306	0.570	0.676	0.794	0.072	0.428	22.053	1.842	1.798	2.439	1.046	0.626	95.600
	1959	0.556	39.25	1.141	0.592	0.720	0.752	0.043	0.432	15.978	1.761	1.767	2.160	1.045	0.594	101.882
	1963	0.552	38.67	1.056	0.594	0.719	0.726	0.050	0.468	12.947	1.717	1.696	1.762	1.042	0.596	101.681
Type 1 units	1949	0.561	38.73	1.580	0.497	0.608	0.845	0.091	0.457	26.347	1.965	1.736	2.534	1.046	0.667	85.983
	1954	0.561	39.21	1.293	0.563	0.676	0.791	0.065	0.438	22.182	1.841	1.796	2.438	1.045	0.626	95.600
	1959	0.549	38.99	1.139	0.584	0.714	0.752	0.036	0.422	16.152	1.763	1.756	2.150	1.044	0.598	100.974
	1963	0.547	38.31	1.048	0.585	0.711	0.723	0.049	0.467	12.949	1.716	1.694	1.743	1.041	0.602	100.550
Type 2 units	1954	0.558	38.99	1.286	0.559	0.671	0.789	0.061	0.440	22.145	1.840	1.796	2.430	1.044	0.630	94.893
	1959	0.544	38.62	1.130	0.577	0.705	0.749	0.039	0.431	16.136	1.762	1.755	2.135	1.043	0.605	99.701
	1963	0.542	37.98	1.040	0.574	0.701	0.721	0.053	0.471	12.849	1.714	1.689	1.711	1.040	0.610	101.964
Type 1 persons	1949	0.592	33.72	1.696	0.422	0.534	0.861	0.021	0.431	48.455	1.964	1.150	2.086	1.045	0.721	75.518
	1954	0.531	34.78	1.393	0.478	0.558	0.812	0.109	0.571	46.361	1.885	1.168	2.095	1.040	0.715	78.912
	1959	0.526	35.35	1.202	0.453	0.577	0.769	0.065	0.515	28.594	1.796	1.149	2.150	1.038	0.704	81.599
	1963	0.519	35.40	1.087	0.477	0.588	0.736	0.279	0.643	22.477	1.741	1.125	2.160	1.036	0.698	83.155
Type 2 persons	1954	0.547	34.45	1.419	0.497	0.577	0.817	0.101	0.526	45.942	1.885	1.169	2.096	1.043	0.700	81.599
	1959	0.528	35.62	1.207	0.457	0.583	0.770	0.065	0.520	28.457	1.797	1.148	2.150	1.039	0.700	82.448
	1963	0.524	35.78	1.089	0.485	0.599	0.736	0.270	0.634	22.353	1.740	1.125	2.160	1.037	0.690	84.710

Sources: As for tables 2.2 to 2.10, and table A7.1.

Table A3.6　*Ranking of all distributions by inequality by type of measure*

Type of distribution	Year	(a) M	(b) R	(c) V	(d) M log	(e) σ log	(f) V(S)	(g) Q	(h) Sk	(i) α₃	(j) δ	(k) α	(l) λ	(m) g	(n) h	(o) C
B.I.R.	1949	4	7	19	1	2	19	20	16	15	22	19	22	5	3	2
	1954	2	4	11	3	5	11	16	6	9	13	20	16	3	5	5
	1959	2	2	3	5	8	3	13	10	8	7	21	5	2	6	8
	1963	1	1	1	4	3	1	19	15	4	1	22	1	1	1	3
C.S.O.	1949	18	16	21	13	12	21	15	9	17	21	12	20	20	12	12
	1954	21	22	16	16	15	16	12	2	10	16	18	19	20	15	15
	1959	16	21	10	21	22	9	4	5	5	8	15	15	17	22	22
	1963	15	15	5	22	21	5	6	13	2	4	10	4	12	21	21
Type 1 units	1949	19	17	20	11	13	20	14	11	16	20	11	21	20	12	13
	1954	19	20	15	15	15	15	9	7	12	15	16	18	17	15	15
	1959	14	18	9	19	20	9	2	1	7	10	14	10	15	20	20
	1963	12	13	4	20	19	4	5	12	3	3	9	3	11	19	19
Type 2 units	1954	17	19	14	14	14	14	8	8	11	14	17	17	15	14	14
	1959	11	14	8	18	18	8	3	3	6	9	13	9	13	18	18
	1963	10	12	2	17	17	2	7	14	1	2	8	2	9	17	17
Type 1 persons	1949	22	3	22	2	1	22	1	3	22	19	5	6	17	2	1
	1954	9	6	17	9	4	17	18	20	21	18	6	7	9	4	4
	1959	7	8	12	6	6	12	9	17	19	11	4	11	7	6	6
	1963	5	9	6	8	10	6	22	22	14	6	1	14	4	10	10
Type 2 persons	1954	12	5	18	11	6	18	17	19	20	17	7	8	13	8	6
	1959	8	10	13	7	9	13	9	18	18	12	3	12	8	8	9
	1963	6	11	7	10	11	6	21	21	13	5	2	13	5	11	11

Source: As for table A3.5.
1 = Least inequality.

α_3 and α had little agreement with other measures or with each other. These groupings confirm similar groupings made by Yntema [72].

The grouping errors of the measures were tested by reducing the number of ranges from fifteen to eight for two of the six sets of distribution. The types chosen were type 1 and per capita distributions. There are two harmful effects that can arise from large grouping errors. The ranking of a number of distributions may be changed. This means that conclusions concerning inequality trends from less detailed data could be entirely misleading. Also changes in the statistic value make comparisons between distributions with different numbers of ranges misleading, as well as producing a spurious absolute index of inequality.

Table A3.7 *Average^a changes in the statistic values when the number of income ranges is reduced (% change with respect to the statistic values in table 3.5)*

Measure	Average change (%)	Maximum change (%)	Minimum change (%)
(a) M	2.46	5.90	0.00
(b) R	3.09	4.16	1.30
(c) V	7.13	12.78	2.78
(d) $M\log$	2.59	7.46	0.00
(e) $\sigma\log$	1.41	2.65	0.19
(f) $V(S)$	3.71	4.93	0.83
(g) Q	74.05	166.67	39.10
(h) Sk	10.68	21.01	3.88
(i) α_3	30.27	66.87	0.40
(j) δ	0.875	3.41	0.00
(k) α	47.58	69.99	19.13
(l) λ	4.20	7.14	0.18
(m) g	0.09	0.19	0.00
(n) h	1.11	2.34	0.13
(o) C	1.41	2.65	0.19

Source: As for table A3.5.
^{a} An average of the proportionate changes in each of the eight distributions analysed.

Most of the fifteen measures recorded large changes in the statistical value as a result of the reduction in the number of ranges (see table A3.7). Three measures recorded changes of over 30% and hence must be considered unsuitable. The measures in question were Q, Sk and Pareto's α. The other skewness measure α_3 also came out badly, with an average change of over 10%. The remaining measures can be grouped by range of proportionate change:

0% to 1%	g and δ,
1% to 2%	$\sigma\log$, C, h,
2% to 5%	M, R, $M\log$ and λ, $V(S)$,
5% to 10%	V.

The measures g and δ appear to be quite insensitive to changes in the number of ranges. The actual variations in changes for those measures are also small. Large differences between the maximum and minimum values would suggest further instability with respect to the nature of the distribution being analysed. This is the case with the α_3, V, $V(S)$ and Sk measures, which all show much larger changes for the per capita distributions. The per capita distributions are, of course, more highly skewed than the units distributions.[1] The same phenomenon is to a much lesser extent evident for δ and R. The reverse holds for α and λ. All other measures would seem to be unaffected by the skewness of the distribution.

In only seven measures was the ranking of both distributions unaffected. These were, δ, λ, α_3 V, $V(S)$, g and h. Three measures indicated unchanged ranking for the per capita distribution only, R, M log and σ log. The other five measures produced different rankings in both cases. Combining the tests on grouping errors, we can conclude that g and δ are by far superior in this respect to the other measures, with λ, and h as good substitutes. However, it will be recalled that on theoretical grounds we have previously rejected both measures; g is not independent of the distribution size and δ is the parameter of an unsatisfactory regression. Also g is an insensitive measure. In table A3.6 there are four occasions, involving ten distributions, on which g registers identical statistic values. A reasonable conclusion would therefore be that all the measures must be rejected.

II

In this section we outline the measures of variation and skewness used in section I.

The following notation is used:

y = aggregate number of persons or units,
I = aggregate amount of income,
Y_i = number of persons or units per range i,
I_i = amount of income per range i,
Y_i = cumulative persons or units up to and including range i,
I_i^* = cumulative income up to and including range i,
x = a given level of income,
$\bar{x}$ = average income, i.e. I/Y,
$\bar{x}_i$ = average income per range i, i.e. I_i/Y_i,
$\log x$ = logarithm of the geometric mean, i.e. the mean of the logarithmic values of the attribute magnitudes.

1. *The relative mean deviation*

$$M = \sum_{i=1}^{n} \frac{|\bar{x} - \bar{x}_i| \cdot Y_i}{Y} \Big/ \bar{x}.$$

---

[1] It is interesting to note that only one of the skewness measures, α_3, reflects this large difference in skewness. See table A3.5.

2. *The concentration ratio*

$$R = 1 - \sum_{i=1}^{n} (Y_i/Y)\left((Y_i^*/Y)+(Y_i^*-1/Y)\right).$$

3. *The coefficient of variation*

$$V = \sqrt{\left(\sum_{i=1}^{n} \frac{(\bar{x}-\bar{x}_i)^2 \cdot Y_i}{Y}\right)} \Big/ \bar{x}.$$

4. *The mean deviation in logarithms*

$$M\log = \sum_{i=1}^{n} \frac{|\log \bar{x}-\log \bar{x}_i| \cdot Y_i}{Y} \Big/ \{\log x\}.$$

5. *The standard deviation in logarithms*

$$\log = \sqrt{\left(\sum_{i=1}^{n} \frac{(\log \bar{x}-\log \bar{x}_i)^2 \cdot Y_i}{Y}\right)}.$$

6. *The coefficient of variation referred to the standard attribute*

$$V(S) = \sqrt{\left(\sum_{i=1}^{n} \frac{(\bar{x}-\bar{x}_i)^2 \cdot Y_i}{Y}\right)} \Big/ \sqrt{\left(\sum_{i=1}^{n} \frac{(\bar{x}_i)^2 \cdot Y_i}{Y}\right)}.$$

The standard attribute is the square root of the average square of the attribute magnitudes. When we have perfect equality it is identical to the arithmetic mean. It is one of the lesser-known moments of a distribution.

7. *Bowley's index*

$$Q = (Q_3-Q_2)-(Q_2-Q_1)/Q_3-Q_1,$$

where Q_i is a quartile value, and $i = 1$, 2 or 3.

8. *Pearson's coefficient*

$$Sk = 3(\text{mean}-\text{median})/\text{standard deviation}.$$

9. *Cubed deviation*

$$\alpha_3 = \frac{1}{Y} \sum_{i=1}^{n} (\bar{x}_i-\bar{x})^3 \cdot Y_i/\sigma^3,$$

where σ is the standard deviation.

III

In this section we analyse further the measures of inequality derived from the theories of income distribution. The six theories used in section 1 can be divided into three types:

(a) empirical laws of distribution – the well-known Pareto and Gini curves,
(b) rational laws of income distribution – the Lydall and Gibrat hypotheses, and
(c) the welfare theories of Dalton and Bernoulli.

The Pareto and Gini theories have been clearly outlined and analysed in many notable works.[1] It is not our intention to add to these comments. For those unfamiliar with the hypotheses, they are:

(i) *Pareto*

$$\log Y_x = \log A - \alpha \log x,$$

where x is a given income level, Y_x is the number of persons (or units) with an income equal to or in excess of x and A is location parameter.

(ii) *Gini*

$$\log Y_x = \delta \log I_x - \log C,$$

where I_x is the aggregate income at and above a given income level x and C is a location parameter.

Almost as widely known is the Gibrat theory, alternatively called the lognormal theory of income distribution. This ingenious formulation hypothesises that the logarithms of income are normally distributed. This in turn results from a number of relative random and stochastic influences acting on all incomes, at any given time, independent of the level of any particular income. If these random shocks were in absolute terms they would produce, eventually, a normal distribution. By defining them as relative, such that the shock consists of a proportionate change in income, then a lognormal distribution can be derived. This is Gibrat's law of proportional effect.[2]

A lognormal distribution, when plotted cumulatively on logarithmic probability graph paper, produces a straight line. The linear formula for such a line is:

$$Z = b \log x + A,$$

where Z is a standardised probability scale with a mean of zero and a standard deviation of one. The measure of inequality is b, which equals

$$b = 1 / \sqrt{(2 . \sigma \log)}$$

from whence the Gibrat index is

$$100/b = C.$$

The goodness of fit of the lognormal theory is estimated by linearising the straight line on the logarithmic probability graph paper. A skewed lognormal

---

[1] See Bowman [9], Dalton [21], Andic [3], Pareto [57], and Gini [27].
[2] For further details, comments and developments of this theory, [2] see Mincer [43], Andic [3], Gibrat [26], Aitchison and Brown [2], Kalecki [32] and Champernowne [17].

distribution can generally be made normal by inserting an appropriate constant minimum level of income (x_0), such that the relative shocks become proportionate to the difference between the level of income and x_0. That is:

$$Z = b \log (x - x_0) + A.$$

This, of course, necessitates the omission of all income below x_0 from the 'explained' variables. Since the aim is to describe a complete distribution this is an unsatisfactory procedure.

The essential criticism of any stochastic model is that it is, in effect, an admission of defeat by the economist. It is not only unrealistic but plainly irresponsible to assert that any distribution of income and changes therein are the result solely of random factors. Random factors obviously play a part. Nevertheless, so do factors such as growth, inflation, trade union power, individual choice, age, sex and so on. The lognormal theory can be dismissed on the grounds that it explains little and 'sheds no light on the process of distribution'.[1]

Lydall's theory is derived from the hierarchy of supervision and the salary arrangements that go with such a structure.[2] It is assumed that persons in one income class are responsible for the supervision of those in the income class below. Furthermore, a fixed supervisor/supervisee relationship is assumed such that

$$Y_i = n Y_{i+1} \tag{1}$$

where Y_i denotes persons or income and i is any given income range.

The income of a supervisor is a function of the number of supervisees and the income of the supervisees, such that:

$$I_{i+1}/nI = p \tag{2}$$

where I_i is aggregate income per income range.

If n and p are constant for all values of i, then $\log Y$ plotted against $\log Y_i$ will produce a straight line

$$\log Y_i = A + \lambda \log I_i \tag{3}$$

where

$$\lambda = -\log n/\log np \tag{4}[3]$$

As Lydall carefully points out, his theory is relevant only to employment incomes. Nevertheless, we have applied it to all incomes. There are two possible justifications for such an application. Firstly investment income may be ran-

---

[1] See Mincer [43] for discussion on this point. Quote from Mincer [43] p. 283.
[2] See Lydall [40].
[3] Proof: The slope of the line

$$\lambda = (\log Y_{i+1} - \log Y_i)/(\log I_{i+1} - \log I_i)$$
$$= \log (Y_{i+1}/Y_i) / \log (I_{i+1}/I_i).$$

Substituting Y_{i+1}/Y_i and I_{i+1}/I_i from (1) and (2) we have

$$\lambda = (\log 1/n)/\log np$$
$$= -\log n/\log np.$$

domly distributed about the earned (i.e. employment) income pattern. We attach little importance to this possibility. In the second case it might be argued that investment income does not affect the coefficient n (i.e. the supervision effect) but only the income effect coefficient, p. Investment income will tend to raise the actual value of p. This case could be further developed by arguing that there may be a two-way relationship between employment and investment income. The opportunity to receive investment income might be a function of savings from earned income and/or the opportunity of becoming a supervisor a function of personal wealth and hence investment income. These relationships will obviously be ill-defined in reality. Nevertheless, the reasonable goodness of fit of the Lydall hypotheses to 'all' income data indicates that there may be some effect of this nature (cf. table A3.8).

The two welfare theories are derived by Dalton,[1] who attributes the first to Bernoulli. Both of these theories are incapable of being empirically evaluated by any statistical technique, since they incorporate an unmeasurable variable – welfare. However, it is possible to derive inequality indices from them. The Bernoulli hypothesis simply states that economic welfare is a function of the level of incomes, namely:

$$w = \log x + x_s,$$

where w is the level of economic welfare, x is the income level and x_s is a subsistence level of income.

The assumption is that proportionate additions to income, above the level x_s, give equal additions to economic welfare, that is that there is a diminishing marginal utility to income

$$dw = \frac{dx}{x}.$$

The corresponding measure of inequality, if $x_1, x_2 \dots x_n$ are individual incomes, is by Dalton's definition

$$\frac{n \log \bar{x}_{ar} + nx_s}{n \log \bar{x}_g + nx_s},$$

where $\bar{x}_{ar}$ and $\bar{x}_g$ are the arithmetic mean and geometric mean of the above individual incomes. If we assume x_s is zero then this measure can be simplified to $\bar{x}_{ar}/\bar{x}_g$.

Dalton's own version of the Bernoulli hypothesis makes two important improvements. Welfare is given a finite limit (L) and the diminishing marginal utility of income is increased, so that more than proportionate additions to income are necessary to bring about equal additions to welfare. Thus the relation between welfare and income becomes

$$dw = dx/x^2$$

so that $w = L - 1/x$ where L is constant. The corresponding measure of inequality now is

[1] Dalton [21] appendix pp. 3–5.

$$\frac{(nL-n)/\bar{x}_{ar}}{(nL-n)/\bar{x}_h}$$

which reduces to

$$\frac{(L-1)/\bar{x}_{ar}}{(L-1)/\bar{x}_h},$$

that is in effect the harmonic mean over the arithmetic mean.

Dalton argues at great length the necessity of presenting a measure of inequality, which will reflect correctly the effect of proportionate additions to income, in the light of the conventional postulate of a diminishing marginal utility of income. It is for this reason that he insists on writing the Bernoulli index as log AM/log GM. In this case he argues that proportionate additions to income would diminish inequality, in terms of economic welfare, whilst with the formula AM/GM they would leave inequality unaffected. We use the logarithmic version in table A3.5.

However, since diminishing marginal utility of income is a dubious postulate except at very high levels of income, and welfare is a nontestable concept, Dalton's arguments lose much of their point. The only practical justification for measures involving the arithmetic, geometric and harmonic means is that they simply indicate, as ratios, dispersion or deviation from the so-called 'perfect' state of equal incomes.

The final comments of this section and this chapter are on the statistical merits of the four theories which are susceptible to statistical testing. In table A3.8 the $\bar{R}^2$ and Von Neuman ratios of each theory for each type of distribution are presented. In all cases the coefficients are significant at the 1% level.

From table A3.8 we see that in all models the $\bar{R}^2$ is high and consistently very high in the cases of the Gini and Gibrat theories. However, this highly satisfactory characteristic is spoiled by the poorness of the Von Neuman ratios. In none of the Gibrat regressions are we able to dismiss positive autocorrelation amongst the residuals at either the 1% or 5% levels. The values of the ratio for this model indicate severe autocorrelation. On this score the lognormal hypothesis must be rejected. Much the same goes for the Gini model, where only three regressions pass the autocorrelation test. These are:

B.I.R. 1963
Type 1 persons 1954
Type 2 persons 1954.

The Pareto model passes the test on four occasions:

B.I.R. 1949   Type 1 Units 1949
C.S.O. 1949   Type 1 Persons 1949

and since the $\bar{R}^2$ of the Pareto models are lower in general than those of the Gini, we are unable to choose between the Pareto or Gini models. Neither of them can be judged satisfactory.

The correlation coefficients are very inconsistent in the Lydall model, varying

Table A3.8   *Statistical evaluation of the theories of income distribution*

Type of distribution	Year	Theory	$\bar{R}^2$	V.N.R.[a]	Theory	$\bar{R}^2$	V.N.R.[a]
B.I.R.	1949	Pareto	0.993	1.247	Lydall	0.934	1.127
	1954		0.979	0.593		0.868	0.489
	1959		0.965	0.317		0.659	1.603
	1963		0.965	0.320		0.599	0.137
C.S.O.	1949		0.954	1.234		0.941	1.169
	1954		0.918	0.851		0.914	0.910
	1959		0.884	0.674		0.769	0.271
	1963		0.855	0.582		0.593	1.260
Type 1 units	1949		0.953	1.219		0.944	1.231
	1954		0.916	0.845		0.910	0.877
	1959		0.883	0.673		0.761	0.263
	1963		0.854	0.581		0.587	1.218
Type 2 units	1954		0.916	0.840		0.906	0.876
	1959		0.882	0.670		0.775	0.257
	1963		0.853	0.577		0.574	1.150
Type 1 persons	1949		0.768	1.016		0.921	0.474
	1954		0.714	0.949		0.958	0.795
	1959		0.666	0.872		0.958	0.805
	1963		0.625	0.781		0.979	1.314
Type 2 persons	1954		0.714	0.951		0.959	0.840
	1959		0.666	0.869		0.983	1.429
	1963		0.624	0.777		0.978	1.255
B.I.R.	1949	Gini	0.998	0.620	Gibrat	0.924	0.275
	1954		0.999	0.789		0.926	0.260
	1959		0.999	0.745		0.954	0.330
	1963		0.999	1.740		0.940	0.438
C.S.O.	1949		0.998	0.704		0.938	0.306
	1954		0.999	0.930		0.944	0.299
	1959		0.999	0.749		0.963	0.369
	1963		0.999	0.688		0.969	0.532
Type 1 units	1949		0.998	0.701		0.933	0.269
	1954		0.999	0.937		0.949	0.327
	1959		0.999	0.744		0.963	0.435
	1963		0.999	0.683		0.970	0.504
Type 2 units	1954		0.999	0.934		0.948	0.301
	1959		0.999	0.741		0.961	0.395
	1963		0.999	0.654		0.969	0.484
Type 1 persons	1949		0.998	0.630		0.938	0.352
	1954		0.999	1.689		0.939	0.266
	1959		0.999	0.854		0.935	0.303
	1963		0.999	0.764		0.950	0.338
Type 2 persons	1954		0.999	1.811		0.929	0.356
	1959		0.999	0.865		0.906	0.403
	1963		0.999	0.777		0.945	0.377

[a] V.N.R. = Von Neuman Ratio.

from 0.574 to 0.984. Nevertheless, in general they are good and are accompanied, in most cases, by Von Neuman ratios superior to those of the other models. There are nine regressions in the Lydall model for which we can assume no autocorrelation among the residuals. They are:

	Type 1 units 1963
B.I.R. 1949	Type 1 persons 1959
B.I.R. 1959	Type 1 persons 1963
C.S.O. 1949	Type 2 persons 1959
C.S.O. 1963	Type 2 persons 1963

The results of the Lydall model are not really satisfactory. However, if a choice were to be made between the four models, then in terms of both theoretical and statistical rigour the Lydall model would be chosen. Our broad conclusion is that both as measures of inequality and as empirical laws of income distribution, the models presented above are quite inadequate.

ESTIMATES OF THE YIELDS OF ASSETS
IN 1954, 1959 AND 1963

Yields were estimated for those assets producing income which would come into the taxable field of unearned income. Where possible the average yield for the year was a weighted average, based on the quarterly death rate. This was to counteract the bias in the statistics on wealth.

The yields used are presented in table A4.1 below.

Table A4.1   *Yields of assets*

Asset	Yields %		
	1954	1959	1963
1. National savings certificates and premium bonds	3.30	3.30	3.20
2. Defence bonds and tax reserve certificates	3.30	4.40	4.20
3. U.K. short term government securities	3.30	4.16	4.75
4. U.K. medium term government securities	3.30	5.07	5.07
5. Northern Ireland and municipal securities; U.K. long-term government securities	3.30	5.22	5.33
6. 2½% Consols and undated U.K. government securities	3.30	4.82	5.62
7. Commonwealth government securities	3.93	4.69	4.59
8. Other government securities	2.53	3.32	3.99
9. U.K. ordinary shares	5.34	4.87	4.23
10. U.K. preference shares	5.34	6.09	6.49
11. Foreign and Commonwealth company shares	4.78	4.06	3.19
12. Post Office Savings Bank and Trustee Savings Bank accounts	2.64	2.64	2.86
13. Deposit accounts	2.64	2.00	2.00
14. Building society shares and deposits	2.73	3.38	2.53
15. Land and Buildings	3.45	2.20	2.60

Source: B.I.R. [19] 105, and same as table 4.2.

The 1959 and 1963 yields were estimated in exactly the same way. The 1954 estimates, because of data inavailability, were rather more approximate. The remainder of this appendix presents a brief discussion of the estimation procedures for 1959 and 1963. The differences from the 1954 estimates are also noted.

For each item the following assumptions or weights were adopted:

1. The yields on premium bonds in 1959 was 4% and in 1963 4½%. The yield on the ninth issue (1951–6) of national saving certificates was 3¼%, after allowance for accrued interest and annual additions. These rates were weighted by the total principal value plus accumulated interest for the national savings certificates and by the amount remaining invested for premium bonds. In both instances end-of-year stock values were used.

2. The grossed up yield on defence bonds in 1959 was 5.6% and in 1963 5.0%. The weighted average yield, i.e. the after-tax actual yield, on tax reserve certificates was $2\frac{1}{4}$% in 1959 and 1963. The weights were the nominal amounts remaining invested at the end of the year for both stocks.

3.–6. The yields on government securities are as published by the C.S.O. in the *Monthly Digest of Statistics*. Similar assumptions to those used in our estimates of capital gains were made with respect to the yields on Northern Ireland and municipal securities.

Up to this stage the procedure for the 1954 yields for each item was identical except that in deriving the composite yields we were forced to use the same weights as for 1959. Furthermore, the inadequacy of the base capital assets data used in the text required that the six items be amalgamated.

7. A simple average of the yields of government securities of Australia, Canada, India, New Zealand and South Africa as presented in the U.N. *International Financial Statistics*.

8. The yield on U.S. Treasury Bills is assumed to be representative of the non-Commonwealth foreign government sector.

9. Yield on industrial ordinary shares as given in the *Monthly Digest of Statistics*.

10. Same source as item 9, but only for preference shares. For all years we were unable to obtain any data suitable for weighting the yields of preference shares and debentures. However, since the two yields are always similar, the error should be slight. For 1954, items again had to be amalgamated and the only basis for weighting was provided by the stock values in the 1960 Inland Revenue data.

11. For the want of more information, Moody's estimate of the yields on 200 U.S. stocks was adopted in this case.

12. The yield on Post Office Savings Bank accounts and ordinary accounts in Trustees Savings Banks was $2\frac{1}{2}$% throughout the three years. The yield on Trustees Savings Bank special Investment Department accounts was 3.15% in 1954, 4.0% in 1959 and 4.78% in 1963. The weights used were the balances remaining deposited in each group at the end of the year.

13. This is the joint stock banks' deposit rate. For 1954 items 12 and 13 had to be amalgamated. The weights were derived from Morgan's data for that period.[1]

14. The average rates paid on shares were 2.61% for 1954, 3.43% for 1959 and 3.56% for 1963 and on deposits 2.01%, 2.87% and 3.15% respectively. The weights were the accumulated value of shares and deposits at the end of the year.

15. This yield is estimated as the ratio of schedule A and B income, in the income surveys, to 'gross landed wealth'. The ratio is somewhat lower than might be expected. This is probably due to the exclusion of some land income from schedules A and B, such as imputed rent in excess of the schedule A and B valuation. Some forms of farm income and other miscellaneous receipts by

[1] Morgan [52] table 30.

occupiers of land are also excluded. These items are normally taxed under cases VI or III schedule D.

The Inland Revenue informed us that all items of schedule D cases III and VI are included in the survey estimates of investment income.

The Inland Revenue income distribution survey data classify investment income into three groups: (e.g. see B.I.R. [19] 105, table 78.)

(1) schedule A, owner-occupied,
(2) schedule B plus other schedule A income,
(3) interest and dividends

The last group, we deduce, comprises schedule C and part of cases I and cases III, IV, V and VI of schedule D.

The cases of schedule D are:

   I   profits of a trade, which includes distributed dividends, etc.,
  II profits of a profession or vocation, which is defined as earned income in the B.I.R. surveys (e.g. see B.I.R. [19] 105, table 76),
III interest on loans, discounts and certain payments connected with the use of land (e.g. way leaves),
 IV income from overseas securities,
  V income from other overseas possessions,
 VI annual profits and gains not charged under any other schedule, including excess rents and other miscellaneous receipts by occupiers of land.

Since in the Inland Revenue income distribution survey data there is no division of income according to schedule case, we cannot make any adjustment to the yield on land for the event that schedule D case III is included as part of overall investment income.

The yields in table A4.1 are then used to estimate the aggregate yield of estates of different sizes and compositions. These aggregate yields we assume to correspond to investment income. We thus have a link-up between the two sets of data.

ESTIMATION PROCEDURE AND SOURCES
FOR TABLE 5.1

1. INCOME IN KIND

The totals for all income in kind produced by the C.S.O. were £193m. for 1954, £206m. for 1959 and £222m. for 1963.[1] This includes five categories of income.[2]

    (a) board and lodging, food, etc. provided by farmers for farm workers,
    (b) free and cheap coal to coalminers,
    (c) food and lodging for domestic servants,
    (d) food and quarters received by merchant seamen and fishermen,
    (e) net cost to employees of meal vouchers or meals provided in canteens.

Categories (a) and (c) are included in the distribution of income by ranges. Therefore unallocated income in kind is the sum of the other three categories. However, we had no data on item (d), so that our estimate of unallocated income in kind consisted only of groups (b) and (e). Item (d) should be very small indeed.

The estimates of free coal were derived from the average proportion of the weekly earnings of coalminers which is supplied in the form of coal. This proportion was grossed up by applying it to the total annual wage bill for the coalmining industry. The work-sheet and result of this particular calculation is given in table A5.1.

Table A5.1 *Cheap or free coal to coalminers*

Year	Average weekly earnings per wage earner (1)	Average weekly value of free or cheap coal (2)	Annual wage bill of coalminers (3)	Annual value of free coal (3)+[(2)/(1)]
1954	235/1d	10/10d	£410.9m	£19.3m
1959	283/9d	16/6d	£456.1m	£26.5m
1963	334/0d	22/1d	£423.0m	£27.1m

Sources: Ministry of Power and Fuel, *Statistical Digest*, 1965, tables 18, 29 and 30.

The data for item (e), net canteen and meal voucher expenditure,[3] was obtained from a number of studies on labour costs in industry, mainly in manufacturing. Throughout we assume that employer cost per employee for the manufacturing industries, which cover approximately 40% of all employed persons, can be applied to all employed persons (less agricultural workers, who are already accounted for in category (a)). We further assume that the net cost to the

---

[1] C.S.O. Blue Book [16] 1965. Table 22.
[2] See Harris and Solly [29] pp. 76 and 138.
[3] Employer expenditure net of receipts from employee purchase.

employer is an indication of the benefit to the employee. Both assumptions are made for pragmatic reasons and no doubt may lead to biased results.

A recent survey by the Ministry of Labour on labour costs [47] indicated an average net cost in 1964 of £6.7 per employee per annum. A similar but less comprehensive study for 1955, again by the Ministry of Labour [48], came out with a figure of £0.95 per employee. It is doubtful whether the change has been so large; in fact it would be quite reasonable to expect that in volume terms the cost has been pretty constant over this period and that any increased money costs are purely inflationary.[1] If the 1964 figure was reduced to 1954 prices, by the index of retail prices of food, it would come to £4.7. A trend of this magnitude is supported by similar estimates made in other surveys for the intervening years. The Glasgow Survey [61] gave a figure of £6 per employee, the I.E.A. Survey [29] £4.6 for 1958 and the I.W.S. Survey [24] £5.3 for 1957.[2]

The 1955 Ministry of Labour enquiry was therefore considered inaccurate for this item. The other surveys, however, displayed insufficient consistency, so it was decided, for our three years, to use the respective deflated value of the 1964 cost. The estimates were as follows:

> 1954   £4.7 per employee per annum
> 1959   £5.9
> 1963   £6.5

These figures were multiplied by the numbers employed in all industries excluding agriculture (and fishing in 1954).[3] A slight error may occur between the 1959 and 1963 estimates on the one hand and 1954 on the other, due to the change in standard industrial classification after 1954. The work-sheets are presented in table A5.2.

Table A5.2 *Net meals and canteen expenditure by employers for employees*

Year	Average cost per employee (1)	Total employment less agricultural employment (2)	Total annual expenditure (1) × (2)
1954	£4.7 p.a.	21,984	£103m
1959	£5.9 p.a.	20,922.8	£125.5m
1963	£6.5 p.a.	22,049.3	£144m

Sources: Ministry of Labour [47] tables 7 and 101 (for 1963 employment data, June figures); *Annual Abstract of Statistics* (various) for average monthly employment data per annum for 1959 and 1954.

[1] The volume of food consumption per head is presumably pretty static, whilst the volume of free or cheap products may have risen. This is probably offset to some degree by the fall in the supply of recreational and medical services (see Reid and Robertson [61]).

[2] In all these surveys, total costs were expressed as a percentage of payroll. These we converted to a per employee basis. This was possible since each survey covered, in general, manufacturing industries. Thus by applying the payroll percentages to the total payroll and employment in the manufacturing industry a per employee estimate was obtained.

[3] Figures on employment in agriculture are not published separately from those for fishing in 1954.

2. *Non-taxable grants.* These estimates are published in the C.S.O. Blue Books [16], e.g. 1965 Blue Book, table 48, items grants to persons for child care, school meals, welfare foods and employment services.

3. *Excess of imputed rent over the Schedule A valuation.* As explained, the 1963 estimate was the whole of imputed rent. A figure for total imputed rent is published by the C.S.O. For 1959 we subtracted from total imputed rent the total value of income assessed for schedule A owner-occupied tax in 1959–60, given in B.I.R. surveys, published in B.I.R. Reports [19]. In 1954 there was no such information. The B.I.R. survey for 1954–5, however, did give data on schedule A and B income classed together. By assuming that schedule A owner-occupied income amounted to approximately the same proportion of schedule A and B as in 1959 we derived our estimate. Some error will be introduced by the use of financial year data, but it should be very small.

4. National saving certificates, post-war credits, and all contributions to national insurance and private superannuation and their investment income data are published in the C.S.O. Blue Book [16], i.e. tables 22 and 36, items 4, 5, 7, 8 and 9 in the 1965 issue.

5. *Income below £50.* The Inland Revenue supplied us with this information.

6. *Labour cost benefits.* Other fringe benefits normally provided by employers for employees are: housing facilities, recreational facilities, free or cheap products, crèches and works transport to and from work. Medical services and educational leave or assistance are sometimes also supplied. These items we shall omit, since both are provided 'free' or at the subsidised rate on the open market.

Therefore the benefits included in this group exclude the latter set of items. From the various labour cost surveys mentioned above, the estimates per employee per annum for the above items were (*n.b.* for manufacturing only):

1964 Ministry of Labour	£3.2
1960 Glasgow Survey	£2.6
1958 I.E.A. Survey	£1.0 (recreational facilities only)
1957 I.W.S. Survey	£1.8 (recreational facilities and housing only)

The coverage of the above surveys varies considerably. The 1964 Ministry of Labour and 1960 Glasgow estimates for housing and recreational facilities only would be £1.6 and £1.5 respectively. The 1955 Ministry of Labour survey gives a figure of £7.4 and includes all items plus education. The comparable 1964 estimate would be £7.1 and the Glasgow survey figure would be £6.0. The 1955 figure again appears to be a poor estimate.

The solution adopted was to accept the 1964 and 1960 estimates. A figure for 1955 was calculated on the assumption that the Ministry of Labour overall total of £9.4 per employee per annum for all welfare and subsidy fringe benefits may be accurate and that 24% of this covered the relevant benefits for this section. The corresponding proportion in 1964 was 24%. This gave an estimate of £2.3. By plotting these estimates against years, the figures for 1954, 1959 and 1963 were graphically interpolated. They were £2.2, £2.5 and £3.0 respectively. The aggregate totals were estimated as for income in kind.

7. *Car subsidy benefits.* This category consists of two groups – running cost subsidies by firms and household or family cars owned by firms. We make no

estimate of the value of cars given to employees by firms, or of interest-free loans or hire purchase assistance by firms for employees purchasing cars.

Table A5.3 illustrates the calculation of average running costs per private car per annum.

Table A5.3   *Running costs per private car*

Year	Number of private cars in use ('000s) (1)	Total expenditure on running cost [a] (£m) (2)	Average running cost per car (£) (3) = (2)/(1)
1954	3,100	191	62
1959	4,966	395	80
1963	7,375	661	90

Sources: Col. (1): Ministry of Transport [49] (Motor Survey) and the *Annual Abstract of Statistics 1965*, table 232. Col. (2): C.S.O. Blue Books [16] (various).

[a] Includes test and driving instruction fees.

From the Ministry of Transport [49] (Motor Survey) for 1961 we know that 71% of private cars are not subsidised in any way at all. Of the remaining 29% 12% belong to self-employed persons and 17% to non-self-employed. It is assumed that these proportions apply for all years. In fact all the data used from the 1961 survey are assumed to hold for each of our years.

The number of subsidised cars for each year, by type of employment, are therefore:

	Self-employed	*Non-self-employed*
1954	373,000	527,000
1959	596,000	844,000
1963	885,000	1,254,000

As explained in chapter 5, full-scale evasion is assumed on the part of self-employed car owners, to the extent that they are able to deduct all running costs from their taxable income. Also this item is a part of item 12 of table 5.1. However, we shall deal with it at this stage. To the extent that part of the incurred costs are genuinely business costs, a straightforward multiplication of average running costs by the number of 'self-employed' cars will be an over-estimate. The Motor Survey [49] reported that 16%[1] of all journeys were business journeys. Therefore all running cost estimates will be reduced by 16% on the assumption of a constant cost per journey. The amounts of car running cost tax deductions, which can be considered as additions to personal income for the self-employed, are: 1954, £18m; 1959, £41m; 1963, £67m.

Table 1 of the Motor Survey [49] gives a distribution of the remaining subsidised running costs by the extent of the subsidy provided by the firm. From this we derived the work-sheets produced below in table A5.4. These subsidies are another form of income in kind or fringe benefit. To preserve

[1] The 16% excludes journeys to and from work, the cost of which is generally considered the responsibility of the employee.

consistency with our treatment of other incomes in kind we did not add on the 'tax avoided' factor.

The total values of subsidies were then reduced by 16% and the personal income element in the subsidy is therefore: 1954, £14m; 1959, £29m; 1963, £34m. This is the first part of item 2 in table 5.1.

Table A5.4   *Employer-subsidised running costs*

Degree of subsidy of total running costs (%)	Number of cars per year by size of subsidy ('000s)			Per cent distribution of cars by subsidy size for all years (%)
	1954	1959	1963	
87	184	295	310	35
62	63	101	106	12
37	63	101	106	12
12	154	246	257	29
NS [a]	63	101	106	12
Average total running costs (£)	62	80	90	—
Total value of subsidies (£m)	17	35	41	—

Source: Motor Survey [49] table 1.
[a] Not stated. We assume a 50% subsidy for want of any information.

The second part consists of the average annual value of cars purchased by firms for employees and left at the sole disposal of the employees. The Motor Survey [49] indicated that 7% of private cars came into this category. Also from the survey we can deduce that on average a car is kept by each owner for five years. Further assuming that firms always purchase new cars, then by multiplying the average value of new cars in each year by the number of registrations in that year for each of the five years and dividing the sum total by the number of new registrations during the five years we can obtain a five yearly average value of new cars. This figure is then grossed up by the number of 'firm-owned' cars in order to deduce the total value of this subsidy. However, it is a subsidy spread over five years on average, therefore a rough indication of the average annual value of this subsidy will be one-fifth of the total.[1] We take no account of the interest payment or hire purchase savings that an employee may make by obtaining a car in this manner. The business use element in the subsidy is covered in the running cost subsidy calculations. The work-sheet for this estimate is presented in table A5.5. Again the estimate of the subsidy is net of tax.

The index of new prices in table A5.6 was cross-checked with an unweighted index of prices since 1955 for a number of popular models, obtained from the *Motorists' Guide*. The similarity in absolute levels and price changes indicated that the estimates in the table were reasonable.

[1] A lack of data restricted this estimate in 1954 to the three previous years only.

Table A5.5   *Average annual subsidy of employer-provided cars*

Year	Number of private cars owned by firms ('ooos)	Weighted average value of the car stock at new car prices (£)	Total value of subsidy (£m)	Approximate average annual value of subsidy (£m)
1954	217	600	130	26
1959	347	723	250	50
1963	516	719	371	74

Sources: Motor Survey [49], and table A5.6.

8. *Self-employed persons' depreciation on cars.* The expenses of self-employed persons have already been considered in the previous section.

From the Motor Survey [49] an age distribution of 'self-employment' cars was obtained. This enabled us to estimate the amount of annual and initial allowances being claimed in any given year. For all years a 20% reducing balance annual allowance and a 30% initial allowance were assumed.[1]

Table A5.6   *Average value of new cars*

Year	Consumer expenditure on private cars [a] (£m) (1)	New registrations of private cars[b] ('ooos) (2)	Average value of new cars (£) (3) = (1)/(2)
1952	111	188	590
1953	177	296	598
1954	234	386	606
1955	310	501	619
1956	268	400	670
1957	320	425	753
1958	425	555	766
1959	506	646	783
1960	568	803	705
1961	515	743	693
1962	564	785	718
1963	715	1,009	709

Sources: *Annual Abstract of Statistics* (various); C.S.O. Blue Books [16] (various).

 [a] This item includes expenditure on motor-cycles, etc. and second-hand cars. However, Silbertson [67] (footnote on p. 257) states that the motor-cycle element is small and Dicks-Mireaux [22] (p. 42) says that this item represented mainly expenditure on new cars. Therefore the error may be small here.

 [b] Estimated via 90% of all new registrations. The Motor Survey [49] claimed that approximately 90% of all new registrations were for private cars.

 [1] The actual allowances were (in percentages):

	1954	1959	1963
Initial	20	30	30
Annual	25	25	25

An example of the estimation procedure for 1963 is given below.

Year of car purchase ('000s) (1)	Number of cars (£) (2)	Average purchase price (%) (3)	Percentage value of deductions (%) (4)	Total value of deductions (£m) (4) = [(2)·(3)]·(4)
1963	142	709	50	50
1962	142	718	10	10
1961	142	693	8	8
1960	71	705	6.4	6
1959	62	783	5.1	3
1958	62	766	4.0	2
1957	62	753	4.0	2
1956	62	670	3.0	1
1955	60	619	2.0	1

The total value of allowances in 1963 is a summation of column (4), i.e. £83m. This figure was reduced by 25%, on the assumption that the Inland Revenue only permitted 75% of this type of expenditure as a business capital expenditure. The estimation procedure was exactly the same for 1959. However, in 1954 a much rougher approximation was forced upon us by the lack of price data for up to eight years previous to 1954. Of the estimated 372,000 'self-employed' cars in that year, 20% were assumed to be new and claiming a 50% deduction of the capital expenditure. The remaining 80% were assumed to be three to four years old and claiming 8.5% of the total expenditure three to four years before.

The results of these calculations are given in table A5.7 below.

Table A5.7 *Net depreciation allowances claimed on the cars of self-employed persons*

Year	Total amount of allowances (£m)	75% of total amount (£m)
1954	27	20
1959	61	46
1963	83	62

Source: Tables A5.5 and A5.6;
Motor Survey [49] table 2.

THE ESTIMATED ALLOCATION OF 'UNALLOCATED' PERSONAL INCOME AND SOME FRINGE BENEFITS TO INCOME RANGES ON THE TYPE 2 DISTRIBUTION OF INCOME BY UNITS

NATIONAL INSURANCE CONTRIBUTIONS

The Inland Revenue survey for 1959 produced data on the deductions from earned income for national insurance employee contributions.[1] This data covered deductions amounting to £249.5m and 18.9 million income units, of which 4.45 million were married couples with a working wife, i.e. a total coverage of 23.35 million persons. The total value of employee contributions for that year was £497m. and from the national insurance statistics presented in the *Annual Abstract of Statistics* we find 24.53 million persons as contributors.

The difference between the two income totals suggests little correlation between employee contributions and deductions. Furthermore the average deduction per person or per unit is far from constant or even similar for each income range. Therefore any index which distributed the total of employee and employer contributions according to the number of persons contributing would be misleading.

The solution adopted was to assume that persons not covered by the Inland Revenue statistics represented contributors with income below the effective exemption limit. There were 1.18 million such persons. It was further assumed that the average deduction for such persons would have been £11 p.a.,[2] which gave a total of £12m of hypothetical deductions for incomes below the effective exemption limit. This £12m was then added to the £249.4m deductions above the exemption limit and the total deductions per range (for all ranges) expressed as a percentage of this total. The resulting index was used to distribute all national insurance contributions by income size. The implicit assumptions are: (1) that deductions reflect employee contributions; and (2) that employee contributions reflect the income size pattern for employer contributions.

For the other years we did not have any data on national insurance deductions. In 1954 these deductions were included as a part of the data on total deductions from earned income.[3] In 1959 national insurance deductions were 37% of this item. This is not a high ratio, but it represented our only source of information. Therefore, after assuming that contributions below the exemption limit were 35% higher than in 1959,[4] the total of contributions for other ranges

---

[1] B.I.R. [19] 101, table 68.
[2] The average deduction for the £180–200 range was £11 p.a.
[3] B.I.R. [19] 99, table 55.
[4] The number of units below the exemption limit in 1954 was 35% higher than in 1959.

was distributed according to the percentage distribution per range of total deductions from earned income.

In 1963 employee contributions were included as part of taxable income. This still left the problem of allocating employer contributions. There was virtually no information available. The solution adopted was to allocate the above total according to the number of persons with earned incomes per range (i.e. including working wives). The allowance for contributions below the exemption limit was made by increasing the 1959 proportion for these by 7.5%, which represents the percentage increase in units below the effective exemption limit. The only rationale for this procedure is that had it been adopted on earned income in 1959 a distribution similar to that actually used would have resulted. A further factor is that errors due to misplacing would be less in 1963 than they would have been in 1959 since the manipulations are restricted to employer contributions.

INCOME IN KIND

The income in kind of table 5.1 (item 1) and the labour cost subsidy of item 10 in the same table are combined in this category. All these types of income result from employment. Reid and Robertson[1] illustrate that there is very little correlation between the size of wage and the size of fringe benefit (which includes income in kind). We therefore assumed an equal amount per recipient, irrespective of income size. Since the control totals for income in kind were constructed on the assumption that most employees received such income, it seemed reasonable to distribute the total according to the number of employed persons per income range. This information was obtained, for each year, from the relevant Inland Revenue survey.[2] No adjustment was made for any benefits that might accrue to incomes below the effective exemption limits. Again, we were following Reid and Robertson,[3] whose data for 1960 indicated that there were unlikely to be any fringe benefits for wages below £200.

SUPERANNUATION CONTRIBUTIONS AND INVESTMENT INCOME OF SUPERANNUATION FUNDS

This group comprises items 8 and 9 of table 5.1.

For 1963 and 1959 the Inland Revenue surveys published data[4] on the

---

[1] Cf. Reid and Robertson [61] table 20, p. 64.

[2] Sources: *Reports* [19] nos.: 99, table 55; 101, table 68; 105, table 76; 108, table 61. The number of employed persons included earning wives. The data on the latter include schedule D earnings. This is unfortunate since that for single persons and husbands is based on schedule E (employment) income. However, the error is likely to be insignificant as schedule D earnings are only about 5% of total wives' earnings.

[3] [61] table 20, p. 64. It may well be asked why we failed to use the tables on the distribution of fringe benefits, etc. presented in Reid and Robertson. These figures were rejected for three reasons: (1) they omitted salary earners, (2) only one year was covered, and (3) the definition of income was unsuitable for our purposes inasmuch as it was confined to main source wage earners, i.e. excluding wives' and other income.

[4] Sources: B.I.R. *Reports* [19] nos.: 105, table 79; 108, table 63.

amounts of income deducted for superannuation contributions and retirement annunity premiums by income status. This we assumed to be an accurate guide to the relative income distributions of the above type of contributions. It was also taken as reflecting the final beneficiaries of the investment income resulting from such contributions. For want of any other data, these assumptions had to be accepted.

For 1954 there was no such detailed breakdown of information on deductions from earned income. Therefore we had to use the distribution of total deductions, as in the case of national insurance contributions. This in effect means that the actual distributions by income range of two items for 1954 (i.e. national insurance contributions and superannuation contributions, etc.) may be inaccurate separately, but together may well be correct (in 1959 the two items amounted to 60% of total deductions). Unlike the index for national insurance contributions, we made no allowance for superannuation contributions, etc. by income recipients below the exemption limit. This was also the case in 1959 and 1963. There are, *a priori*, likely to be only an insignificant number of very low income earners contributing to superannuation schemes.

SCHEDULE A EXCESS INCOME

The imputed excess over schedule A was allocated according to the distribution of schedule A income, as reported in the Inland Revenue surveys[1] for 1954 and 1959. By 1963 schedule A had been abolished and the imputed rent in table 5.1 included the 'old' schedule A evaluation. In 1963 distribution was determined by extrapolating the trends per range from 1954 to 1959 onto 1963 by the percentage change in the 1959 valuation over that of 1954, and finally prorating to obtain an index distribution for 1963. The results compared favourably in the middle income ranges with a similar index constructed from data on house-ownership by income size, published by the Co-operative Permanent Building Society [20].[2] These data, however, were not used on account of the bias in the sample in favour of middle and lower-middle income groups. No allowance was made for incomes below the exemption limit.

SELF-EMPLOYED EXPENSES AND DEPRECIATION ALLOWANCES ON CARS

This category of income was allocated to ranges according to the distribution of schedule D income by total net income size, as published in the Inland Revenue surveys.[3] The majority of self-employed income is taxed under schedule D. Again no allowance was or could have been made for incomes below the exemption limits.

NATIONAL SAVINGS CERTIFICATES AND POST-WAR CREDITS

These items were allocated to ranges in proportion to the relative distribution

[1] Sources: *Reports* [19] nos.: 99, table 55; 105, table 78.
[2] Cf. Ministry of Labour [46] table 3.
[3] Sources: B.I.R. *Reports* [19] nos.: 105, table 55; 105, table 76; 108, table 61.

of income from dividends and interest taxed at source, again as published in the Inland Revenue surveys.[1] As in some previous cases, the lack of data prevented adjustments with respect to incomes below the exemption limits. This procedure may have produced an underestimate of the allocation of the lower income groups.

CAR AND CAR TRAVEL SUBSIDIES BY EMPLOYERS

Ideally, in order to allocate this item we should have data on the distribution of car ownership (including car size) by the income status of the owner. However, the only data approximating our needs for the U.K. are for 1953,[2] which unfortunately were presented in such a manner that it was impossible to extrapolate for other years. The 1953 data, which related the proportion of all cars owned by each income group, were adopted as the basis for the distribution of the car and car travel subsidy for 1954. For 1959 and 1963 the relative expenditure on the running costs of cars by each income group was used to determine the allocation of this item. This information was obtained from the *Family Expenditure Surveys*.[3] The surveys also produced data on the net purchases of cars by each income group. This might have been considered a good index for the car subsidy element. However, it is misleading in that it is sensitive to second-hand car prices and hire purchase down-payments. The running cost item, it was assumed, would be a better indicator of car ownership and car travelling expenses, with the further assumption that greater running costs per household represent either a larger car or greater travel or both and hence the possibility of larger employer-provided subsidies. The distribution of running costs by income size in 1953–5 [46] furthermore, was very similar to that of the 1953 distribution of car ownership.

NON-TAXABLE GRANTS

For want of any information it was assumed that these items would be allocated in a similar way to the non-taxable income brought into the Inland Revenue income distribution. Thus they were distributed by an index of the net addition of income per income range for each year, which we derived from data supplied by the Inland Revenue.

INCOMES BELOW £50 P.A.

There were no data at all on these incomes, which could be an extremely heterogeneous collection. It seems probable, since no person could live on £50 p.a., that they are incomes of persons dependent on some other income unit or persons with other major sources of income. Therefore it was decided that the most reasonable allocation was according to the number of persons per income

---

[1] Sources: B.I.R. *Reports* [19] nos.: table 55; 105, table 78; 108, table 62.
[2] Source: Dicks-Mireaux [22] table 3.
[3] Sources: *F.E.S.* [45], *Report* 4 (for 1957–9), tables 6, 7, 8 and 9, and *Report* 5 (for 1963), table 2.

range. As our final manipulations are to be carried out on the type 2 distribution, these incomes were allocated according to the number of persons per range in the type 2 distributions by income units.

Where relevant the above allocations were then subjected to the adjustments described in chapter 5 (pp. 133–4). This produced the range allocation for each item for the type 2 distributions by income units – see table A6.1.[1]

It is evident from what we have done so far that all our estimates for fringe benefit income have been made in terms of the amounts of income only. For all except one case, national insurance contributions, we had no data on the corresponding number of income units involved. Even in that one exception the data were such that for our purposes they were virtually useless. Therefore all the adjustments made in order to include fringe benefits in the overall income distribution were from the 'income' side. Basically the procedure was to add the total of fringe benefits income per range to the total of income from other sources for that range and re-estimate the average income per income unit. The percentage increase between the pre- and post-addition average income was noted and the income limits of each range were increased by the same percentage. The final step was then to use the Pareto interpolation technique to recalculate the income distribution back into the conventional ranges. These manipulations were carried out on all our type 2 distributions – see tables 5.2 to 5.6.

This is a technique of 'income incorporation' frequently used by the Inland Revenue when estimating the income distributions for the C.S.O. Blue Books [16] (i.e. where there are no data on the number of income recipients) and is probably the best procedure available. It nevertheless implies certain strong assumptions. These assumptions are: first, that all units in each range are in some way recipients of the newly 'brought-in' income; secondly, that all units in each range receive the average additional income for that range, and finally that as a result of the additional income no unit is moved up more than two income ranges and in general the move up is only by one range. In view of the types of income under consideration it is unlikely that many incomes would benefit to the extent of the £300 or more necessary for a three-range movement. The danger in the procedure and in the other underlying assumptions is the possibility of over- or under-estimating the upward movement of units. If an error in either direction were consistent for all ranges, then over- or underestimation in a given income range would be partly offset by a similar error in the higher income ranges. However, to justify any error, consistent or not, is difficult. An underestimation of the upward movements would imply that the beneficiaries in any given range were the highest incomes in that range and *vice versa* for overestimation. Without any data, we can only argue that there is no clear-cut or even dimly hidden explanation for the prominence of these biased patterns

[1] The original distributions outlined in this section can be worked out, if desired, by working backwards from Table A6.1 with the use of table 6.3.1 in Stark [69].

Category of income	|	Income range (£)															
		50–250	250–300	300–400	400–500	500–600	600–700	700–800	800–1,000	1,000–1,500	1,500–2,000	2,000–3,000	3,000–5,000	5,000–10,000	10,000–20,000	20,000+	Total
1954																	
National insurance contributions		56.4	29.0	58.5	78.4	74.0	60.7	47.5	47.6	34.6	11.8	13.4	10.7	4.3	4.1	1.0	532
Income in kind		18.1	13.0	25.4	29.6	25.9	20.5	15.3	13.6	6.8	1.5	1.2	0.7	0.3	0.1	—	172
Superannuation contributions and investment income of these funds		58.6	47.6	118.1	158.6	149.4	122.4	95.9	95.9	69.0	23.9	26.9	21.6	8.6	8.3	2.2	1,007
Schedule A excess		6.7	5.5	10.9	13.2	13.2	11.6	9.7	13.1	15.8	8.1	10.0	9.6	6.9	3.2	1.5	139
Self-employed expenses and depreciation		0.7	0.8	2.4	2.7	2.7	2.4	2.2	3.2	5.0	3.2	4.3	4.2	2.8	1.1	0.3	38
National saving certificates and post-war credits		0.6	0.6	1.1	1.0	0.9	0.8	0.8	1.1	2.3	1.6	2.5	3.2	3.3	1.9	—	23
Car subsidy		5.0	1.4	3.3	2.4	2.0	2.0	2.2	5.6	9.4	2.8	2.0	1.2	0.6	0.1	—	40
Non-taxable grants		64.3	1.9	1.2	1.8	2.3	3.3	3.4	4.5	1.3	—	—	—	—	—	—	84
Incomes below £50 p.a.		13.5	2.8	7.4	9.3	9.3	7.6	5.3	4.6	2.5	0.8	0.5	0.3	0.1	—	—	64
Total		223.9	102.6	228.3	297.0	279.7	231.3	182.3	189.2	146.7	53.7	60.8	51.5	26.9	18.8	6.3	2,099
1959																	
National insurance contributions		13.9	7.0	141.0	100.0	117.4	115.5	102.3	139.7	107.4	21.7	15.3	9.0	4.7	1.5	0.6	897
Income in kind		2.0	1.0	25.2	22.5	26.2	26.7	24.8	36.5	29.5	4.8	2.9	1.3	0.5	0.1	—	204
Superannuation contributions and investment income of these funds		2.8	1.5	26.3	64.9	115.7	148.6	171.3	315.6	377.3	126.3	110.8	87.3	57.5	18.9	4.2	1,629
Schedule A excess		0.7	0.3	14.5	15.4	20.3	23.7	24.3	41.1	51.0	19.0	17.2	12.5	7.4	2.6	1.0	251
Self-employed expenses and depreciation		—	—	2.4	4.1	5.7	5.8	5.6	9.5	14.8	8.7	10.2	9.8	6.4	2.0	1.0	86
National savings certificates and post-war credits		—	—	2.1	2.0	2.1	1.7	1.8	3.6	7.2	5.3	7.6	9.7	9.8	5.3	3.8	62
Car subsidy		0.2	1.2	1.7	3.6	4.0	2.1	2.7	4.8	13.1	11.3	8.5	16.9	7.0	1.5	0.4	79
Non-taxable grants		43.5	10.1	6.4	6.9	3.2	2.4	5.2	7.9	3.4	0.9	0.1	—	—	—	—	90
Incomes below £50 p.a.		7.8	2.4	4.2	5.2	6.8	8.0	7.5	10.9	8.0	1.5	1.0	0.5	0.2	—	—	64
Total		70.9	23.5	233.8	224.6	301.4	334.5	345.5	569.6	611.7	199.5	173.6	147.0	93.5	31.9	11.0	3,362
1963																	
National insurance contributions		16.6	7.3	15.5	65.4	52.6	53.7	53.0	109.0	167.8	40.0	17.8	8.2	3.4	0.5	0.2	611
Income in kind		1.0	0.5	1.0	24.9	20.4	21.5	22.1	46.3	72.4	16.6	6.4	2.5	1.0	0.2	0.2	237
Superannuation contributions and investment income of these funds		2.1	1.0	1.8	26.6	63.7	106.5	135.9	343.6	788.6	361.5	231.7	126.0	91.4	23.6	13.0	2,317
Schedule A excess		2.1	1.0	1.9	18.3	25.4	45.6	59.1	120.3	164.8	44.9	29.9	17.0	8.0	2.0	0.7	541
Self-employed expenses and depreciation		—	—	—	3.4	4.9	5.6	6.5	13.2	22.8	14.5	18.6	17.2	13.2	3.9	2.2	126
National savings certificates and post-war credits		—	—	—	0.7	0.5	0.6	0.6	1.0	2.5	2.2	3.7	5.3	6.3	4.2	2.4	30
Car subsidy		0.4	0.2	1.1	1.4	1.4	1.9	2.2	6.9	36.3	25.3	17.9	8.1	3.9	0.6	0.4	108
Non-taxable grants		58.2	11.0	7.9	5.7	3.6	1.6	5.6	10.8	7.6	0.2	0.5	0.2	0.1	—	—	113
Incomes below £50 p.a.		6.9	2.5	4.4	4.7	5.4	6.7	7.4	15.6	20.4	5.4	2.1	1.0	0.4	0.1	—	83
Total		87.3	23.5	33.6	151.1	177.9	243.7	292.4	666.7	283.2	510.6	328.6	185.5	127.7	35.1	19.1	4,166

Sources: As for table 5.1, and [6] table 6.3.1.

APPENDIX 7

STATISTICAL TABLES

Table A7.1 *Taxable and non-taxable income distribution*

Income range (£)	Year 1949				Income range (£)	Year 1954			
	Taxable units ('000s)	Taxable income (£m)	All units ('000s)	All income (£m)		Taxable units ('000s)	Taxable income (£m)	All units ('000s)	All income (£m)
50–	—	— ⎫	—	—	50–	—	— ⎫	—	—
135–	6,700	1,300 ⎭	12,190	1,920	155–	3,140	630 ⎭	8,750	1,440
250–	2,940	810	2,990	825	250–	1,590	425	1,680	460
300–	4,500	1,555	4,600	1,590	300–	3,350	1,175	3,400	1,190
400–	2,440	1,085	2,540	1,130	400–	3,350	1,505	3,400	1,525
500–	1,300	710	1,350	735	500–	2,800	1,535	2,850	1,565
600–	640	415	660	428	600–	2,100	1,355	2,160	1,395
700–	360	270	390	292	700–	1,400	1,045	1,450	1,085
800–	390	345	400	355	800–	1,225	1,075	1,280	1,125
1,000–	400	480	400	480	1,000–	725	861	735	871
1,500–	150	255	150	255	1,500–	230	394	230	394
2,000–	118	284	118	284	2,000–	161	389	161	389
3,000–	68	255	68	255	3,000–	97	363	97	363
5,000–	33	224	33	224	5,000–	44	292	44	292
10,000–	9	117	9	117	10,000–	11	143	11	143
20,000–	2	70	2	70	20,000–	2	73	2	73
Totals	20,050	8,175	25,900	8,960	Totals	20,225	11,270	26,250	12,310

Table A7.1 (*Continued*)

Income range (£)	Taxable units ('000s)	Taxable income (£m)	All units ('000s)	All income (£m)	Income range (£)	Taxable units ('000s)	Taxable income (£m)	All units ('000s)	All income (£m)
	Year 1959					Year 1963			
50-			5,759	953.7	50-			4,459	859
180-	1,617	347.7							
250-	1,200	329.4	1,713	469.7	250-	925	253.3	1,400	384.2
300-	2,416	843	2,679	933.3	300-	1,999	700.1	2,319	816.7
400-	2,420	1,090.7	2,635	1,186.0	400-	2,083	993.5	2,272	1,018.8
500-	2,631	1,445.2	2,715	1,491.6	500-	2,046	1,123.9	2,140	1,176.5
600-	2,502	1,620.8	2,558	1,657.2	600-	1,241	1391.2	2,190	1,422.8
700-	2,157	1,613.4	2,256	1,687.6	700-	2,074	1,553	2,108	1,578.3
800-	2,853	2,537.1	2,970	2,642.2	800-	3,732	3,343.3	3,823	3,424.8
1,000-	2,212	2,593.1	2,247	2,634.0	1,000-	4,413	5,287	4,545	5,446.0
1,500-	436	743.6	443	754.7	1,500-	1,185	1,988.5	1,249	2,097.9
2,000-	287	688	287	688	2,000-	356	1,683.3	456	1,085.7
3,000-	156	588	156	588	3,000-	210	789.4	210	789.4
5,000-	65	430	65	430	5,000-	105	697.7	105	697.7
10,000-	14	181	14	181	10,000-	20	264.6	20	264.6
20,000+	3	99	3	99	20,000+	4	129.9	4	129.9
Totals	20,969	15,150	26,500	16,396	Totals	21,393	19,538.7	27,300	21,192.3

Source: These tables were supplied to us by the Inland Revenue. They are a breakdown of the data published in the C.S.O. Blue Books.

Notes: All units = taxable plus non-taxable.

These numbers are not 'rounded', hence the slight discrepancy with the figures given in the C.S.O. distributions.

Table A7.2 Capital gains cross-classified with taxable income ranges, 1954

Taxable income range (£)		Capital gains by range of investment income (Investment income range £)														Totals	
		<200	200–300	300–400	400–500	500–600	600–700	700–800	800–1,000	1,000–1,500	1,500–2,000	2,000–2,500	2,500–3,000	3,000–4,000	4,000 and over	Amounts (£m)	Persons ('000s)
50–	Amount (£m)	362	—	—	—	—	—	—	—	—	—	—	—	—	—	364	—
	Persons ('000s)	6,462	—	—	—	—	—	—	—	—	—	—	—	—	—	—	6,462
155–	Amount	117	19	—	—	—	—	—	—	—	—	—	—	—	—	136	—
	Persons	2,089	21	—	—	—	—	—	—	—	—	—	—	—	—	—	2,110
250–	Amount	45	18	—	—	—	—	—	—	—	—	—	—	—	—	63	—
	Persons	802	20	—	—	—	—	—	—	—	—	—	—	—	—	—	822
300–	Amount	73	12	48	—	—	—	—	—	—	—	—	—	—	—	133	—
	Persons	1,307	14	43	—	—	—	—	—	—	—	—	—	—	—	—	1,364
400–	Amount	68	6	11	100	—	—	—	—	—	—	—	—	—	—	185	—
	Persons	1,223	7	10	67	—	—	—	—	—	—	—	—	—	—	—	1,307
500–	Amount	60	4	6	21	71	—	—	—	—	—	—	—	—	—	162	—
	Persons	1,080	5	6	14	38	—	—	—	—	—	—	—	—	—	—	1,143
600–	Amount	47	4	5	11	10	34	—	—	—	—	—	—	—	—	111	—
	Persons	848	4	4	7	5	18	—	—	—	—	—	—	—	—	—	886
700–	Amount	35	3	4	8	7	2.5	18	—	—	—	—	—	—	—	80	—
	Persons	628	3	3	5	4	6	7	—	—	—	—	—	—	—	—	652.5
800–	Amount	44	5	6	12	9	6	1.7	57	—	—	—	—	—	—	143	—
	Persons	790	5	6	8	4	3	4.5	20	—	—	—	—	—	—	—	837.7
1,000–	Amount	45	7	9	17	14	8	4.5	18	70	—	—	—	—	—	192.5	—
	Persons	808	8	7	11	8	4	1.8	6	18	—	—	—	—	—	—	870.8
1,500–	Amount	18	4	5	10	8	4	2	6	13	56	—	—	—	—	129	—
	Persons	331	4	4	7	4	2	1	9	13	11.4	—	—	—	—	—	370.4
2,000–	Amount	15	5	10	15	10	5	3.5	12	15	18	52	87	—	—	243.5	—
	Persons	279	5	10	10	4.5	2.5	1.4	4	4	3.5	7.1	11.7	—	—	—	337.2
3,000–	Amount	7	2	4	10	8.7	4.5	3	11	15	17	19	48	64.8	40	255	—
	Persons	121	2	3	6	4.3	2.3	1.3	3.6	5	3.4	2.7	6.6	6.5	2.8	—	170.5
5,000–	Amount	2	1	1	2.5	2.9	1.5	1	3.5	6	8	10	26	21	200	286.4	—
	Persons	31	1	1	1.6	1.5	0.7	0.4	1.2	1.6	1.5	1.4	3.6	2.1	9.9	—	58.5
10,000–	Amount	—	—	—	0.5	0.4	—	—	0.5	1	1	1.4	3.7	3	143	155.5	—
	Persons	—	—	—	0.5	0.4	—	—	0.5	1	1	0.2	0.5	0.3	4.4	—	—
20,000+	Amount	—	—	—	0.4	0.2	—	—	0.2	0.4	0.2	0.6	0.5	0.2	38	39.1	—
	Persons	—	—	—	—	—	—	—	—	—	—	0.1	0.3	0.2	0.9	—	7.2
Total	Amounts	938	90	105	207	141	68	37	111	121	100	83	165	89	421	2,676	
	Persons	16,700	90	91	137	73	25	15									

Table A7.3 *Capital gains cross-classified with taxable income ranges, 1959*

Taxable income range (£)		Capital gains by range of investment income (Investment income range £)																Totals	
		<100	100– 200	200– 400	400– 500	500– 600	600– 700	700– 800	800– 1,000	1,000– 1,250	1,250– 1,500	1,500– 1,750	1,750– 2,000	2,000– 2,500	2,500– 3,000	3,000– 4,000	4,000 and over	Amounts	Persons
50–[a]	Amount (£m)	90	61	2	—	—	—	—	—	—	—	—	—	—	—	—	—	153	—
	Persons ('000s)	3,084	137	1.9	—	—	—	—	—	—	—	—	—	—	—	—	—	—	3,222.9
250–	Amount	23	30	2	—	—	—	—	—	—	—	—	—	—	—	—	—	55	—
	Persons	796	67	2.2	—	—	—	—	—	—	—	—	—	—	—	—	—	—	865
300–	Amount	46	43	52	—	—	—	—	—	—	—	—	—	—	—	—	—	141	—
	Persons	1,575	93	43.7	—	—	—	—	—	—	—	—	—	—	—	—	—	—	1,712
400–	Amount	45	28	29	69	—	—	—	—	—	—	—	—	—	—	—	—	171	—
	Persons	1,524	61	24.5	37	—	—	—	—	—	—	—	—	—	—	—	—	—	1,647
500–	Amount	43	23	24	27	45	—	—	—	—	—	—	—	—	—	—	—	162	—
	Persons	1,456	50	20.3	19	16	—	—	—	—	—	—	—	—	—	—	—	—	1,360
600–	Amount	40	22	12	26	16	39	—	—	—	—	—	—	—	—	—	—	155	—
	Persons	1,355	47	10	14	6.5	13	—	—	—	—	—	—	—	—	—	—	—	1,446
700–	Amount	36	20	9	14	16	14	49	—	—	—	—	—	—	—	—	—	158	—
	Persons	1,219	43	6.9	7	6.5	4	12	—	—	—	—	—	—	—	—	—	—	1,298
800–	Amount	58	37	15	20	12	17	30	46	—	—	—	—	—	—	—	—	235	—
	Persons	1,964	80	12.7	10	5	6	8	12	—	—	—	—	—	—	—	—	—	2,098
1,000–	Amount	73	56	35	37	24	17	24	28	75	59	—	—	—	—	—	—	429	—
	Persons	2,489	123	29.2	30	10	6	6	12	13	9	—	—	—	—	—	—	—	2,712
1,500–	Amount	23	23	19	23	15	14	18	16	18	30	51	61	—	—	—	—	311	—
	Persons	779	50	15.4	12	6	5	5	4	3	5	7	6.4	—	—	—	—	—	898
2,000–	Amount	14	18	17	21	15	14	18	22	3	30	7	39	148	103	—	—	498	—
	Persons	474	38	14.3	11	6	4	5	3	4	4	3	14	14	8	—	—	—	594
3,000–	Amount	5	8	10	12	10	10	14	14	18	23	16	29	55	71	76	75	492	—
	Persons	186	18	7.7	7	4	3	3	4	3	3	2	3	5	5	5.6	2.8	—	262
5,000–	Amount	1	1	2	5	4	3	5	4	3	9	14	29	29	43	45	347	529	—
	Persons	34	2	2.2	5	4	3	3	4	6	9	9	9	2.7	3	2.1	9.9	—	69
10,000–	Amount	—	—	—	—	—	—	—	1	1	1	1	1	4	5	5	237	256	—
	Persons	—	—	—	—	—	—	—	1	1	1	—	0.2	0.3	1	0.3	3.6	—	7.4
20,000+	Amount	—	—	—	—	—	—	—	—	—	—	—	—	—	—	—	310	310	—
	Persons	—	—	—	—	—	—	—	—	—	—	—	—	—	—	—	1.7	—	1.7
Totals	Amounts	497	371	288	254	157	129	158	127	140	152	97	144	236	222	174	969	4,055	—
	Persons	16,935	813	191	135	64	42	40	33	24	23	13	15	22	17	8	18	—	18,393

Sources: B.I.R. [19] 105, table 106; and chapter 4.

[a] Estimates below £180 are based on Inland Revenue figures for incomes below the exemption limit.

Table A7.4 *Capital gains cross-classification with taxable income ranges, 1963*

Taxable income range (£)		Capital gains by range of investment income (Investment income range £)														Totals	
		200	200–300	300–400	400–500	500–600	600–700	700–800	800–1,000	1,000–1,500	1,500–2,000	2,000–2,500	2,500–3,000	3,000–4,000	3,000 and over	Amounts (£m)	Persons ('000s)
50–	Amount (£m)	151	20	—	—	—	—	—	—	—	—	—	—	—	—	171	
	Persons ('000s)	1,567	27	—	—	—	—	—	—	—	—	—	—	—	—		1,594
275–	Amount	41	7	—	—	—	—	—	—	—	—	—	—	—	—	48	
	Persons	425	10	—	—	—	—	—	—	—	—	—	—	—	—		435
300–	Amount	190	16	38	—	—	—	—	—	—	—	—	—	—	—	244	
	Persons	1,972	22	42	—	—	—	—	—	—	—	—	—	—	—		2,036
400–	Amount	129	34	16	27	—	—	—	—	—	—	—	—	—	—	206	
	Persons	1,334	47	18	19	—	—	—	—	—	—	—	—	—	—		1,418
500–	Amount	119	18	37	10	30	—	—	—	—	—	—	—	—	—	214	
	Persons	1,228	25	42	7	18	—	—	—	—	—	—	—	—	—		1,320
600–	Amount	112	13	19	23	8	32	—	—	—	—	—	—	—	—	207	
	Persons	1,158	17	21	16	5	16	—	—	—	—	—	—	—	—		1,233
700–	Amount	98	10	12	11	19	10	14	—	—	—	—	—	—	—	174	
	Persons	1,015	14	13	8	12	5	6	—	—	—	—	—	—	—		1,073
800–	Amount	204	18	18	12	16	35	13	45	—	—	—	—	—	—	361	
	Persons	2,112	25	19	8	10	17	5	16	—	—	—	—	—	—		2,212
1,000–	Amount	358	34	36	22	20	23	12	46	45	—	—	—	—	—	596	
	Persons	3,708	47	40	16	12	12	5	17	13	—	—	—	—	—		3,871
1,500–	Amount	133	19	20	14	14	18	7	20	22	88	—	—	—	—	355	
	Persons	1,382	26	23	10	8	9	3	7	7	18	—	—	—	—		1,493
2,000–	Amount	95	16	21	13	14	17	7	24	19	70	65	45	—	—	404	
	Persons	980	22	19	10	8	8.5	4	9	6	15	10	6	—	—		1,099.5
3,000–	Amount	43	13	14	10	10	14	3	9	14	37	25	36	103	38	376	
	Persons	449	13	13	6	6	7	3	6	6	8	4	5	12	3		541
5,000–	Amount	10	3	5	4	3	6	1	9	9	25	18	19	38	199	352	
	Persons	106	5	5	4	3	6	1	3	5	4	3	2.5	4	11.3		158
10,000–	Amount	—	—	—	—	—	—	—	3.5	2.7	5	3	3	7	186	205	
	Persons	—	—	—	—	—	—	—	1	1	4	3	3	7	7		11.8
20,000+	Amount	—	—	—	—	—	—	—	—	—	—	—	—	—	77	77	
	Persons	—	—	—	—	—	—	—	—	—	—	—	—	—	1.7		1.7
Total	Amounts	1,683	218	233	146	135	156	62	162	110	224	110	103	148	500	3,990	
	Persons	17,436	300	258	105	82	78	27	59	33	47	18	14	17	23		18,497

Table A7.5a *Family size distribution of taxable units, 1949 (percentage per range)*

Income range (£)	1 person	2 persons	3 persons	4 persons	5 persons	6½ persons	7 persons	Total
			Per cent of units by number of persons per unit					
135–	73.55	16.93	5.70	2.42	0.87	0.52	0.01	100
250–	48.00	27.60	15.17	6.33	1.96	0.93	0.01	100
300–	26.39	31.31	22.31	13.55	4.39	2.10	0.03	100
400–	16.29	33.81	23.16	16.54	4.56	3.59	0.05	100
500–	12.63	38.10	22.71	15.94	6.56	3.97	0.09	100
600–	12.42	40.51	22.02	15.67	5.81	3.45	0.12	100
700–	14.17	40.82	21.60	15.61	5.22	2.47	0.11	100
800–	16.36	40.89	21.00	15.24	4.77	1.58	0.16	100
1,000–	18.69	40.22	19.36	14.97	5.00	1.62	0.14	100
1,500–	20.44	40.89	17.10	14.49	5.21	1.71	0.16	100
2,000+	20.15	43.15	15.32	13.32	5.82	2.12	0.12	100

Source: B.I.R. [19] 95, table III.

Table A7.5b   *Family size distribution of taxable units (excluding dependent relatives), 1949 ('000s of units)*

Income range (£)	Number of units (in '000s) by number of persons per unit							Total units	Income (£m)
	1 person	2 persons	3 persons	4 persons	5 persons	6½ persons	7 persons		
135—	4,928	1,135	382	162	58	34	1	6,700	1,300
250—	1,411.2	811.4	446	186.1	58	27	0.3	2,940	810
300—	1,187	1,409	1,000	609.7	198	95	1.3	4,500	1,555
400—	397	825	5,651	404	160.1	87.6	1.2	2,440	1,085
500—	164	496	295	207.2	85	51.6	1.2	1,300	710
600—	80	259	141	100	37.2	22	0.8	640	415
700—	51	146.9	77.8	56.2	18.8	8.9	0.4	360	270
800—	64	159	82	59.4	19	6	0.6	390	345
1,000—	75	161	77	60	20	6.4	0.6	400	480
1,500—	31	61	26	22	7.8	2	0.2	150	255
2,000+	46.3	99.2	35	31	13.4	4.8	0.3	230	950
Total								20,050	8,175

Sources: As for tables A7.5a and A7.1.

Table A7.6a *Family size distribution of taxable units (excluding dependent relatives), 1954 (percentage per range),*

Per cent of units by number of persons per unit

Income range (£m)	1 person	2 persons	3 persons	4 persons	5 persons	6½ persons	7 persons	Total
155—	84.7	10.1	2.8	1.3	0.6	0.5	—	100
250—	74	17.1	4.7	2.2	1.1	0.9	—	100
300—	54.7	25.7	10.12	5.45	2.41	1.61	0.01	100
400—	34.53	31.33	16.8	10.51	4.1	2.7	0.03	100
500—	16.68	37.45	22.24	14.61	5.28	3.7	0.03	100
600—	14.2	37.76	22.42	15.62	6.32	3.64	0.04	100
700—	7.81	40.61	23.24	17.83	6.52	3.93	0.06	100
800—	8.46	44.13	21.37	16.39	5.98	3.61	0.06	100
1,000—	15.75	41.42	19.39	16.08	5.23	2.03	0.10	100
1,500—	19.87	38.85	16.73	16	6.09	2.34	0.12	100
2,000+	19.33	41.62	14.76	15.37	6.29	2.51	0.12	100

Source: B.I.R. [19] 99, table 82.

Table A7.6b *Family size distribution of taxable units (excluding dependent relatives), 1954 ('000s of units)*

Number of units (in '000s) by number of persons per unit

Income range (£)	1 person	2 persons	3 persons	4 persons	5 persons	6½ persons	7 persons	Total units	Income (£m)
155—	2,659	317	88	41	19	16	—	3,140	630
250—	1,176	272	75	35	18	14	—	1,590	435
300—	1,832.4	861	339	182.6	80.7	54	0.3	3,350	1,175
400—	1,157	1,050	563	352	137	90	1	3,350	1,505
500—	467	1,049	622.7	409	147.8	103.6	0.9	2,800	1,535
600—	298.2	793	471	328	133	76	0.8	2,100	1,355
700—	109	568	326	250	91.2	55	0.8	1,400	1,045
800—	103	541	262	201	73.3	44	0.7	1,225	1,075
1,000—	114	300.3	140	117	38	15	0.7	725	861
1,500—	45.7	89.4	38.5	36.8	14	5.3	0.3	230	394
2,000+	60.9	131.1	46.5	48.4	19.8	7.9	0.4	315	1,260
Total								20,225	11,270

Sources: As for tables A7.6a and A7.1.

Table A7.7a *Family size distribution of taxable units (excluding dependent relatives), 1959 (percentage per range)*

Income range	Per cent of units by number of persons per unit								Total
	1 person	2 persons	3 persons	4 persons	5 persons	6 persons	7 persons	8 persons	
180–	90.5	6.5	1.3	0.7	0.5	0.3	0.1	—	100
250–	86.2	9.9	1.9	1	0.5	0.3	0.1	0.1	100
300–	76.8	16.5	3.5	1.6	0.8	0.4	0.2	1.1	100
400–	57.5	25.6	9.5	4.6	1.7	0.7	0.2	1.3	100
500–	37.3	31.4	16.8	9.6	3.3	1.1	0.31	0.19	100
600–	22.8	33.7	20.9	12.7	6.4	2.2	0.7	0.5	100
700–	15.8	33.7	22.7	17.6	6.9	2.6	0.8	0.4	100
800–	11.2	35.1	23	18.3	7.5	3.1	1.1	0.7	100
1,000–	10	41	21.6	17.1	6.5	2.4	0.8	0.6	100
1,500–	14	38.7	18.5	17.9	8.5	1.8	0.4	0.2	100
2,000+	17.3	39.3	16.1	16.9	7.4	2.3	0.5	0.2	100

Source: Information from Inland Revenue.

Table A7.7b   Family size distribution of taxable units (excluding dependent relatives), 1959 ('000s)

Income range (£)	Number of units (in '000s) by number of persons per unit								Total units
	1 person	2 persons	3 persons	4 persons	5 persons	6 persons	7 persons	8 persons	
180–	1,463	105	21	12	8	5	3	—	1,617
250–	1,034	119	23	12	6	4	1	1	1,200
300–	1,855	398	84	39	19	9	4	8	2,416
400–	1,392	620	230	111	41	17	5	4	2,420
500–	981	826	442	252	87	29	8	6	2,631
600–	563	843	521	328	161	55	18	13	2,502
700–	340	726	489	379	148	55	14	6	2,157
800–	320	1,002	656	522	214	88	31	20	2,853
1,000–	221	907	478	378	144	53	18	13	2,212
1,500–	61	169	80	78	37	8	2	1	436
2,000+	91	206	85	89	39	12	2	1	525
Total									20,969

Sources As for tables A7.7a and A7.1.

Table A7.8a *Family size distribution of taxable income units (excluding dependent relatives), 1963 (percentages per range)*

Per cent of units by number of persons per unit

Income range £	1 person	2 persons	3 persons	4 persons	5 persons	6½ persons	Total
275–	85.28	9.76	2.15	1.58	0.58	0.65	100
300–	82.92	11.91	2.24	1.37	0.86	0.70	100
400–	73.51	19.16	3.81	1.70	0.74	1.08	100
500–	56.06	27.37	7.54	5.36	2.14	1.53	100
600–	42.88	29.13	14.39	8.66	3.49	1.45	100
700–	33.13	30.87	16.76	11.20	5.18	2.84	100
800–	20.18	32.88	20.08	15.77	6.77	4.32	100
1,000–	9.88	39.41	20.41	18.21	7.42	4.74	100
1,500–	10.22	42.78	19.9	16.86	6.91	3.33	100
2,000–	13.95	40.12	17.34	17.87	7.58	3.14	100
3,000–	16.72	39.53	15.97	15.57	8.77	3.43	100
5,000+	16.92	43.4	14.05	14	7.97	3.66	100

Source: B.I.R. [19] 108, tables 67–71.

Table A7.8b *Family size distribution of taxable income units (excluding dependent relatives), 1963 ('ooos)*

Income range (£)	Number of units (in 'ooos) by number of persons per unit						Total units	Income (£m)
	1 person	2 persons	3 persons	4 persons	5 persons	6½ persons		
250-a	788.8	90.3	19.9	14.6	5.4	6	925	253.3
300-	1,657.5	238.1	44.8	27.4	17.2	14	1,999	700.1
400-	1,531.2	399.1	79.4	35.4	15.4	22.5	2,083	933.5
500-	1,147	560	154.3	109.7	43.8	31.2	2,046	1,123.9
600-	918.1	623.7	308.1	185.4	74.7	31	2,141	1,391.2
700-	687.1	640.7	347.6	232.3	107.4	58.9	2,074	1,553
800-	753.1	1,227.1	749.4	588.5	252.7	161.2	3,732	3,343.3
1,000-	436	1,739.2	897.6	803.6	327.4	209.2	4,413	528.7
1,500-	121.1	506.9	235.8	199.8	81.9	39.5	1,185	1,988.5
2,000-	63.6	182.9	79.1	81.5	34.6	14.3	456	1,083.3
3,000-	35.1	83.1	33.5	32.7	18.4	7.2	210	789.4
5,000+	21.8	56	18.1	10.3	10.3	4.7	129	1,092.2
Total							21,393	19,538.7

Sources: As for tables A7.8a and A7.1.

a £275-300 distribution applied to the £250-300 units in the calendar year data.

REFERENCES

JOURNAL REFERENCES

A.E.A.   American Economic Association
B.O.U.I.S. Bulletin of the Oxford Institute of Statistics
J.P.E.   Journal of Political Economy
J.R.S.S.   Journal of the Royal Statistical Society
L.B.R.   Lloyds Bank Review
N.B.E.R.   National Bureau of Economic Research
N.I.E.R.   National Institute of Economic Research
Restat.   Review of Economics and Statistics
S.J.E.   Scottish Journal of Economics or Scottish Journal of Political Economy

A. NUMBERED REFERENCES

[1] Abel-Smith, B. and Townsend, P. *The Poor and the Poorest*, Occasional Papers on Social Administration, no. 17, London, 1965.

[2] Aitchison, J. and Brown, J. A. C. *The Lognormal Distribution*, Cambridge University Press, Cambridge, 1957.

[3] Andic, F. M. *Distribution of Family Incomes in Puerto Rico*, Caribbean Monograph Series, no. 1, Rio Piedras, 1964.

[4] Atkinson, A. B. *Poverty in Britain and the Reform of Social Security*, Cambridge University Press, Cambridge, 1969.

[5] Barna, T. *The Redistribution of Income through Public Finance in 1937*, Oxford University Press, London, 1945.

[6] Beveridge, W. H. *Report on Social Insurance and Allied Services*, Cmnd. 6404, H.M.S.O., 1942.

[7] Bowley, A. L. *Change in the Distribution of National Income 1880–1913*, Oxford University Press, London, 1920.

[8] Bowley, A. L. *Elements of Statistics*, 6th edition, P. S. King, New York, 1937.

[9] Bowman, Jean. 'A Graphical Analysis of Personal Income Distribution in the United States', A.E.A. Readings in the Theory of Income Distribution, Allen and Unwin, London, 1950.

[10] Brady, Dorothy. 'Research on the Size Distribution of Income', Conference on Research in Income and Wealth Studies, Vol. 13, N.B.E.R., 1951.

[11] Brittain, S. 'Some Neglected Features of Britain's Income Levelling', *A.E.A. Papers and Proceedings*, 1959.

[12] Campion, H. *Public and Private Property in Great Britain*, Oxford University Press, London, 1939.

[13] Campion, G. P. M. and Daniels, G. W. *The Distribution of National Capital*, Manchester University Press, Manchester, 1936.

[14] Cartter, A. M. *The Redistribution of Income in Post-War Britain*, Yale, 1955.

[15] Cartter, A. M. 'A New Method of Relating British Capital Ownership and Estate Duty Liability to Income Groups', *Economica*, August, 1955

[16] Central Statistical Office [C.S.O.]. *National Income and Expenditure Books*, [Blue Books], H.M.S.O.

[17] Champernowne, D. G. 'A Model of Income Distribution', *Economic Journal*, June 1953.

[18] Chiozza-Money, L. G. *Riches and Poverty*, London, 1905.

[19] Commissioners of Her Majesty's Inland Revenue [B.I.R.], Report nos.: 61 (1919), 63 (1921), 64 (1922), 83 (1939), 95 (1953), 99 (1957), 101 (1959), 105 (1963), 107 (1965), 108 (1966). H.M.S.O.

[20] Co-operative Permanent Building Society. 'Who Buys Houses' (1963). Occasional Bulletin, no. 59, November 1963.

[21] Dalton, H. *The Inequality of Incomes*, Routledge, New York, 1929.

[22] Dicks-Mireaux, L. and others. 'Prospects for the British Car Industry', N.I.E.R., September 1961.

[23] Dow, J. C. R. *The Management of the British Economy 1945–60*, Cambridge University Press, Cambridge, 1964.

[24] Durham, W. *The £s.d. of Welfare in Industry*, Industrial Welfare Society, London, 1958.

[25] *Economic Trends*, 'Survey of Personal Incomes for 1959–60', H.M.S.O., August, 1963.

[26] Gibrat R. *Les Inegalities Economiques*, Paris, 1931.

[27] Gini, C. 'On the Measure of Concentration with especial Reference to Income and Wealth', Cowles Commission, 1936.

[28] Gough I. and Stark T. 'Low Incomes in the United Kingdom, 1954, 1959 and 1963', Manchester School, June 1968.

[29] Harris, R. and Solly, M. *A Survey of Large Companies*, Institute of Economic Affairs, 1959.

[30] Hemming, Mrs M. F. W. 'Social Security in Britain and Certain Other Countries', *N.I.E.R.*, August 1965.

[31] Jackson, J. M. 'Poverty, National Assistance and the Family', *S.J.E.*, June 1966.

[32] Kalecki, M. 'On the Gibrat Distribution', *Econometrica*, April 1945.

[33] Kendall, M. G. *Advanced Theory of Statistics*, Vol. 1., Griffin, London.

[34] Kendall, M. G. *Rank Correlation Methods*, Griffin, London, 1962.

[35] Klein, L. R. 'Savings and Finance of the Upper Income Classes', *B.O.U.I.S.*, November 1956.

[36] Langley, M. 'The Distribution of Capital in Private Hands in 1936–68', *B.O.U.I.S.*, December 1950. 'The Distribution of Capital in Private Hands in 1946–47', *B.O.U.I.S.*, February 1951.

[37] Little, I. M. *A Critique of Welfare Economics*, Oxford University Press, 2nd edition, London, 1958.

[38] Lydall, H. F. *British, Incomes and Savings*, Blackwell, Oxford, 1955.

[39] Lydall, H. F. 'The Long Term Trend in the Size Distribution of Income', *J.R.S.S.*, 1959, Series A, Part 1.

[40] Lydall, H. F. 'Distribution of Employment Incomes', *Econometrica*, January 1959.

[41] Lydall, H. F. and Tipping, D.G. 'The Distribution of Personal Wealth in the U.K.' *B.O.U.I.S.*, February 1961.

[42] Mallet, B. 'A New Method of Relating British Capital Ownership and Estate Duty Liability to Income Groups', *J.R.S.S.*, 1938.

[43] Mincer, J. 'Investment in Human Capital and Personal Income Distribution', *J.P.E.*, August 1958.

[44] Ministry of Education. *Grants to Students*, Cmd. 1051, H.M.S.O., 1960.

[45] Ministry of Labour. *Family Expenditure Surveys* [F.E.S.], 1957–9 and annually since 1961, H.M.S.O.

[46] Ministry of Labour. *Report of an Enquiry into Household Expenditure in 1953–4.* H.M.S.O., 1957.

[47] Ministry of Labour. 'Labour Costs in Britain in 1964: Manufacturing Industries', *Gazette*, December 1966.

[48] Ministry of Labour. 'Wages and Related Elements of Labour Costs', *Gazette*, August 1957.

[49] Ministry of Transport. 'Motor Car Ownership and Use' in *New Contributions to Economic Statistics*, H.M.S.O., 1964. (Reprints from *Economic Trends*, February 1962, February 1964.)

[50] Mogridge, M. J. H. *Planning, Incomes and Increasing Prosperity*, Centre for Environmental Studies, Working Paper, London, 1969.

[51] Morgan, J. N. 'The Anatomy of Income Distribution', *Restat.*, August 1962.

[52] Morgan, E. V. F. *The Structure of Property Ownership in Great Britain*, Oxford University Press, London, 1960.

[53] Nicholson, J. L. *Redistribution of Income in the United Kingdom in 1959, 1957 and 1953*, Bowes and Bowes, London, 1965.

[54] Nicholson, R. J. 'The Distribution of Personal Income', *L.B.R.*, January 1967.

[55] Orshansky, P. 'Counting the Poor: Another Look at the Poverty Profile', *Social Security Bulletin*, January 1965.

[56] Paish, F. N. 'The Real Incidence of Personal Taxation', *L.B.R.*, January 1957.

[57] Pareto, V. *Cours d'Economie Politique*, Lausanne, 1897.

[58] Prais, S. J. and Houthakker, H. S. *The Analysis of Family Budgets*, Cambridge University Press, Cambridge, 1955.

[59] Pilch, M. and Wood, V. *New Trends in Pensions*, Hutchinsons, London, 1964.

[60] Prest, A. R. and Stark, T. 'Some Aspects of Income Distribution in the U.K. since World War II', Manchester School, September 1967.

[61] Reid, G. L. and Robertson, D. J. (eds.). *Fringe Benefit, Labour Costs and Social Security*, Allen and Unwin, London, 1965.

[62] Revell, J. *Wealth of the Nation*, Cambridge University Press, Cambridge, 1967.

[63] Robbins, Lord. *Robbins Report on Higher Education*, Cmnd. 2154, II, H.M.S.O., 1963.

[64] Rowntree, B. S. *Poverty and Progress*, Longmans, London, 1941.

[65] Royal Commission on Taxation. *Final Report, Annex, Taxation of Capital Gains and Memorandum of Dissent*, Cmnd. 9474, H.M.S.O., 1955.

[66] Seers, D. *The Levelling of Incomes since 1935.* Blackwell, Oxford, 1951.
[67] Silbertson, Z. A. 'The Motor Industry 1955–64', *B.O.U.I.S.* November 1965.
[68] Simons, H. *Personal Income Taxation,* University of Chicago Press, Chicago, 1938.
[69] Stark, T. *A Survey of Income Distribution in the U.K. since World War II,* Ph.D. Thesis, Manchester University, 1967.
[70] Titmuss, R. M. *Income Distribution and Social Change,* Allen and Unwin, London, 1962.
[71] Vaizey, J. *Cost of Education,* Allen and Unwin, London, 1958.
[72] Yntema, D. 'Measures of the Inequality in Personal Distribution of Wealth or Income', *Journal of the American Statistical Society,* December 1933.
[73] Yule, G. U. and Kendall, M. G. *An Introduction to the Theory of Statistics,* Griffin, London, 1958.

B.   ADDITIONAL STATISTICAL SOURCES FOR TABLES

Annual Abstract of Statistics, H.M.S.O.
International Financial Statistics, U.N., annual.
Investors' Chronicle, London, weekly.
Monthly Digest of Statistics, H.M.S.O.
National Assistance Board, *Reports.*

INDEX